Foreword - Fred Eyre

Fred Eyre

It is a truly wonderful feeling to think that you have been blessed with the best job in the world. I know because I once was one of those fortunate people, many years ago, when I was a professional footballer for Manchester City.

Not just a professional footballer, it was "......for Manchester City" that elevated it to the level above all else. So I know exactly how Ian feels, and his book captures not only his love of football and his devotion to Manchester City, but also the sheer zest for his own working life as he takes us through it virtually on a day to day basis.

As his co-commentator and travelling companion, I am with him almost every step of the way so I can personally vouch for the authenticity of his adventures.

From the remote, but beautiful Faroe Islands with Manchester City and hundreds of puffins, across Scandinavia and Europe, and all the corners of the Premier League "Cheesy" takes us through it all. Surely there could be no better time to be the Manchester City correspondent for BBC Radio Manchester than at the dawn of an exciting new era at the club.

The Club is backed by untold wealth, led by a "smart cookie" recruited from one of the world's leading sports companies, and a manager intent on bringing only top class players to the City of Manchester Stadium.

It's an exhilarating new chapter in the history of Manchester City Football Club and all Ian has to do is sit alongside me, and watch the match and tell his listeners all about it.

Best Job in the World

You know what?

I reckon Ian Cheeseman really has got "The Best Job in the World"!

Fred Eyre
Worsley 2009

Introduction - Colin Bell

Colin Bell

Soon after Ian had finished working with me on my autobiography, "Reluctant Hero", I expressed my wish that this would only be the first of many, and here is the second; long may it continue.

I could not have been more pleased by that first book, into which he put so much care, time and effort. I don't believe that anyone else could have captured my personality better than Ian did.

During the three years we worked together, we became close friends and I know that his love for Manchester City is second to none. He lives and breathes City and that comes across in everything he says and does. His enthusiasm and passion for the club, which I represented with such pride, is there in his radio commentaries, at every City function he's involved in and in everything he writes.

I've discovered that his passion for football is not just limited to City and he has told me many stories of his trips far and wide to watch a wide range of games from the lower levels of the game right up to the highest standards.

I wish him well with "Best Job in the World", which is full of fascinating tales of his travels and know it will be well received by football supporters throughout the north west and all those who share his passion for the beautiful game.

Colin Bell
July 2009

Rodney Marsh

I was born to be a footballer. It has been my love all of my life. I felt privileged to be able to work at the thing I loved. I would not have wanted to do anything else.

The Best Job in the World is a compendium of anecdotal recollections of Ian Cheeseman, who had the incredible fortune to not only be a massive football fan, but be lucky enough to be a broadcaster and media professional following, amongst others, the team that he loves.

What football fan wouldn't want to live this labour of love.

Rodney Marsh
July 2009

Introduction

This project started as a series of blogs, on the BBC Manchester website, from the different venues Manchester City were sent during their UEFA Cup run of 2008 – 2009. I'd wanted to give people an insight into the trips, the places and the people that make these journey's more than just football matches. I received fantastic feedback from all those who read them, urging me to do more.

I know, from my years as a paying spectator (I was a "normal" fan for over thirty years), that half the fun of being a football fanatic, are the events and incidents around the game. Let's face it, there are so many disappointments on the pitch, whoever you support, that it would drive you crazy if you didn't have friendships, adventures, banter and moments of humour along the way.

This is my blog of a season, an extraordinary season, with thousands of miles of foreign and domestic travel mixed in with one typical season which was typically packed with fun and drama. Through the "window" of that one season, during which I attended 116 games, I have told my own story from a boyhood dream through obsessive fandom to the fulfilment of my goal of becoming the Manchester City commentator for the BBC.

The season I selected also happened to be the start of an exciting new phase in the history of Manchester City, who had new mega-rich owners and another new manager. Droylsden captured national headlines with their controversial and thrilling run in the FA Cup, there was the return of Joe Royle to Oldham Athletic and Stockport County's financial troubles plus exciting promotion campaigns for Bury and Rochdale and a highly impressive season for Wigan Athletic.

As the season progressed I often pinched myself as the many fascinating, incident packed journeys took place; at times I felt like I was in a book. I'd fancied writing something about my transition from fan to journalist for a while, as I feel my story is unique.

As a child, like so many others, I had no idea what I wanted to be. I wouldn't have minded being a tram driver, maybe an astronaut or be permanently on tour with Abba. Then on 12th November 1975, a dream came into my mind, "I'd love be the City commentator on the radio". On that day I was listening to the radio. City were playing United in the League Cup. It was the day Colin Bell suffered that terrible knee injury, which effectively ended his career.

My mum wouldn't allow me to go to the game because it was a midweek match, a derby and potentially too dangerous. As I listened intently, something clicked inside me and suddenly I knew that was what I wanted to do. Reality quickly set in and I came to the conclusion that it was an impossible dream, so my mind went back to the action.

I was worried for Colin as he was carried off, but by the end of the game I was delirious, as City had hammered United 4-0.

I was born in Manchester, at St.Mary's hospital, which was opposite the Palace Theatre (there's a Sainsbury's there now).

I grew up in Radcliffe, attending Radcliffe County Primary School, where I had many great friends and very happy times. I did well, as did most of my class mates. Almost all of us passed our eleven plus exam, which was unheard of. Typically about five or six children per class would normally gain a pass, but for us, it was thirty out of thirty five, thanks to a combination of talented pupils and brilliant teaching from Mr Booth, Mrs Thirkell and Headmaster Mr Shakeshaft.

I also took entrance exams for Bolton School, Bury Grammar and Canon Slade Grammar School in Bolton, passing them all, but not gaining a big enough percentage to be offered the free place that my parents had hoped for. They chose to send me to Canon Slade, where my best mate Graham Mason also decided to go.

After two terms, my dad got a promotion at work, and we moved to Norwich (I'm an only child) to a village called Hethersett. My new school was

Wymondham College. It was a nice enough area and I made friends quickly and even picked up a bit of the "ooh ahr" accent, but I wasn't really happy there. My mum, who was born in Germany and only moved to England when she met my dad, was also homesick for the north west.

Twelve months after our move south my dad's work circumstances changed and there was a chance for him to return to his Manchester office, so we came "home". We lived in Whitefield and I attended Stand Grammar School, where many of my junior school friends had gone.

I achieved seven "O" levels (now GCSEs) and two "A" levels. I'm sure I would have also passed Maths and maybe even Physics, if my mum hadn't been battling cancer for nine months during my study years.

Sunderland Polytechnic was my next stop, where I started a degree in geography, but after a few weeks I moved to Manchester Polytechnic to study social science. At the end of the first year of the course I dropped out and started working for the Co-operative Bank as a clerk.

I met the girl who was to become my wife in those early years. I married Irene in 1984 and moved to Oldham. By then I realised I was never going to be a very good banker and was looking for something more exciting, but just as a hobby; I wasn't planning a new career.

I joined Radio Cavell (Oldham's hospital radio), inspired by Fred Eyre, who I thought was fantastic when appearing each morning on Dave Ward's breakfast programme on Piccadilly Radio. He used to do the day's sports news from his own unique, witty perspective.

Meanwhile Irene and I started a family and she left the bank to become a full-time mother. My involvement at Radio Cavell, where I was now presenting a weekly magazine programme, had brought back into my mind that boyhood dream, as I met the guys who commentated on Oldham's home games.

I started to expand my involvement in extracurricular broadcasting - just for fun. I commentated for "Clubcall", a premium rate football phone service and I described the City games for the club video.

There were many other things I tried, which included an article for "Shoot magazine", editing and writing for a City supporters club magazine, presenting, on camera, a video documentary for Oldham Athletic, conducting interviews for "Signal Cheshire", a Stockport based independent radio station and many other small projects.

In 1994, Andy Buckley, BBC GMR's head of sport, who I'd met at City, invited me to apply for a job in his sports team. I was offered the position of broadcast journalist and joined the BBC in May that year. I will always be indebted to Andy and Colin Philpott, the station editor, for giving me my first job in broadcasting.

Twelve months later we added to our family with a second son. By 1998 I'd picked up an award in the category "North West Sports Journalist of the Year" and could see that my boyhood ambition was now within reach. In November 2001, after years of self doubt, hard work, luck and determination my dream came true and I was the BBC's City correspondent.

During the Commonwealth Games of 2002, I persuaded Colin Bell to allow me to write his life story, which was published in 2005 as his autobiography "Reluctant Hero". It may also have extended his life. When a surgeon read it and spotted a potential health problem, inherited from his mother, he advised investigative surgery which in turn led to surgery to remove early cancerous growths from his bowel.

Over the years I've been asked to speak about my job at many functions and to tell some of the stories of how I made the transition from fan to journalist. I hope that this chronicle of many seasons, through one season, that those who're interested, will now have a clearer idea of the bigger picture, and I hope my story acts as an inspiration to those who want to fulfil there dreams and ambitions. Nothing comes to you, you have to make things happen.

I was a very committed fan, and have always kept meticulous records of every football match I have been to. I've attended over 1600 competitive first team City games, plus many more friendlies, youth cup and reserve games and over 800 matches which don't feature City; the vast majority of those being before I was paid to attend games! When my time as a professional is over, I'll return to be being a fan. Once you've got the bug, or should that be obsession, it never goes away.

Introduction - Ian Cheeseman

Thanks

I'd like to take this opportunity to thank Fred Eyre for being an inspiration and great friend and Charlie Hadfield and Chris Bailey for their support, friendship and good company.

My deep gratitude also goes to Michael Jones, Gail Cooke and Optimum Publishing Solutions for their support and enthusiasm with this project, to Emily Brobyn, Nigel and Colette Gleghorn and of course to my wife Irene and my sons Steven and Daniel for their love and understanding.

Thanks to Eddie Garvey and Roland Cooke for the use of a couple of their excellent photographs - the others, which are not quite as good, are mine.

There are many others, too many to name individually, to whom I owe a debt of gratitude, including Colin Bell and Rodney Marsh for their contributions to this book.

First published in Great Britain in 2009 by:

Optimum Publishing Solutions, OPS LLP
The Cottages, Regent Road, Altrincham, Cheshire WA14 1RX

Paperback edition 2009

ISBN 978-0-9563274-0-6

Printed and bound in Great Britain

Best Job in the World
From the football specials to the press box

Ian Cheeseman

July

Tuesday 1st July

Like many other Manchester City fans, I woke up excited by the prospect of finding out, later that day, who City would be playing in the first qualifying round of the UEFA Cup. City had qualified via the fair play league, the final gift of outgoing manager Sven Goran Eriksson.

As EB Streymur of the Faroe Islands was confirmed, I have to admit I had only a vague idea where the Faroe Islands were. I thought they were close to Scotland and didn't realise they were quite so isolated. I discovered they were famous for puffins, whaling, and buildings that looked like the lawn was on the roof; and I thought mowing the back garden was tricky.

It would definitely be a step into the unknown for everyone. I felt certain it would be a gentle opener to the new season, for the City players at least, but for me it was going to be a round trip of over 1800 miles. I've always said I'd follow City to the ends of the earth!

To say they won the fair play league, which is how it's often explained, is a bit misleading as they actually finished as the fifth best behaved English team, but the teams above them had already qualified for Europe. City entered the competition at the first qualifying round.

The first problem was how to get there. I could have flown via Copenhagen, but the prices were shooting up by the minute, as I studied my options on the internet and I was keen to keep costs to a minimum. I had to persuade my bosses at the BBC that this was a game we must provide commentary on, so after a bit of research I decided that the cheapest way to do it, without swimming, was to fly direct from Stansted Airport. The problem was that the only flights were on Monday's and Friday's.

I booked basic accommodation and reckoned I'd saved a few hundred pounds on what it would have cost to go via Denmark, so they agreed and I was booked and raring to go.

Monday 14th July 2008

My week started with the drive down to London to catch the Monday tea-time flight to the Faroe Islands. I wasn't quite sure what to expect; would it be full of City fans wanting to sample the Faroes' culture before Thursday's game?

The two other Brits on board were tourists, who admitted they would attend the game, but were not football fans.

So who would sit next to me? Well, I couldn't have handpicked my companion better. Not only was Magni Arge the president of Atlantic Airways, the only airline to fly in and out of the islands, but he'd been a football commentator for 20 years. He'd also hosted former US Vice-President Al Gore and former President Bill Clinton on their visits to the Faroes and spoken at the Transatlantic Climate Conference in April!

We chatted for two hours, by which time I had a far better idea of what to expect, though before arriving, there was the small issue of landing. I'd been told that touching down in the Faroes was like coming in on an aircraft carrier.

"It is challenging because the topography is not very well suited for building airports", is how Magni succinctly put it. "The one we will be landing at, the only one on the islands, was built by British soldiers during their friendly occupation during the second world war. The runway is just 1200 metres long, so only smaller aircraft can land here. The weather conditions can be somewhat adverse - maybe it would be more interesting for your story if it is a bit challenging today."

I disagreed and was grateful for the gentle landing a few minutes later. It was fascinating nevertheless. We came down through low cloud to eventually see the mist shrouded islands – it put me in mind of 'Lost', the cult US TV programme, or Isla Sorna in 'Jurassic Park', with Magni serving as my very own Richard Attenborough.

On landing I spotted Christian Mouritsen, a Faroese footballer who'd spent three years at City, until released just a few weeks earlier, at the age of 19. What were the odds of him being there to wave off his relatives on holiday?

He'd played in the same under 18's team as Michael Johnson and in the Youth Cup with Micah Richards, so knew City well. I could tell he was excited about the upcoming game, a chance to see one or two familiar faces, but clearly it was also a chance for him to reflect.

After seeing his family through passport control, he told me, "I left City because they said I wasn't good enough, so I've returned home to try something new. I think it will be a very slow game here on Thursday, and the standard will be like League Three in England."

Despite being released by the club, he told me he'd be supporting City and was in no doubt they would win easily.

I was expecting to catch the bus from the airport to Torshavn, the capital of the Faroe Islands, but Magni offered me a lift, though it proved to be a personal introduction rather than a simple road journey. I discovered that the airport, to my surprise, was 49 km from Torshavn; I'd imagined everything would be smaller.

In his 4x4, he took me there via the scenic route, up narrow, twisting roads, with sheer drops on both sides. The views, and the road, were breathtaking. Although there was no snow, the quickly ascending road weaved between, what looked like, the poles that slalom skiers race between when descending the Austrian mountains on Ski Sunday.

I must admit I felt a little anxious, but trusted my driver who had presumably made this journey many times before and in much worse weather conditions. Magni's aim was to show me the breathtaking view of the island of Koltur, which I suspected was the most iconic of the islands, just because it looks so unusual.

I think most people, when imagining an island think of it being round and rising out of the sea to a perfect peak in the middle, like Tracey Island in "Thunderbirds". This one starts low to the sea at one end and rises, evenly, at what looks like a 25 degree angle to reach high cliffs at the far end and is green with no trees. In fact Thunderbird two could have used it to take off from!

As we continued to climb my excitement grew as Magni told me we'd get a perfect view right around the next corner, but then the mist closed in. What an anticlimax! All I could see was the hand in front of my face – just about – and that's not a pretty sight at the best of times.

This situation had happened to me once before on a family holiday to Austria, many years ago, when we'd spent half a day driving around numerous gravity defying hair-pin bends to the top of Grossglockner, the country's highest mountain. Once again, it was a beautiful ascent, until 10 minutes from, what I'd been told would be, the gorgeous view of the Pasterz glacier. In came the clouds and the nearest I've got to see of this alleged stunning panorama, was the post card I bought at the gift shop.

Still, the Faroes are known for their atmospheric fog, and I was here for a week, so there might be another chance – third time lucky? Eventually Magni's fascinating tour came to an end and he dropped me off at the hostel I'd booked, a clean and tidy little place, close to the port and the stadium. If everyone on the Faroe Islands was to be as friendly as Magni, the City fans following me there later in the week would have no fears.

I had made it my task to visit both home grounds of EB Streymur, as the City game had been switched to the national stadium in Torshavn. The club had two home venues because, as the name might suggest, the two original clubs, EB and Streymur, are from two different villages. They joined together in the 90's with the philosophy that one small club is stronger than two very small clubs.

To visit both grounds I'd have to visit both villages, which were some distance apart and on different islands. I was now beginning to understand the scale of the place, and was a little worried that it might not be as easy to get around, without a hire car, as I had expected.

I made my way into Torshavn, the centre was only five minutes away by foot, making the tourist information centre my first port of call. I'd heard, through a friend, that someone called Solfrid Ikroki, who had spent the last year on an exchange with the tourist office in Preston, worked there. I didn't know if that name was male or female, but I knew they'd be able to speak English.

The first person I met was the boss, a lovely lady called Ingigero, who also spoke perfect English, as well as Faroese (the native tongue) and Danish, the second language of the islands. I got the feeling that she'd been expecting me, perhaps the work of Magni, who I suspect had told them I might be in.

Before long we were leafing through maps of the islands and scanning the bus timetables. It quickly became apparent that it would be almost impossible to visit both grounds in one day. Ingigero picked up the phone and got in contact with someone at EB Streymur, though of course she could have been on the other end of a "phone a friend" on "Who Wants to be a Millionaire" for all I knew, because I couldn't understand a word. As she replaced the receiver, I was told I'd be picked up by car in about half an hour.

While I waited, Ingigero introduced me to Solfrid, a pretty young woman in her 20's, who told me about her trip to Preston. I arranged to record a radio interview with her, later in the day, before being whisked off to my waiting car ride.

My driver was a lifelong EB Streymur fan, Esmar Olsen, and he took me on the trip of a lifetime from one end of the biggest two islands to the other. We travelled through a 5km tunnel, carved through solid rock, and along the side of a breathtaking fjord to the club's normal home ground. This was the "stadium" originally used by Streymur.

The main stand was modern, but small, with multi-functional office space designed for use by the local community. It had about ten rows of seats spread along two thirds of the length of one touchline. On the opposite side of the pitch was a steep sided hill, scattered with loose rocks, this only allowed room for a small fence, which stretched behind both goals. It looked like something from the old subbuteo table football game I'd had as a boy.

I was pretty handy at that game, and used to play regularly against my pal Barry, a big Man United fan. I usually beat him. My team was called "World-Wide City", quite prophetic given the players in the current City squad. Back in April 1974 I'd been beating Barry at subbuteo, as we listened to commentary of City beating United at Old Trafford 1-0, thanks to that Denis Law back heel. I was already dreaming that one day I might be the City commentator.

Two years later, I was at Wembley with my dad, watching City win the League Cup, never suspecting it would be their last major trophy for such a long time. By contrast EB Streymur's most recent trophy had been the Farosese Cup, which had earned their place in the UEFA Cup. Esmar gave me the chance to lift it high, like Mike Doyle had done that day at Wembley.

Being at Streymur's tiny ground put everything into perspective. City's opponents, later that week, were surely going to be the smallest club they'd ever played in a serious competition, but as Jimmy Cricket might say, there's more. Next Esmar took me to EB's ground, which is only used for youth football, but had previously hosted first team fixtures.

To get there we had to cross the relatively new bridge between the islands of Streymoy and Eysturoy and go as far north as possible to the village of Eidi. Just like the Streymur stadium, the surface was artificial, and next to a steep incline. This was far more spectacular though, being surrounded on three sides by the north Atlantic and the other by the rugged, rock strewn hills. It seemed to be the only flat spot for miles and was just big enough for the pitch and small, wooden changing rooms.

There were a few footballs lying around near the dugouts so I kicked one against the advertising hoardings for a few moments. I could now claim I'd played at one of football's most remote and stunning venues.

If ever that expression, "it's a stones throw from...." was true, this was it. I can't imagine how many misdirected goal kicks have resulted in footballs floating out into the Atlantic, heading for Iceland. It made me think of Shrewsbury's old Gay Meadow, and City's embarrassing FA Cup defeat in 1979, when I'd been told that if the ball went over the stand roof, there were ball boys waiting in a boat on the nearby river Severn ready to fish the ball out of the water. That would have been a risky job in the Faroes.

Having seen the two stadiums, I then had the pleasure of meeting Rolant Hojsted, EB Streymur's larger than life Chairman, who greeted me with, "What an amazing draw it was. Someone asked me, before I went to Geneva for the draw, who we wanted and I said Manchester City. It was our lucky time this time. I was never off the phone to fans after that! It's the biggest game in Faroese football. Yes, we've had France and Germany here playing Internationals, but never a club side as big as City."

After another spectacular forty five minute drive, back through our awesome surroundings, we were in Torshavn again, at the Torsvollur stadium which would stage the game. I collected my press pass and was led to my commentary position, which was in a bedroom! I was told the room, overlooking the pitch, which was to be my vantage point, was one of many used as a dormitory for young players on training camps there. At least I'd be able to have a lie down after the game, and I'd be dry, as the rest of the stadium was open to the elements.

By now I was missing the Manchester rain, at least it stops occasionally! There had been almost continuous rain falling since my arrival. I was told Thursday, matchday, would be dry, which seemed hard to believe.

As promised I returned to the tourist information office for more advice from the ever cheerful Ingigero, and to interview Solfrid live on BBC Radio Manchester. Ingigero then told me that a Faroese cultural evening I'd hoped to attend that evening, which promised local poetry, dancing and cuisine, had been rearranged for Thursday, which ruled me out, so she booked me in at the fish buffet where I was promised a chance to sample the specialities of the islands.

As well as all the usual offerings like sole, cod, plaice and salmon, there was whale meat - and blubber. The meat was black and chewy - but with a slice of blubber to smooth its passage down my throat, it was tolerable.

Not a delicacy I will be trying again though, especially when chef Niels told me, "It's got quicksilver [mercury] in it so you can't eat too much. Quicksilver pollutes your body and doesn't go out again." Another reason to leave whale meat to the Faroese!

I spent the late evening updating my blog on the BBC website, sat in my room at the hostel, with no need for artificial light, as the sun was still shining, or at least occasionally breaking through the blanket cloud cover, as late as 11.30pm.

Wednesday 16th July

I didn't spend enough time in the hostel to get to know many of my fellow guests, but there didn't appear to be any football fans in the breakfast room but it was full to bursting with young families in hiking boots.

I'd awoken early, to start my day with an appearance on the breakfast show, back home, from my room in the Skansen Hostel, thanks to a laptop and wireless connection. I then took the bus to Vestmanna where I boarded a sightseeing boat to the bird cliffs, to see the much heralded native bird, the puffin. I was told that eating puffin meat was seen as a treat in these parts, but I can't say that thought appealed to me.

Among my fellow passengers were a group of Danish policemen who had travelled over from Copenhagen for the game but had a bit of spare time to see some of the sights. Our boat journey took us along another spectacular fjord until we reached a stunning set of caves and entrances cut out of the rock by the surging sea water.

I felt close to nature. The skipper spoke some English and allowed a few of us to sit in his private area, watching him expertly steer the boat and enjoy the best views away from the freezing spray.

Once back in Torshavn, I met up with Jonathan Warner, a City fan who lived on the southern island of Sandoy with his Faroese wife and children. As well as explaining what it felt like to be a Blue in such an unlikely footballing outpost, he told me about his expeditions to hunt puffins for food.

"They are such friendly birds, they look great on the postcards, but actually, I have to say, they're even better in the stomach. I've been puffin catching with my brother-in-law. We had to climb down the cliffs holding onto a single rope, and you have to have a good head for heights."

After my non-footballing adventures and nearly two days in the Faroes, it finally started to feel like the football match I'd come to see might actually happen. The City team arrived for training at the Torsvollur stadium and their obligatory pre-match press conference. They'd flown directly from Manchester.

It was the first time I'd properly met the new manager Mark Hughes and he spoke about his knowledge of the Faroes from his previous visit with Wales: "It's one of those games where they've got nothing to lose and everything to gain. We don't want to be back page news, we need to be fully professional, as I expect us to be."

Since I was the only member of the local media to make the trip, and there were hardly any other journalists interested in the press conference, I also spoke to Micah Richards, who told me his early thoughts on the new boss: "He's a bit more disciplined and has been good in the short time we've had him." Micah also reiterated his commitment to City, despite summer rumours he'd be off: "I wouldn't have signed a five and a half year deal, which shows there's only one place I want to be and that's at City."

All the time I'd been in the Faroes, and even before I'd set off, I was aware that a group of City fans were planning to travel to the game by road, ferry and a hired fishing trawler, to make the trip a bit more affordable. At one stage I'd even considered making the journey with them, but my fear of seasickness and worries about arriving too late to do my job properly and then taking too long on the trip home had made me decide against it.

I was in constant contact with them through the trip organiser, Leighton Gobbit, and a friend of mine, Dave, who was one of the passengers. On my outbound flight I'd told Magni all about the "trawler 12", as I called them, and he was fascinated by their adventure.

You can imagine how worried I was when Magni called me, while I was watching the City players train, to tell me that he'd heard they were stranded in Lerwick, in the Shetland Islands, due to bad weather.

It came as no surprise to me, though, that he'd helped organise a "rescue flight" to collect them and fly them to the islands. I hot-footed it to the hostel, where they were to stay, so I could be there to meet them. Eventually Dave and there rest of them staggered, travel weary, towards me. Dave and his mate Mike told me, "The weather was too rough for us to set out from Lerwick, so we spent the day praying that somehow things would sort themselves out. The next thing you know there's a free flight laid on for us, and here we are. It's typical City, we got here eventually!"

I could relate to their story more than most because, as a supporter, I'd gone to great lengths to make sure I didn't miss a game, once turning down the role of best man at my mate's wedding because City were playing – in the second division! I'd been a steward on the notorious "football specials" for many years, selling pies, sandwiches, drinks and snacks on behalf of the official supporters club, in the mail section of the rear carriage which we called "the cage".

Howard Yeats had run the City travel club for many years and I'd become involved after hitching a lift back, after a 1-1 draw at Wolves in March 1978. My Dad worked for British Rail and had been helping my away trips by getting me free tickets, due to his job, but I wasn't entitled to go on the special trains, as they were a private charter.

Howard and his two mates Charlie and John told me I could go back with them, as their train was due in before my scheduled service. I felt guilty that I had the wrong ticket to be on their train, so offered to "work my passage" by helping sell raffle tickets. Within weeks I'd been enrolled as a steward, a voluntary position, but with free transportation to away games. It sounded good to me as my entitlement to my Dad's tickets was soon to end, as I would no longer be a dependant.

For years I spent the away trips in "the cage" selling food and drink, even taking responsibility for a special of my own, when 13 trains were chartered for the 1981 FA Cup final and it's replay a few days later. I learnt a lot about the game during those years, spending many happy hours discussing football philosophy with Charlie Hadfield, who slowly became one of my best friends.

Thursday 17th July – Matchday 1
EB Streymur v Manchester City - UEFA Cup

After reading the morning's sports bulletins, via the laptop in my room at the hostel, on BBC Radio Manchester, I was picked up by a lady from the Faroes' tourist board by car, and rushed to the quayside in Torshavn where I boarded schooner Nordlysid, for a trip around the Island Nolsoy, which was to take three hours. I wasn't the only person invited, it seems that the Manchester City officials, corporate guests and press had all been offered the trip, so I decided another adventure was well worth the rush.

It seems the City people had either not got the message or had opted for the bus tour instead so I travelled in an elite party of four. My companions were three Danish students, Christian, Dorte and Mette. Christian, sadly, was a rugby fan.

Captain Enni couldn't have been a better host and first officer Henrik Hansen told me that, "this boat is built for the North Atlantic conditions, so you need have no fears. The boat is 63 feet long and can reach speeds of nine knots."

I even got to steer the schooner briefly. I'd like to say it was great to feel the wind blowing through my hair, but that would be poetic licence, as most of my hair has receded to nothing during my years watching City.

I saw hundreds of puffins diving into the sea, or in the case of the young ones, learning to fly, and it was a truly exhilarating experience. I'd never prepared for a football commentary like that before!

Once my sailing exploits had concluded I headed for the stadium, to check that everything was in position. I'd learnt to double check things as much as possible after being told I'd be broadcasting off the top of a bus in Lokeren, a few years earlier, during City's last European adventure.

On that occasion I'd arrived mid-afternoon to find that the bus was still en route, I was visualising Cliff Richard driving it through Belgium. It eventually arrived two hours before kick-off and it had been a race against time to get everything in place and working by kick-off time.

The Faroe Islands experience was starting to be following the same route, not the bus route, but the broadcasting nightmare route. It was 1pm, and despite my repeated attempts to connect my broadcast equipment to our Manchester studios, it wouldn't work.

Two and a half hours later, and with a rumbling stomach keeping me company, my new best friend Louis, a Faroese telephone engineer, got me connected. What a relief. If Louis had failed, the national TV and radio stations had offered help by bringing me some of their equipment. I'd like to think we'd have been as helpful in England if the problems had been the other way around.

I rushed back my accommodation to get the rest of what I needed, gulped down a burger in the "Torshavn Mall" and just made it back in time to start the on-air pre-match build-up. Just ahead of kickoff, Jonathan joined me in my bedroom commentary box to act as my summariser, and proved to be very good, especially as he'd never done anything like that before.

The match was something of an anticlimax after the week-long build-up, a straight forward 2-0 win thanks to goals from Martin Petrov and Dietmar Hamann, who later told me that he, "didn't notice the seagulls flying around the stadium until the crowd got excited by them, in the second half. My goal fell nicely for me and I hit it perfectly and fortunately it went in."

The match provided another first for me, a female referee - Nicole Petignat from Switzerland, who seemed a bit fussy but essentially no different from a male official.

Before the game, the "Trawler 12" were introduced to Mark Hughes and got T-shirts from Magni, who promised to visit England for the second leg. I knew that if there was to be any problem with his flight to Manchester, the boys would have sent a fishing boat to collect him.

I just had time for a quick snack, before packing up for the journey home, so I popped along to the burger bar near to the hostel. Can you imagine how shocked I was when an EB Streymur fan, stood ahead of me in the queue, welcomed me with… "You're Ian Cheeseman, I've been reading your blog."

My co-commentator Jonathan and his family, who by coincidence were flying to London on my early flight the next day, gave me a lift back to the airport a few hours later and my Faroes adventure was over.

Thursday 31st July – Matchday 2
Manchester City v EB Streymur – UEFA Cup

Between the first leg in the Faroes and the second leg in Barnsley, I'd spent a week with my family in Austria, but for one City fan the Faroes adventure had lasted much longer than mine. As the other eleven of the adventurous "trawler 12" prepared for their return journey, my mate Dave Scally complained of stomach cramps and was rushed to hospital.

He reluctantly waved his mates on their way, telling them he'd be OK and the next thing he knew he was waking up from an emergency operation to remove his appendix. It must be bad enough going through that experience when you're close to home, but I can only imagine how isolated Dave must have felt.

The only comparison I can draw was when I had a hernia repaired. I spent one night in hospital and a couple of uncomfortable weeks walking around like Quasimodo. Dave was visited by Sigfriour Clementsen, the manager of EB Streymur, who brought him a shirt signed by all the players. Once sufficiently recovered, he organised a sightseeing trip of the islands for Dave, on the same schooner I'd enjoyed with the Danish students.

Flying was still out of the question, so he had to stay another week on those remote North Atlantic islands before being picked up by the Streymur boss on his way to the airport for the trip to Manchester for the second leg. Dave arrived back on the Monday of the return leg, having listened to Clementsen's tactical talk during the flight, but not giving anything away about City's approach to the game – very loyal as you'd expect.

The EB Streymur players spent as long in Manchester as I did on their islands, taking the opportunity to do some sightseeing with Dave helping to organise a stadium tour at the City of Manchester Stadium, which was the nearest they would come to playing there, as the match had been moved to Barnsley's Oakwell Stadium, as the playing surface at Eastlands hadn't recovered from the Ricky Hatton fight and a Bon Jovi concert.

I'd been to see New Jersey's finest myself, so it would be hypocritical of me to criticise the necessary switch of venue. City's assistant groundsman Lee, had told me weeks earlier, when City had qualified for the UEFA Cup, that the first round match would have to be played elsewhere. Preston, Huddersfield and Everton had all been considered as alternatives, with Barnsley eventually being chosen. Oakwell was to be City's third home ground in just over five years.

I received a call from someone in the Barnsley press office, on the morning of the game, asking if I had a copy of "Boys in Blue" and the Supra version of "Blue Moon" so they could play it on their PA system before the game. I was happy to oblige and delivered the CD's to their PA box, behind the goal, when I arrived at the ground, a couple of hours before kickoff.

It was interesting to be back in that environment because I'd spent a couple of years being City's on-pitch PA man in the late 1990's until I became the City radio reporter in November 2001. It's a role I felt very proud to fulfil. I believe that a good PA announcer should be clear and concise and not feel like they're there to entertain. George Sephton at Liverpool is one of the best I've heard. Anyone who's been to Anfield will recognise his clear, tenor-like voice instantly.

My proudest day on the pitch was the derby on 18th November 2000. To wear the club suit meant a lot to me anyway, but to stand in the centre circle at Maine Road announcing the arrival of two teams made the hairs on the back on my neck stand on end – shame there aren't any on the top of my head to follow suit.

I'd discussed my match tactics, at around midday, with Chris Bird, City's Chief Operating Officer, and Dave Unsworth, who did all the technical stuff. We agreed my plan and waited for the teams to come out. I stood at pitch-side, looking up at Dave in the PA box as the teams entered the tunnel. As I raised my thumb, he played the entrance music, right here right now, and I announced, "Please welcome Man United and Manchester City", and the placed erupted.

Having shortened United's title deliberately, I proceeded to run through their team at a speed just too quick for their fans to cheer each name, simply listing the players without their appropriate squad numbers, Dave even faded me down slightly so it was harder to hear. Not that he needed to, the booing from the City fans made sure even I couldn't hear me, let alone the crowd. I'd finished long before the crowd realised, and then I launched into the City team, with squad numbers.

"In goal, number one NIICCKKY WEEAAVER!", and so on. What a feeling to be stood on the centre spot as the crowd roared their appreciation. The only other time I felt quite so exhilarated was when I introduced the "parade of legends" at City's last game at Maine Road.

Loaning my CD's to the Barnsley PA announcer hardly compared to those experiences but it was a nice feeling to be back in the box.

As I took my place in the press box for match commentary, I saw my pal Dave limping around the touchline, saying hello to the EB Streymur players and their manager. It must have been a very special match for him. There were a fair number of Faroese fans at the game, they sat in the stand just behind the press box. I felt a special bond with them too, having been treated so well by their countrymen, during my stay.

For that reason, I wasn't too disappointed with City's fairly ordinary performance. Streymur's aptly named Torgard, which translates to mean goalkeeper, kept plenty of early City shots at bay and it became more and more frustrating to watch.

Martin Petrov eventually broke the deadlock early in the second half but it took until the final minute to add respectability to the scoreline when Darius Vassell added a second. I'd have loved to see EB Streymur score a consolation goal, just so they could have enjoyed some reward for their determination over the two legs.

August

Saturday 2nd August – Match 3
Stockport County v Manchester City – Friendly

I've covered lots of games at Edgeley Park, during my years as a sports journalist, and also attended, from time to time, as a paying spectator, when County played regularly on Friday nights. I worked alongside a big County fan called Tom Gibson when I was at the Co-operative Bank. I'd spent the last 18 months of my time as a bank clerk delivering post all over the north west, including the Stockport branch, so I always feel at home in the area.

This game offered an opportunity to see how some of City's Youth Cup winning team would compare alongside first teamers like Dietmar Hamann, Stephen Ireland, Rolando Bianchi and new signing Tal Ben Haim. Last time I'd seen County was their 1-0 playoff semi-final win against Wycombe in May.

Winger Vladimir Weiss, who'd starred as an under 18, impressed me and was full of inventiveness. I was also interested to see how good County's loan signing Stephen Gleeson would fit in, he'd just joined for six months from Wolves. He hit the post early in the game to leave me with a good first impression.

I'm not a big fan of friendlies and I've learnt not to make snap judgements on players in these games. I remember seeing new City striker Lee Bradbury score on his debut at Burnley and thinking he was a world beater and my first impression of Gelson Fernandez on a pre-season trip to Sweden was also good.

Tal Ben Haim seemed keen and sharp, and sounded full of enthusiasm, when I got the chance to interview him after the game. If words were anything to go by, Ben Haim seemed a sensible signing.

Not that the score mattered, but it was a 2-2 draw with Anthony Pilkington and Peter Thompson scoring for County and Valeri Bojinov and a late Ched Evans penalty earning the draw for City.

Tuesday 12th August – Match 4
Bury v Burnley – League Cup

Midweek football usually means I'm out reporting on a game and presenting and producing a three hour radio programme of match coverage. If I'm lucky, I'll get a day to prepare, which might involve going out to a couple of clubs, to record interviews with managers or players. Alternatively, I might spend my time pre-arranging interviews to be conducted live on the night.

There'll be a fair bit of editing too, and I try to make sure that our coverage of the games, and the way they're previewed, is even-handed. Sometimes that's easier said than done because there's only a limited amount of time and resource at my disposal. Fortunately we have a very knowledgeable, willing and flexible team of freelancers who're only too keen to contribute on the night.

I try to avoid long rambling chats and predictable content, so I'm always trying to plan ahead and seize every opportunity that comes along. Whenever I'm around football people, I try to make sure I have a recorder with me so that I can grab a few words, even if there's no immediate programme to broadcast it in. As long as the chat is interesting, it can be stored for future us.

I interviewed the sprinter Darren Campbell at an event publicising the AAA Athletics Trials at Sport City one summer. He's a man I've admired for years. If I ran a bath I'd come second, but his successes have been breathtaking. I chatted to him about the Manchester derby, which I saved until the game came around, months later. Imagine how difficult it would have been to arrange that interview nearer the time of the game, he might have been anywhere in the world.

One of the great pleasures of going to Bury is that the visiting scouts and managers tend to sit within view of my position on the back row of the press box, in the main stand. Just over the fence I usually spot Paul Futcher, father of Bury centre-half Ben Futcher.

Bury's ever-cheerful commercial manager Peter Young rarely fails to say hello. I used to enjoy bumping into former director Iain Mills, who you might remember left the club after complaints that he wore shorts. What a daft reason to let a passionate man like that leave.

I used to go to Gigg Lane with a neighbour of mine, when we live in Whitefield, back in the 1970's and saw some great games. Bury played Middlesbrough twice in the same season, losing in the League Cup but beating them 3-2 in an FA Cup replay in January 1976.

I stood on the terraces, opposite the main stand, and bumped into a few of my school mates. I knew that I'd get a bit of kudos the following day for being there. Several of my Bury heroes played, with John Forrest in goal, Keith Kennedy at left back, Brian Williams in midfield and Derek Spence and Andy Rowland in attack.

I'm pretty sure David Armstrong played for Middlesbrough. His baldness made him look old to me, even though he was probably in his mid 20's. These days I think of thinning hair as a sign of wisdom.

It was, like many of the other Bury games I attended at that time, a night match, which made it all the more special. Over 11,000 were packed in with the chanting usually initiated by the Cemetery End on my right, or the "semi end" as it was, and still is.

When Bury went 2-0 down within the first quarter of an hour, I expected another battling defeat, like the one in the league cup, but this was going to be a night I would never forget. Andy Rowland got one back and deep into extra-time, as I was wondering if my mum would shout at me for getting home so late, Jimmy McIlwraith scored the winner and the place erupted.

I've collected football programmes from every game I've been to, and of course that edition still sits proudly in my collection. Bury programmes always seemed bigger than the others and yet thinner, but still very special to me.

Back in the twenty first century, I usually leaf through the programme as I finalise my preparations for the evening's broadcasting, and once seven o'clock comes it's like a switch goes on in my head and suddenly I'm alive with adrenalin. Joanne, back in the Manchester studio, opens the fader to my microphone at Gigg Lane and we're up and running.

Bury lost the game 2-0, with Burnley's Martin Patterson scoring both goals and the former United player Chris Eagles impressing. One of our other games, Rochdale against Oldham, went all the way to penalties, so it was a late finish.

Thursday 14th August – Match 5
Manchester City v FC Midtjylland – UEFA Cup

This wasn't the most inspiring of games. It was played at a relatively slow tempo and there didn't seem to be much desire from the City players. The Danish side seemed better organised and it came as no great surprise to me when they took the lead through a shot from Danny Olsen.

In many ways this game reminded me of the visit of the Polish side Groclin, in 2003, when Mila's freekick had meant City had to win the away game, which they didn't. Just like that game, City seemed to have more quality, but the opposition seemed to want to win more. I must admit, I feared that home defeat might mean the end of City's UEFA Cup campaign, despite the bravado of everyone at City, who blamed a lack of competitive games for their lacklustre performance.

I just thought it was poor.

Saturday 16th August – Match 6
Rochdale v Barnet – League Two

Just behind the main stand, inside the ground, next to the turnstiles, is Spotland's tea/coffee and refreshments cabin. They do a fantastic pie and mushy peas for a very reasonable price. I'd sussed out the pies at Rochdale when I made my first visit there in 1975 to see a 3-0 win against Crewe.

I can't deny that I'm a "glass full" kinda guy, so the Rochdale manager Keith Hill and his number two David Flitcroft are my kind of people. I can understand why their players do so well, in fact probably better than they should do. If Hill and Flitcroft were my bosses I'd be more than keen to do my best for them, every week.

Most of the people I interview professionally, especially in the Premier League, have been trained to say as little as possible, so it's always a pleasure to pop up to Spotland and chat to the two of them both on the record, and off it. Jack, the kitman, is another of football's great characters. Always pottering around, often given the thankless tasks of fetching and carrying, going to the shop for sandwiches and, of course, having to sort out the smelly left-overs after training. He never complains.

It was a big disappointment, therefore, when Dale fell a goal behind in the opening couple of minutes. Hilly didn't last long in his position at the top of the stairs just behind the press box. He was down on the touchline barking out encouragement to his players and slowly but surely they started to turn it around.

Goals from Adam Rundle and Chris Dagnall put Dale ahead by the break. Impressive striker Jon Shaw, stylish and effective, completed the scoring and was a pleasure to interview after the game. He was as modest as they come. Overall the team had been well organised and full of character, just like their management team.

Sunday 17th August – Match 7
Aston Villa v Manchester City – Premier League

A day later than most of the other teams in the top flight, City got their league season off to a disappointing start at Villa Park, usually a happy hunting ground for the Blues.

I usually park my car in the playground of a local school. You might be surprised to learn that parking spaces are not handed out to the press very liberally in the Premier League, but Villa always oblige and are one of the few who send details through to our secretary Anne in advance. It's a short walk across the car park behind the North Stand, to the press entrance.

This is the ground where Micah Richards scored the last minute equaliser in the FA Cup, before swearing on live TV when talking to Garth Crooks. Normally I'd just laugh at an incident like that, but since I'd given Micah media training a few months earlier, I felt as though it was partly my fault. It wasn't of course, I never told him **!!** swear.

I remember doing some filming, outside Villa Park, during the summer of 1996 when the Holland supporters were there, during Euro 96 for a game against Switzerland. I'd been asked by North West Tonight, for BBC television, to compile a fan's view of the tournament, because I'd bought tickets for eleven games at venues all around the country, including the final.

The Dutch fans were certainly the most colourful I saw at the tournament and my mate Charlie, who'd I'd known since those days as a travel steward on the football specials, worked with a Dutch fan called Ruud, who we met up with outside the ground. Charlie played along with my filming, complaining to me as I held the camera, about the high price of the programmes, which seemed a bit of a rip-off.

By the time Euro 96 came to an end, with the Germans beating the Czech Republic at Wembley, thanks to a golden goal from Oliver Bierhof, Charlie had become a bit of a star. We'd played football at the museum which had been built at Elland Road, and for the grand climax he dug out his 1966 World Cup Final programme and ticket for comparison with the 1996 prices.

Charlie is still one of my regular travelling companions to away games and he was there with us at Villa Park for City's opening game of the new season. He buys a seat in the away end and consequently has a long wait after games while I do post match interviews.

It gives him a chance to study people, something I enjoy too. He usually has a wry observation to share with us on the return journey. His analysis of the game, often from a seat behind the goal, is free from media influence, and is always spot on, I rarely disagree with him; he is my football soulmate.

The press box at Villa Park has always been one of the best, with a big area to spread out my equipment and bags with good access in and out of the seats. To my surprise, for this game, things had been moved around a bit. This was another example of the prime seats being given over to the high paying corporate customers. Don't get me wrong, the facilities are still good, but a bit more squashed in than they'd been in the years before.

The real drama of the day came before the game even started. Valeri Bojinov suddenly pulled up during the warm up and it was immediately apparent that he was in serious trouble. He'd looked impressive during the preseason friendlies, making it even more heartbreaking as he was helped down the tunnel with a ruptured achilles.

I feared this might mirror the drama of Paul Lake's premature comeback at Middlesbrough's Ayresome Park in August 1992, which proved to be his last game. From the moment I saw Paul go down that day, I knew that was it for him, I hoped it wouldn't be the same for Bojinov.

Brad Friedel was making his Villa debut in goal, he'd been close to signing for City just a few weeks earlier, but apparently chose the midlands club because of their financial stability. Ched Evans replaced the unlucky Bojinov in attack and Gareth Barry, who'd took some persuading to stay at Villa, after suggestions he might go to Liverpool, was in Villa's midfield.

Just like City, Martin O'Neill's team had already played in the UEFA Cup, so both sides started brightly but it was Villa who maintained the pace and ran out 4-2 winners in a highly entertaining game. Gabriel Agbonlahor made a name for himself, with an eight minute hat-trick.

Saturday 23rd August – Match 8
Oldham Athletic v Cheltenham Town – League One

I moved to Oldham, from Radcliffe, when I got married in 1984. My relationship with Irene, was all very traditional, we didn't live together before the big day and I carried her over the threshold. We chose to live in Chadderton because my dad had a car and her mum and dad didn't, so it was easier for everyone if we were nearer to her parents.

The location appealed to me because it had good transport links to Manchester and the motorway system and being quite close to Boundary Park was nice too, because it would be easy to walk over for games, when City weren't playing. Back then I was working at the Co-op Bank in Manchester, and it was soon after I moved to Oldham that I joined the hospital radio station, Radio Cavell. It was well known in the area and had a really good reputation.

I didn't think I'd be particularly good as a DJ, but had dreamt of being involved at a radio station since I'd been a little boy. My professional inspiration was Fred Eyre, who was doing a regular sports spot with Dave Ward on Piccadilly Radio. Fred was well informed and witty and I hoped I could be a little bit like that.

I remember the first time I met Fred, it was at the Granada TV studios where I'd been asked by Howard Yeats, from the City supporters club, to attend the recording of a lunchtime TV programme, on which Fred was to be a guest to promote his new book "Kicked into Touch". He seemed a genuine guy and I was impressed with his attitude to everyone.

Perhaps a little naively, I went along to Radio Cavell and hoped to be able to replicate Fred's spot during their more limited broadcasts, within the hospital. Quickly I realised that I wasn't Fred and nor should I try to be. I must learn to walk before I could run, or maybe just jog.

I started by helping to gather requests from patients and their visitors on weekday evenings. It was great experience for me because I was quite shy and it forced me to interact with people, often in difficult circumstances. Many of those lying in their beds didn't really want to talk to a 24-year-old kid who was wandering up the ward towards them. It forced me develop a "larger-than-life" personality.

I was determined to remain sincere, I'm not a big fan of broadcasters who put on an act when they are in the public eye, so it was more a case of extending the personality I already had. Within a couple of months, I'd made a rather hurried debut as a presenter – someone hadn't turned up – and gone from doing it "by numbers" to a bit more of a rounded personality.

Although I enjoyed contributing to the request programmes, I wanted to challenge myself by trying different things and so when the chance came to take over the Sunday morning show, I grasped it with both hands.

I inherited a programme called "Pyjama Party", which had a format that was flexible. I selected my own music and could add in whatever content, within reason, that I felt was appropriate. I changed the title to "All Kinds of Everything", which gave me the scope to try just about anything and paid tribute to the Irish singer Dana, who won the Eurovision Song Contest with a song of that title in 1970.

A few years later I met her and asked her to record an introduction to my show which I played every week for several years. Dana is one of the more genuine celebrities I've ever met. I like that trait in people.

During the ten years that I presented that show on Radio Cavell, I slowly developed the contents from a very basic music show to a speech format, with music here and there.

I was constantly trying to think of new things to include and did everything from sport and politics, travel features, celebrity guests and comedy. In 1989 I ran the London Marathon, in a respectable (for me) time of 3 hours 24 minutes, while carrying a small recorder and interviewing runners around me. I later edited this into a 90 minute show. My friend Dave, who had a pilot's licence for light aircraft, flew me over Oldham, while I recorded another.

My studio guests included the three prospective candidates for the Oldham seat at the general election, a guy who told me he'd been visited by UFO's and an astrologer. The Oldham actress Sally Ann Matthews, who played Jenny Bradley in Coronation Street, was a lovely guest, as was the Oldham manager Joe Royle, who I remember picked "Live to Tell" by Madonna as a favourite record, but the best of all was the morning after City's promotion at Bradford, Sunday 14th May 1989, when David White and Andy Hinchcliffe joined me at 9am for two hours.

Can you imagine two Premier League footballers agreeing to do that and then turning up, on time, these days? Even if the players agreed, the PR people would probably not allow it anyway. Clive Allen also made the effort to come over to Oldham one Sunday morning. Genuine people do that sort of thing.

My first visit to Wembley (as a commentator) was scheduled for Sunday 29th April 1990. It was the League Cup final between Oldham Athletic and Nottingham Forest. Irene was heavily pregnant after a miscalculation on my part had left her expecting our first child during the football season!

I'd worked out that full term is nine months, but it turns out it's just eight and a half months from conception to birth. I didn't know that, or we would have left it another four weeks before trying! My second son, Daniel was born during the month of June, I didn't make that mistake twice.

I didn't want to miss a game, so I became more and more anxious each time a match approached, particularly as I set out for Norwich, just a week before the due date. Fortunately, the trip to Carrow Road came and went without incident, and before long I was anxiously counting down to Everton at home. Once that one had been played I was convinced Irene would have the baby before the next game, when she'd be a week overdue and City played Derby County.

As Saturday 28th dawned I feared the contractions would start at any moment. I wanted to be at the birth, supporting her, but I didn't want to miss a match. Eventually I set out for Maine Road and the game was played out as a 1-0 defeat to the Rams and I was back home beside her as quickly as possible after the final whistle. Only one more City game to go now, Crystal Palace a week later, surely the baby would be home in our new cot by then?

Later that evening, as I planned my trip to Wembley with Oldham, the first contractions started and I accepted that I wouldn't be going to the Littlewoods Cup Final, but at least I hadn't missed a City game. We went to the hospital at about 3am and were told it would be lunchtime before the baby was born.

Irene gave birth at about 9am, two hours after we'd listened to the Latics fans gathering on Sheepfoot Lane, just outside our hospital window, next to Boundary Park, followed by the silence after they'd all gone.

We took pictures, I made the phone calls to the family and we shed a few tears before she said to me, "If you set off now, could you still get there?" I felt guilty to even consider the possibility of leaving her, but she insisted I should, as long as her mum and dad were with her, and they'd just arrived.

I was off like a flash, there was no traffic on the M6 and M1 because everyone else was well ahead of me. I arrived at Wembley at 2pm, shared the commentary with fellow Radio Cavell volunteer Kent Wells, and arrived back at about 11pm that night. Irene had listened to my commentary via the hospital radio headsets next to her bed. What a day, I was father to my first son Steven, I'd been at the birth and commentated on Oldham Athletic at Wembley, all on the same day.

Now he's a grown man, Steven is not really interested in football, but as a youngster he was a Junior Blue and had acting parts in the annual City pantomime such as Aladdin, Friar Tuck and he was a dwarf in Snow White. It must have ignited a passion within him for acting because he has gone on to many more successes since then, has been studying performing arts at University and may well become a professional actor.

I remember him telling me he'd got a part as a man who'd been happily married for 25 years, and I said, "Don't worry son, I'm sure you'll get a speaking part next time!"

Whenever I'm at Boundary Park, I always say hello to the volunteers who, to this day, still commentate on Oldham's home matches for the patients in the neighbouring hospital. I'll never forget my roots.

This visit of Cheltenham was my first game of the new season at Boundary Park, so after a few words with Tom Hill and Kent Wells, who sit to my right in the press box, I plugged in my equipment and waited for kick-off, only interrupted by Roy Butterworth, Oldham's matchday press officer, to sign the attendance book and share some banter and laughs with.

The game was sheer perfection. A 4-0 home win, including a hattrick by Lee Hughes. The side had a lovely balance to it. The experienced Sean Gregan captained from central defence, Andy Liddell and Chris Taylor played wide and Hughes was up front alongside rising star Lewis Alessandra. The victory took Latics into top spot in League One.

Sunday 24th August – Match 9
Manchester City v West Ham United – Premier League

My early broadcasting experiences at Radio Cavell had led to my next break, into the media world, when City embraced the new media called video, by filming their home games. They decided they needed a commentator, but couldn't afford to pay – well decided they didn't want to pay, was probably more accurate.

It was down to a straight choice between me and Vince Miller, a singer who'd spent years acting as MC in the City social club, during it's glory years under the management of former player Roy Clarke. By now, Vince was the on-pitch announcer at Maine Road, and so they gave the chance to me. Although it seemed irresistible, I had concerns about suffering from vertigo on the TV gantry, perched precariously over the directors' box on a vantage point only accessible via a narrow wooden gangplank with flimsy looking handrails.

I was also a little concerned that I'd no longer be able to sit with my dad among the normal supporters. I decided that I couldn't let this chance pass me by, so a week later I was preparing like a professional rather than just making sure I hadn't forgotten my scarf and flask of tea.

I'm sure I was terrible during those early games, but slowly I improved. One week, I asked City's commercial man, Geoff Durbin, who'd given me the "job" in the first place, if I could have an ex-player sat with me to act as my summariser/expert. He felt it was a bit radical at the time, because it wasn't even the norm on TV or radio, but I persuaded him, "as long as there was no cost implication", and during the coming months I had a variety of ex-players fulfilling the role, including Mike Summerbee, Glyn Pardoe, Mike Doyle and the one and only Fred Eyre.

Fred did loads of games with me, before David Pleat, then manager at Luton, got a copy of our video, and took exception to Fred saying that one of their defenders was a carthorse, which he was! Pleat's complaints meant City had to appease him by asking Fred to step down.

My most dramatic day up on the gantry, was alongside Buzzer (Mike Summerbee) when Paul Lake swallowed his tongue in a collision on the pitch, I think it was against Aston Villa. We both feared the worst when his body went into spasm for 4 to 5 minutes as the medics tried to save his life. It was such a relief when Lakey eventually recovered. I later lent my copy of that video to Lakey – and have never seen it since!

On the day City beat Huddersfield 10-1 I was sat among the supporters watching, because Granada were filming the game for TV coverage and I wasn't needed. Due to public demand, City wanted to sell copies of the match, but Granada wouldn't allow their commentary on the commercial release, so I was asked to dub on a commentary in a studio, in Sheffield, a few days later.

I bumped into John Motson, a day or two before the recording, and he advised me to ask the studio to play the crowd noise into my headphones very loudly, so I would feel like being there again and would therefore commentate naturally. Good advice, except that when I received my copy of the final version I'd under-reacted to each goal, because I expected the crowd noise to be loud on the recording too.

I never liked my commentary on that video and haven't listened to it since.

The matchday programme for this 2008 visit of West Ham, the first home league game of the new season, included a welcome from the chairman, Thaksin Shinawatra, and an expression of his pride at bringing in a new manager, Mark Hughes, a new executive chairman, Garry Cook, and record signing Jo, who was at the Olympics with Brazil.

Despite the disappointment of the home defeat against Midtjylland, the stadium was buzzing with optimism. Everyone I bumped into was raring to go, and as usual I was looking forward to commentating from the best seat in the ground – mine in the press box!

Vincent Kompany made an impressive debut, in a much changed team from the one that lost at Aston Villa, with Micah Richards wearing the captain's armband in the absence of the suspended Richard Dunne.

Elano was the star of the show, a 3-0 win, bagging two goals and also being involved in one scored by Daniel Sturridge.

Tuesday 26th August – Match 10
Wigan Athletic v Notts County – League Cup

Having been at the JJB Stadium, a year earlier, to see a weakened team go out of the League Cup to Hull City, I was hoping for something better from the Latics this time, and they duly obliged. Henri Camera was the star of the show, scoring twice and buzzing around throughout the game.

It was a first chance, for me, to see Amr Zaki, who came on at half-time and scored within fifteen minutes. The press box at Wigan is, just like most others, just above the players' tunnel, on the half-way line, but Radio Manchester's facilities are high up on the TV gantry, which is nothing like the one I'd frequented during my learning days at City.

My position at Wigan is accessed by climbing step after step after step - they seem to go on forever. I usually have three bags with me when I'm working. The first contains the ISDN mixing box, which controls microphones, headphones and the connection back to the studios, the second has all my paperwork and recording equipment and the third has backup items, plus the second pair of headphones and microphone, for use by my summariser.

I don't mind carrying them, even though I have to lurch along with them from many far-flung car parks and side streets, but I always dread carrying them up to the press box at Wigan. There's a young steward, who nearly always challenges me for ID as I reach the door to the last flight of stairs to the gantry. I then have to, as I'm trying to open the door, and juggle three bags, show him my match day pass at the same time. I often feel like I'm taking part in some sort of game show as I balance on one foot, holding all three bags in one hand, while searching out my pass with the other.

Still, at least the pies are good in Wigan, and there's a record breaking selection of multi-coloured foil trays to select from at half-time, if I've got the stamina to go there and back during the break. I'm not a fan of cheese and onion pies, despite my name, I'd rather have a steak and kidney, but I usually end up with the former in my haste to grab something quickly before mountaineering back into position for the start of the second half. I must remember to take some grappling hooks next time.

On this day, it was worth all the trouble because the Latics won impressively 4-0. Carlo Nash was in goal and hardly had a shot to save.

Thursday 28th August – Match 11
FC Midtjylland v Manchester City – UEFA Cup

My journey to Herning, the small rural town where FC Midtjylland are based, started with a flight from Manchester to Copenhagen, in the company of the City reporter for the Manchester Evening News, Chris Bailey. There were similarities to the last European trip we'd made together, a year earlier. We'd gone to Sweden to meet the new manager Sven Goran Eriksson and had travelled backwards and forwards to Varberg, from Gothenburg, by train.

Scandinavian trains are clean and modern, and like most trains in mainland Europe, run to time. In Sweden they have the added bonus of having the prettiest ticket collectors I've ever seen.

It was a four hour journey, with one change of train and Chris and I sat through the bulk of the journey in a four seat arrangement, with a table, opposite two young women who'd just returned from a trip to South Africa.

Their excited recollections of their travelling experiences, in perfect English, helped pass the time until we reached the highlight of the trip. It was the highlight for me. Chris and our travelling companions simply yawned as we headed out over the Great Belt Bridge.

It joins the islands of Zealand and Fyn and has the third largest main span in the world. I love bridges. The only disappointment was that I never got to see it because we were on it!

Our hotel was quiet, and far from full, with the proprietors explaining they'd refused to allow football fans to book with them, because of problems they'd had with ice-hockey fans in the past. We were located at the less busy end of the main Herning shopping street.

As I was woken up at 7am the next morning, I realised that the hotel was not quite as quiet as it seemed. Two men were digging up the road, next to my bedroom window, with a pneumatic drill. Both of them looked over the age of 70, in contrast to most of the other natives, whose average age seemed more like 18. It felt like a set from "Village of the Damned", being inhabited only by teenagers.

It seems that Herning has one of the biggest student populations in Denmark; you see there's always a reason. The two elderly diggers had the keenness of youth. I'd wished they were longer in bed, like basketball players!

Earlier than normal, I went jogging, heading out into the countryside, in the approximate direction of the stadium. I got lost, but pleasantly lost, and eventually retraced my route back to the hotel before heading to the stadium by bus for the pre-match press conference.

Since there were suggestions that some of the Danish hooligans might turn up to bait the City fans, Chris and I spent match day observing the arrival of the day trippers, in case of trouble. Fortunately everything seemed well ordered and we chatted to some of the fans before heading back out to the stadium for the game.

During the afternoon, the news came through that Shaun Wright-Phillips had re-signed for City from Chelsea, prompting lots of chanting from the City fans, and giving me a chance to interview the club's new head of communications Vicky Kloss - her radio debut - in the build-up to kick-off. She was a bit nervous, but did very well. Vicky had succeeded Paul Tyrrell. She had been at City for years, since switching careers. She'd previously been a policewoman in London; not someone to mess with, but a lovely, genuine person, nonetheless.

I'd feared that the home defeat to the Danish side might mean City would go out of the UEFA Cup, so I wasn't as optimistic as usual. As I described the action with Fred Eyre adding his comments from the studio back in Manchester, my fears of City failing increased.

Then, with just seconds to go, Michael Ball crossed deep, from a position just below my commentary position, and Ched Evans, threw himself into a challenge with the Midtjylland defender Danny Califf, who steered the ball past his own keeper for the equaliser. Extra-time was dominated by City, but the night belonged to Joe Hart, who saved twice in the decisive penalty shoot-out to send City through 4-2.

The flight home wasn't until the evening, so I had a couple of hours to explore Herning. Chris didn't join me, as is usual for him, he hardly left his bedroom, constantly writing stories on his laptop, or at least that's what he tells me.

The big tourist attraction in Herning is the Elia sculpture. Every now and again huge flames shoot out of the top. Getting there and back in the time I had, would have been nearly impossible, but the kindness of the head of tourism for the town solved the problem. He took me there and back in his car.

He told me he'd only seen the spectacular flame once, during his years in the town, and that had only been when he asked what time it was due to perform. It's supposed to burst into flame randomly. Being a curious soul, I peered over the edge when I climbed it and was thankful it was in hibernation.

Our trip back to Copenhagen coincided with the timing of the draw for the next round, when City would be going to Cyprus.

Saturday 30th August – Match 12
Hull City v Wigan Athletic – Premier League

I love visiting new grounds, and had yet to see a game at the KC Stadium, so this was a trip I was really looking forward to. In years gone by, you could locate a stadium by looking out for floodlight pylons, but these days they look more like superstores from the outside.

It was, therefore, fairly predictable that I would come off the A63 too early, upon seeing the local shopping complex, which looked like a new stadium from a distance – honest.

Once I arrived at the correct concrete and steel venue, I dragged my baggage up to the top of the stand and watched Wigan demolish newly promoted Hull City with a masterclass of perfect football. Amr Zaki scored twice and looked like a world beater, but then again they all did.

The Wigan boss Steve Bruce was understandably bubbly afterwards while Phil Brown, wearing a goatee beard and moustache, in support of a charity, seemed to have the weight of the world on his shoulders. It proved to be just what Hull needed, they quickly bounced back and rode high in the table for quite a while after that, and for Wigan it just confirmed that the 4-0 win in midweek hadn't been a flash in the pan. I fancied Wigan might be in for a good season.

Sunday 31st August – Match 13
Sunderland v Manchester City – Premier League

The return of Shaun Wright-Phillips, this was his second debut, and his contribution was exhilarating. He scored twice in the second half and tormented Sunderland throughout. It was also the Premier League debut of Jo, now back from Beijing and Michael Johnson looked impressive throughout.

Trips to the north east always include a stop at the Little Chef on the A19, and this was no exception. The Olympic Breakfast is a must and sets up the day perfectly. There's not always time to eat at away games, because we start work as soon as we arrive. Fred has it particularly tough, as he settles into his seat from the moment the build-up to the match starts, usually two hours before kick-off, until the end of the post-match phone-in. He must have a strong bladder!

My day usually involves adding the finishing touches to my commentary notes, getting the team news, plus the gossip and stories doing the rounds from the other journalists and club staff. It is amazing how quickly the last couple of hours before the match pass by.

At the end of City's 3-0 win I watched defender Vedran Corluka walk over to the City fans. His body language suggested to me that he was waving goodbye, amid rumours that his collapsed move to Tottenham had been re-initiated and that he would move there the following day, transfer deadline day. The suggestions of his departure had been prompted by rumours of the club having financial problems. I didn't want to see him leave and felt it was a backward step by City.

Monday, the last day of the summer transfer window, wasn't a day, as a City fan, that I was particularly looking forward to.

September

Monday 1st September – Transfer deadline day

It was supposed to be my day off, so I was relaxing in the jacuzzi at my local gym when one of the staff came to me and told me I had to call the office as soon as possible. City had new owners.

There had been suggestions that the Abu Dhabi royal family might be getting close to buying the club from Thaksin Shinawatra, but I didn't think they'd be making the move, if indeed they ever made a move, for a few more weeks. Everyone was caught by surprise. The biggest development in Manchester City's history, and no-one knew about it!

Within an hour I was in the BBC and the story was developing by the minute. Not only were the new owners looking to complete the takeover in record time, but by 10.30am it was becoming clear that £30 million had been made available immediately, to spend in the remaining hours of the transfer window.

It was decided that there had to be a City phone-in to let the fans have their say on the incredible events that were unravelling, but there was little knowing then that the day was going to get more and more dramatic.

All sorts of names were being thrown around. According to rumour, bids had been made for Arsenal's Cesc Fabregas, Liverpool's Steven Gerrard and Fernando Torres, David Villa of Valencia and Mario Gomez from Stuttgart. While all this was gathering momentum, Mark Hughes was playing golf and looked as bewildered as anyone when he was interviewed on TV. The only player NOT linked with a move to City was Flora, but even that one was starting to spread like a knife through butter.

Suddenly the rumours that City could hijack Dimitar Berbatov's move from Spurs to Man United sent everyone into frenzy.

I managed to track down a telephone number for Dr Sulaiman Al-Fahim, the self-appointed spokesman for City's new owners. It was a bizarre conversation, with all sorts of names being banded about, including a suggestion that Cristiano Ronaldo was now a possible target for City too, and that money was no object.

As a journalist I was excited to be covering such a huge story and to be right at the cutting edge of developments – as a fan I was giddy and running on adrenalin. I really didn't know what to think or what to believe. By late afternoon Spurs confirmed they'd accepted City's bid for Berbatov and yet all the reports suggested he was at Old Trafford.

I decided to present the phone-in from the City centre, as it would give me a chance to approach non-football fans, who might not be aware of what was going on. Typically phone-ins attract only by a certain type of fan, the critical and vociferous, but this one would be different.

We took our radio car to Exchange Square, in the centre of Manchester, and parked right under the BBC big screen, next to the big wheel. My plan worked a treat, because as well as a flood of callers, I talked to passers by, who were flabbergasted by the news coming out of Manchester City.

Towards the end of the hour-long broadcast, as we approached seven o'clock, there was a new rumour, City had made a late bid for Robinho, who'd seemed certain to go to Chelsea and team up with his former Brazil manager Luiz Felipe Scolari – surely it was too late for City to hijack that deal?

As we went off air, I have to confess that my head was in a spin. For the rest of the evening I followed events by every means possible, not going to sleep until the ink had dried on the signing of Robinho for £32.5 million – a record British fee.

Some might argue it had been the most momentous day in the history of Manchester City. This wasn't just a big story in the city of my birth, I was born at St.Mary's Hospital, now a Sainsbury's opposite the Palace Theatre, but all over the world.

Tuesday 2nd September – Match 14
Oldham Athletic v Morecambe – Johnstone's Paint Trophy

This was the classic "after the lord mayor's parade" game – no offence meant to Oldham and Morecambe. It's hardly the most glamorous competition anyway, but coming the day after all the head-spinning activities of transfer deadline day, it felt a little surreal to be there.

City's signing of Robinho was the subject on everyone's lips with some expressing disgust and saying it was an "obscene" amount of money to pay, both for and to, a footballer, whilst others were still excited by the unexpected rollercoaster of a day that it had been.

It certainly reminded me of what football is supposed to be about, not that I really need reminding. Football is, well it was when I was growing up, the people's game. Most youngsters supported their home town team or the club their father's supported, with only the odd few latching onto the big clubs like Liverpool and United.

I can even remember a time when the majority of United fans were from the immediate area around the city. Whether it's right or wrong that the demographics of football support are changing, is up for debate, but the fact cannot be ignored. If City's new-found wealth brings success, I'm sure their support base will change too.

Oldham Athletic might not expect to play in the Champions League or even have realistic ambitions of winning anything but promotion, now and again, but they have their heart and soul firmly planted in the local community, and for that they're just as valuable as any of the so-called glamour clubs.

I love my trips to Boundary Park, and our other lower league football venues, every bit as much as to the Premier League games I'm lucky enough to see every week. Each of these stadiums is full of passionate, loyal supporters who plan their lives around the fixtures of their club.

There are many advantages to being a fan of one of the smaller clubs. You're more likely to meet you heroes and the club officials on a regular basis, you can get autographs when you want, and you can usually afford the better seats in the ground, if that's where you want to be.

There are many benefits to the journalist too. Although most clubs have press officers, even those in the lower leagues, the smaller clubs realise the value of publicity and are far less suspicious about the motives of the press. Generally, visits to Oldham, Rochdale, Stockport and the rest of our smaller local clubs, are a pleasure.

I admit that some of the protectionist measures Premier League "communications officers" use are based on keeping certain types of journalists at arms length – the sort that believe the story is often more important than the truth, or that being fair doesn't get their reader/listener/viewer as excited.

Sadly there's always another story to be had, a day later, even if it's just to reveal the first one had no truth to it - two for the price of one! Not everyone is like that though, but it seems that the policy of more and more press officers is to treat all the media with the same level of contempt. In some ways I don't blame them.

Once all the talk of Robinho made way for the game, even the most committed Latics fan would have found this match hard to get excited about. Danny Whittaker gave Oldham the lead early in the second half but an equalizer, soon after, meant the game had to be settled by a penalty shoot-out, which Morecambe won 5-4.

Saturday 6th September – Match 15
Rochdale v Wycombe Wanderers – League Two

This was one of the most emotional matches of my season. I'd never met Rochdale's sports scientist, Paul Conway, though I must have passed him in a corridor or sat at his desk, on the many occasions I've been up to Spotland to interview Keith Hill or David Flitcroft. He'd been struck down by a brain haemorrhage on the Monday leading up to the game, while most of the football world had been worrying about transfer deadline day. He passed away on Wednesday evening.

I was well aware that the club was going to be in mourning and that his wife and young sons would be at the game, but despite suffering bereavements myself, I was overwhelmed by the effect it had on everyone at the game that day.

I remember travelling to Nottingham on the day of 9/11, to watch Manchester City's League Cup tie at Notts County, having just watched the fall of the twin towers on TV. I felt empty and emotionless as the most surreal of days passed me by, like I wasn't really there. The other time I'd felt that way at a match was when a family friend, Marjorie, had gone with me to Maine Road for City against Leeds in April 1977, the day after my mum had died.

All the Rochdale staff, and of course Paul Conway's family, must have been living through the same feelings of inner numbness, and despite being a so-called hardened journalist, I felt their pain.

The match felt "wrong" from beginning to end and yet I think it had been the right decision to play. Rochdale lost 1-0. I spoke to Keith Hill after the game and without ever using it as an excuse, he paid his tribute to his lost colleague in the most eloquent way he could.

Saturday 13th September – Match 16
Manchester City v Chelsea – Premier League

A day of debuts, but the player everyone wanted to see was Robinho. Since the first World Cup I'd been fully aware of, the 1970 finals in Mexico, I've idolised the Brazilians. As far as I'm concerned their team from that tournament, which included Jairzinho, Rivelino, Carlos Alberto and Pele, is the greatest team of all-time. It was poetry in motion.

It was a winning team too, but that's never been the most important thing in football as far as I'm concerned though I'm sure that's not a sentiment shared by all. The modern game seems to have developed a mentality of winning at all costs, and I'm sure most coaches and managers would say the perfect performance is a 1-0 win, with no shots against and just the one killer shot going in at the other end.

We all want to see our team win, but I'm realistic enough to know that only one team, in each country or competition, is successful each season, every other team fails by differing degrees, but they all fail. There must be more to it, therefore, than just winning. I want to see something that excites me, whether that is great dribbling, wonderful goals, slick passing or just the joyful exuberance of attacking creative play.

Simply put, I want to watch football with a smile, and that's what the 1970 Brazilians brought to the game, and indeed their 1982 compatriots Zico, Socrates, Falcao and Eder. They didn't win, they were beaten by the cynical Italians, thanks to a hattrick from Paulo Rossi, just back from a two year ban for being involved in match fixing, something he'd always denied.

My childhood dream had been to see a great Brazilian footballer or footballers pulling on the blue shirt of Manchester City. There was already Elano and Jo, of course, and City had apparently tried to sign Ronaldinho in the summer, but here was one of the very best, making his debut, Robinho. The danger was that too much expectation would be put on his shoulders, firstly because of the price tag and also because of his nationality, because I'm not the only person who sees the Brazilians as the true masters of the beautiful game.

There will always be supporters and coaches who believe that flamboyance is unproductive, and that "closing down" and "working back" is more important than nut-megging an opponent or doing a step over now and again, but I'm not one of them. Showboating is the derogatory term used and of course I realise that the tricks employed by the creative players mustn't be overdone, but for the most part it's those drag-backs and flicks that leave me excited and glad that I went to the game.

I'd been watching Barcelona, on TV, for the previous four or five years and was rarely disappointed by what I saw. The rise to prominence of Lionel Messi has been a joy, as was my weekly fix of Andres Iniesta, Xavi, Samuel Eto'o and Ronaldinho. The critics judged them by the number of trophies they'd won and not by the entertainment they provided. I'd be happy to watch a Barcelona team like that every week, even if City's trophy room remained empty, as it had been since a thief was seen running away from the City of Manchester Stadium with the entire contents under his arm; a roll of sky blue carpet.

So, out he came from the tunnel, down below my commentary position, the great, if unpredictable and sometimes inconsistent talent of Robinho. I didn't care, he was playing for Manchester City.

I had already decided that if Robson De Souza scored, I'd pay my own tribute by celebrating with an elongated description, in the classic Brazilian style. Sure enough, my chance came early on, as Jo was hauled down on the edge of the Chelsea box for a free-kick. As Robinho curled it home I yelled out, "goal for Robiiiinnnnhhhhoooooooooo....".

It wasn't to be City's day though, Chelsea came back to win 3-1, perhaps thanks to the inspiration of their own Brazilian, Luiz Felipe Scolari, the manager who'd guided his country to victory in the 2002 World Cup. It was a highly entertaining game, with Nicolas Anelka, who I'd always enjoyed watching at City, scoring their third and John Terry being sent off for pulling back Jo.

It was still a great day as far as I was concerned, I'd just seen Robinho play for Manchester City!

Tuesday 16th September – Match 17
APOEL Nicosia v Schalke 04 – UEFA Cup

It was to be a long journey to Cyprus, especially as the cheapest route I found was via Prague, which involved a stopover of nearly three hours. What could I do in an airport, for so long, when I couldn't leave? Now I knew how Viktor Novorski - the character Tom Hanks played in "The Terminal" felt. There's only so long observing the drunken antics of returning stag-dos and hen parties can keep your interest - and where's Catherine Zeta-Jones when you need her?

I left home, in Oldham, at 2pm and eventually arrived in Cyprus at 3am local time. My weariness from the journey was not helped by an air temperature of 26c, even at that hour, and my first task was to find my hire car - and then the hotel. On the positive side, the Cypriots drive on the left and my car was a small fiesta, so no problems there.

Once I left the airport I drove through the deserted streets of Larnaca for twenty minutes or so, looking for the signs and street names I'd memorised from my map. The road signs were in Greek and English, but they might as well have been in Swahili because I ended up back at the airport forty five minutes later.

It took me two hours from the moment I set off in my car until I was finally parking in the hotel car park. There were times, during that middle-of-the-night journey that I could feel the onset of panic as I fretted and nearly gave up, in equal measures. Never has getting into a bed felt so sweet. Maybe that's pushing things beyond credibility. Never has getting into bed felt so sweet, when Irene's not been waiting for me!

I awoke, after my brief sleep, drew back the thin curtains to reveal clear blue skies and I could now feel 34 degrees of humid heat. After a very enjoyable breakfast, personally served up by an enthusiastic waiter from India called Matthew, I decided to get my bearings, so I strolled along the beach. My hotel was cheap because of its remote location, but was perfectly acceptable.

People were few and far between, but I met a lovely retired couple from Reading called John and Maureen. Their daughter had introduced them to Cyprus 20 years ago, as she was based there with the British Army. They'd been here every year since.

They told me that they usually visited Cyprus in mid-September and revealed that the temperatures I was enjoying were hotter than usual. They looked after my belongings while I took a dip in the Aegean. When it comes to swimming in the sea or a swimming pool, I'm the biggest wimp around and it's usually 10 minutes of ssss - aaaah - ooooh before eventually I'm in! There, I glided in without problem - the water was lovely and warm.

Further along the beach I met Andreas - a retired Greek man, who lived in a house right next to the sea. I watched him setting fishing traps. He had a couple of, what looked like, washing up bowls, which had a cloth with a small hole in the middle, stretched over them.

He then rubbed flour on the inside rim of the opening, before taking it a few yards into the sea and standing the bowl on its edge. Ten minutes later, after a few puffs on his pipe, he collected it with two or three fish in. He told me they were called 'head fish' in English and tasted delicious – I took his word for that.

By the time I'd stretched out by the hotel pool for forty winks, it was late afternoon and I had plans to watch my second favourite team, the German side Schalke 04. By a very pleasant co-incidence, they were also in Cyprus and would play, that evening, in the same stadium that City would be going to.

As I considered the journey ahead of me, six scuba divers suddenly invaded my tranquillity. They were preparing for a "real" dive, and were under instruction. I wondered if my fellow sun worshippers were as surprised, by their sudden appearance, as I was.

Graham, from Stroud told me, "It's quite normal around here. There's a dive centre next door and they have them all over the island." It turned out that 50 year-old Graham was a regular under the waves, "Along with my friends, we were down at the wreck of the Zenobia this morning, and on other days we've been looking at the wildlife and underwater plants - it's fascinating".

The Zenobia was a roll-on roll-off ferry, carrying lorries and passengers, which was allowed to sink, after springing a leak, half a mile outside Larnaca harbour, back in 1980, once all the passengers had been safely taken off.

I took one more dip in the refreshing pool, though I had to hold my breath when I went under water, before asking my ever-helpful waiter friend Matthew how to get to Nicosia. "Just turn right at the lights, and then straight down the highway - you can't go wrong!" Don't you just hate those words, 'you can't go wrong'.

An hour later I was desperately ringing the rental company and stopping the rare passer-by, which included an 80-year-old woman buying melons from a roadside stall, to ask, "How do I get to Nicosia?" I had only seen the occasional sign for the Cypriot capital.

Another hour later, a fast food seller, just packing up for the day, told me, "Just follow the signs for Levkosia - it's the Greek name for Nicosia." Why did no one tell me that earlier? It was easier after that and took me just 30 minutes from Larnaca to the stadium; I just made the kick-off.

I was impressed by the ground. It was a comfortable win for the 'Royal Blues' and afterwards I met Schalke's German International Kevin Kuranyi, who hadn't played because of injury. He told me he didn't think City would have too many problems emulating their 4-1 victory, as long as they quietened the crowd down early on.

At least I had no problems getting back to Larnaca after the game and I knew the way for next time!

Wednesday 17th September

I awoke to find a City flag hanging from one of the balconies, overlooking the hotel pool. It belonged to three of the nicest lads I've ever met (who says all football fans are hooligans?). After chatting to Duncan, Adam and Nick for a while, and cooling down in the pool, I headed back to the stadium to meet up with the City squad who arrived during the afternoon for their training session and press conference.

The first person I stumbled across was a City fan called "Kippax", who I seem to bump into at every game, including Youth Cup ties. He was as cheerful as ever and told me the groundsman had allowed him a good look around behind the scenes.

Mark Hughes was in relaxed mood and seemed unconcerned by the dry pitch and heat. "We respect them and know that Cypriot football is on a high at the moment", he told me. There had been speculation that Robinho would be rested. When I asked if he would play, Hughes replied with a wry grin, "That's what we signed him for!"

Former City and Wigan player Peter Beagrie was one of those watching the training session, so I took the opportunity to talk to him about the upcoming game and about his memories of playing under Brian Horton at City and briefly under Steve Bruce at Wigan, during Bruce's first stint at the JJB Stadium. Peter's always worth listening to - good company and a great entertainer in his playing days.

I'd always enjoyed watching City when Brian Horton had been manager. He used two wingers, Beagrie and Nicky Summerbee and had added flair and passion with Paul Walsh and Uwe Rösler.

With all the football stuff done, I decided I'd drive down to that well-known town for ravers, Ayia Napa, to see what all the fuss was about. It was about half an hour away from my hotel by car. The Moulin Rouge strip club, near one of those slingshot fairground-type experiences, was the first thing I saw, along with a huge nightclub. I parked, down by the harbour and went for a wander. It was a lot busier than I'd seen elsewhere. I was told that the number of tourists in Cyprus generally had dropped since they converted to the Euro, because of price increases.

All the usual tacky souvenir shops were there. I bought my son a small vase with Cyprus on it. The centre of the town surrounded a beautiful church, with plenty of choices for food, and by now I was starving. I walked past the glass bottomed boats and a yellow submarine, as I studied the menus pinned up outside the pubs and restaurants.

I strolled into the 'Zorba the Greek' and ordered the mixed kebab - well you have to don't you? It was wonderful, the best I've ever had. I sent my compliments back to the chef, Fanos, who rushed out to thank me. With that I left Ayia Napa (the holy wooded valley) to the clubbers, and at the early hour of just 11pm, just as the place was coming alive.

Thursday 18th September – Match 18
Omonoia Nicosia v Manchester City – UEFA Cup

I prepared for the game by jogging along the beach, passing by sunbathing City fans and holidaying Schalke fans. I sat by the pool (it's a tough life) making a few notes for my commentary and then it was back to Nicosia, giving a lift to the three lads from my hotel. They thanked me by presenting me with one of those half-half scarves of the match.

It was a cracking atmosphere at the game, but one thing I didn't anticipate was that the dry, hot weather would affect my throat as much as it did. The best decision I made was having two drinks on hand during the commentary. I constantly sipped them throughout the game.

I've only encountered that type of heat, while working, once before. I travelled to Las Vegas to report on Ricky Hatton's fight against José Luis Castillo in June 2007 and by adding a few extra days onto my working visit, I made it into a short holiday.

What an adventure it proved to be. I flew over the Grand Canyon, helped the magician David Copperfield make a car disappear, and went to the press conference celebrating one year of Cirque De Soleil Beatles, which was attended by Paul McCartney, Ringo Starr, Yoko Ono and Olivia Harrison.

I'll never forget the weigh-in for the Hatton fight. I was trying to interview some of the celebrities, who were in the huge crowd at Caesars Palace, and Bryan Robson was going to be my latest victim. He told me he was in a hurry, but would talk as we walked. After leaving the room, we stopped briefly in the corridor; my back turned to the two hundred or so fight fans that were stood behind a small metal fence.

As I concentrated on my questions, I notice Robson had a puzzled expression on his face, and I started to notice a chant from the crowd. "One Ian Cheeseman, there's only one Ian Cheeseman......." He smiled, I felt a bit embarrassed. We completed the interview and he went on his way. It was a moment I'll never forget.

The day after the fight I had booked to see Celine Dion at Caesars Palace. I'm not particularly a fan, but it was the biggest show in town. To get to the theatre I had to go through the casino. Within a few seconds of entering, I noticed Ricky Hatton, and his brother Matthew, playing roulette. Ricky was wearing his trademark floppy "fishing" hat. No-one seemed to notice them, despite Ricky's well publicised fourth round knock-out of Castillo, so I said hello and watched them play for a few minutes, while talking about the fight and City.

Ricky is a terrific guy, as most people know; down to earth and genuine. Matthew took a picture of the two of us and I joined the queue to see Celine, who was fabulous.

I presented two radio programmes from Vegas, one from the Thomas and Mack Center, where the fight was staged, and the other from Caesars Palace. Despite the furnace-like heat in the city, my voice held up. Then again, there was air conditioning there, unlike Cyprus.

As far as that game in Nicosia is concerned, City made hard work of it, missing a hatful of clear-cut chances, but in the end the two goals from Jo, one off his heel, proved to be enough to earn a 2-1 win. What a contrast my trip to Cyprus had been from the venture to the Faroes, but one thing I was finding, wherever I went, was the friendliness of the locals.

Saturday 20th September – Match 19
Rochdale v Chesterfield – League Two

A spectacular late free-kick from Tom Kennedy won this game for Rochdale, proving that great goals are not just reserved for the top flight or the

Champions League. Dale won 2-1. There were several players in the Dale team that were worth watching including Will Buckley and Adam Le Fondre, who I remember first bursting through at Stockport County.

As usual, I watch Messrs Hill and Flitcroft communicating to each other by phone as the manager stood at the back of the press box and his assistant was in position on the touchline. Can you imagine being "Flicker" and getting an erroneous call in the middle of the game, in between chatting with the Boss?

"Hello, is that Mr Flitcroft? My name is Jane, I'm ringing on behalf of a timeshare company called......" click (followed by lots of swearing).

I always feel welcome at Rochdale, from the moment I walk in through the front door. Usually the first thing I see is the smiling face of Gerry Dawson, for whom nothing ever seems too much trouble, whether you're there to buy a ticket or are a corporate guest. In one man he sums up what the club is, friendly approachable and down to earth.

The club's supporters have asked me, from time to time, to go along to one of their meetings, and I remember presenting their "Who wants to be a Dale millionaire" on one of those occasions. It was great fun.

Sunday 21st September – Match 20
Manchester City v Portsmouth – Premier League

"Poetry in Motion" – could make a catchy song title that one. Three Brazilians in the starting line up with Elano, Jo and Robinho immediately involved in a sweeping move that also featured Javier Garrido and almost led to the first goal.

Jo's rounding of the keeper got things up and running before Elano's corner was turned in by "Dunninho" for number two. After the break Ireland and Jo set up Robinho for the third with Zabaleta passing to Shaun Wright-Phillips who made it four. The scoring was completed by substitutes Ched Evans and Gelson Fernandez, and even my Brazil-sceptic sidekick Nigel Gleghorn was waxing lyrical about the entertainment on show.

Only the Pompey boss Harry Redknapp failed to fully appreciate the show he'd seen, merely claiming it was a bad performance by his team rather than anything special by City.

Nigel sits alongside me for all City's home games and I find him a pleasure to work with. By his own admission he was never one of City's superstars, making just 34 appearances and scoring seven goals during the management of Mel Machin in the late 1980's.

His full season at City, was a promotion campaign, which saw him play in goals a couple of times when Andy Dibble had to go off. He's one of those people who "just gets on with it", and it didn't surprise me when he proved a hero in both those games, a 3-3 at Walsall and 1-1 at Crystal Palace, when he'd scored too.

He also played at Bradford City, the day City's 1-1 draw, and that Trevor Morley goal, took City back into the top flight – a day when City looked like snatching defeat from the jaws of promotion.

Because his early days in non-league football had meant also being a firefighter, he's seen all sides of football. I've worked with many ex-City players down the years including Peter Barnes, Ian Bishop, Earl Barrett, Mark Lillis, Andy Hinchcliffe and Andy May and all of them are great, in their own way.

I first met Nigel at a charity cricket match, when I made a guest appearance for Franny Lee's team. I arrived late and was sent in to bat with nine wickets down. Nigel was bowling. I hadn't played cricket for years.

He quickly worked out that I was unpractised but I defiantly blocked every delivery, Boycott-esque. With every ball he was wincing more and more at the pain of not getting me out and reminding his team mates just how poor I was. I slowly grew in confidence, even as three or four of his team-mates gathered around my bat, looking for the slightest nick to catch me out.

I remained stubbornly at the crease without scoring or even attempting a scoring shot, until the end of the over at which point the heavens opened and it rained like a tropical storm and we all headed for the pavilion.

So much rain fell during the next half an hour that the game had to be abandoned – but I could proudly say I had remained not out, and Nigel remained frustratingly without my wicket. Years later, I've reminded him of that day on several occasions, especially because he's a huge cricket fan.

The next time I spent any time with Nigel was at a meeting of the Bredbury Blues, when he'd been invited, like me, as a guest speaker, taking questions from the supporters. He was knowledgeable, entertaining, funny and engaging – all the qualities I look for in a radio summariser and on our phone-ins.

I've heard players who can rightly claim to be bigger club legends, up and down the country, on various radio stations or even in TV studios, but often their reputation is bigger than their intellect and they don't have anything interesting, challenging or entertaining to say. I'd rather have the wit and good humour of Nigel any day, and I believe, in these ever more competitive times for the media, that's what makes him stand out from the rest.

We do often disagree though, not that it bothers me because it's better than a sycophantic love-in between the two of us. This was one we totally agreed about though, a feast of attacking, entertaining football and City winning 6-0, what more could you wish for on a Saturday afternoon?

Wednesday 24th September – Match 21
Brighton & Hove Albion v Manchester City – League Cup

My other City summariser is Fred Eyre, who surely needs little introduction. As an accomplished after-dinner speaker, former player, coach, chief scout and just about every other footballing title you could give him, good and bad, he's a commentator's dream.

His knowledge is encyclopaedic and not just about football. On long away journeys, like a Wednesday night trip to Brighton, he'll suddenly pepper the conversation with references to any song or performer from the 1950's and 60's or TV programmes old and new and just about every other subject. You've only got to mention a name or phrase and his mind could lead us off anywhere.

Football supporters, up and down the country, have paid royally to be entertained by Fred since his book "Kicked into Touch" first shot him to fame in the 1980's. I have to pinch myself sometimes that he's sat alongside me hour after hour, each season. He certainly makes those long car journeys seem to pass by very quickly.

This was to be a long day, despite the presence of Fred, because this was a match that had to be settled by extra time and penalties. I was only surprised that with a player called Virgo appearing in the Brighton side, that it didn't go to snookers too.

We arrived early enough to take a walk along the Brighton prom, Fred bought some rock for his granddaughters and I reminisced about this being the venue for Abba's Eurovision Song contest victory with Waterloo in 1974. I'm a huge Abba fan and got to interview Benny and Bjorn at the West End opening of Mamma Mia, which has to be one of the highlights of my career, if not my life.

One of the entertainment producers at BBC Radio Manchester knew I was a big fan, so I asked him if he could help me get tickets for one of the preview showings in Manchester. He offered me the chance to stand on the red carpet (which was actually blue) in Leicester Square at the World Premiere.

I travelled down early, for a private screening, before waiting for the stars to arrive at the Odeon Cinema. I was determined to interview Benny and Bjorn and I was waiting patiently behind the railing, with the other journalists, when a PR woman offered me a chance to speak to Meryl Streep, one of the stars of the film. "No thanks, I'm waiting for Benny", was my unhesitating reply. He was two places down the line, and I knew that if I spoke to Meryl he'd be leap-frogged passed me and my chance would have gone.

Benny was worth waiting for. He's a humble genius and my all-time hero.

Back in Brighton, after taking in the bracing air for an hour, I decided it might be useful to visit the fortune telling gypsy who has a small chalet on the prom. As we arrived she told me she was packing up and I'd have to come back the following day. I'd have thought she'd have known I was going to be stopping by, so she couldn't have been very good so we concluded our stroll.

We decided to sample traditional fish and chips at a sea front establishment before heading up to the ground. The Withdean Athletics Stadium was

Brighton's temporary home, and it immediately struck me that the City fans would have a terrible view, not least because they'd be so far back from the pitch and at such a flat viewing angle.

To my huge disappointment, City had made six changes from the team that had done so well at the weekend, and I have to admit I feared the worst for this cup tie, having seen City slip up against lower division opposition on so many occasions down the years.

City were leading in normal time, Brighton during extra time, but only the home team led through the penalties with Michael Ball's missed spot kick proving decisive.

The last time I'd left Brighton, feeling so disappointed, was back in January 1983, John Bond's last match in charge, when City lost 4-0 in an FA Cup fourth round replay. I'd watched the debacle from the "meccano stand", as many of us called the temporary visitors seating being used at the time. We must have been nuts to sit in there.

It would have been much worse had I been stood in the away end. Apart from the terrible performance, it was an open air section and the rain never stopped falling, throughout the game.

As Charlie and I prepared to serve the five hundred hungry City fans queuing towards the "cage" on the football special, we noticed that many of them were only wearing underwear. I'd never seen anything like it. Their sopping wet clothes were hanging on every British Rail heater in sight.

I can't begin to imagine what the travellers, standing on the platforms at Crewe station, thought when our train rolled in later that evening. It must have looked more like a streakers' convention than a train full of football fans. Who'd have thought that twenty five years later I should be returning from Brighton to Manchester, after suffering another cup defeat and feeling just as stripped of any pride in my team.

Saturday 27th September – Match 22
Cheltenham Town v Stockport County – League One

Michael Raynes doesn't look like the archetypal footballer/athlete, but he's one of those wholehearted players who makes things happen and will play anywhere, in any role, to help his side win. He reminds me of County's former captain Mike Flynn.

When Raynes first broke into the County team he was just a boy, and a weedy looking one at that. He must have been eight stones wringing wet, but at least six foot tall. Since then he'd added muscle and experience and had become the heartbeat of the team. This was one of many days where he made the vital difference, scoring a last minute equalizer, to earn his team a 2-2 draw.

The first time I'd seen his name, in 2004, I'd wondered if he was related to a man I'd met on County's end of season trip to China that year, who I knew simply as Mr Raynes. He wasn't, it was just a coincidence.

That was when County bought Stockport Tiger Star and installed John Hollins as manager. I joined up with the trip halfway through, as they changed plans en route to Urumqi, a city nestled between the Taklamaken Desert and the Tianshan, or Mountains of Heaven, near the western border with Kazakhstan – a city which has the distinction of being further from the sea than any other on the planet.

It was an amazing trip, with County playing two games on successive days, much to the annoyance of manager Sammy McIlroy, who was only made aware of the schedule in the early hours of the morning, on the day we arrived there.

His compromise had been to field a team, largely made of County staff, rather than genuine players, in the game against the Kazakh military team. Sammy played too, to lessen the need for others to play, typically leading by example on a pitch he later described as the worst he'd ever seen. Richard Landon, the club's kitman, scored a goal during one of those games in Urumqi, a few days later, back in Beijing, I was sat next to him on a cable car, climbing up and over the Great Wall of China.

Sunday 28th September – Match 23
Wigan Athletic v Manchester City – Premier League

My favourite episode of "Whatever happened to the likely lads" is the one where they try to avoid the score of the England game until "Match of the Day". I can relate to that story. Whenever there's a Grand Prix at the same time as a match I'm covering, I try to avoid the result. It's impossible if I'm presenting the programme, but I always ask that I'm only passed the information I need.

This was the day of the first night race in F1, in Singapore, and despite the potential pitfalls, I managed to remain unaware of the result until I got home, so I was able to watch it - "as live" – later that evening.

I love Formula One and often set my alarm clock for the early hours, to watch it as it happens. It's illogical really, but on one of the occasions when I recorded one of those "middle-of-the-night" races, my eldest son, Steven, quite innocently, like Brian Glover's character "Flint", wanted to let me know he knew, by saying something like, "Don't worry, I won't tell you the result, but it doesn't end the way you'll expect it to!".

My mind started to race – an unintended pun! – just like Terry and Bob, when they read the newspaper headline "England F" and they tried to second-guess the rest of it. "England fail? England five?" It turned out to be England flooded out, match postponed, while in my case, with ten laps of the race to go, Schumacher was in the lead, so, as a Schumacher fan, I assumed he'd get a puncture with one lap to go. I can't remember what happened, but Schumacher didn't win. That clue had spoiled the climax, so now I get up at 3am instead!

Wigan against City was more important to me than the first Singapore night race, so what would be would be, and City were back to the side that had beaten Portsmouth. But, as seemed usual at the JJB Stadium, they were out-battled by Wigan, who'd never lost to City in the Premier League.

Wilson Palacios caught my eye in the Latics team, though it was the equally impressive Antonio Valencia who scored the opener with a super shot past Joe Hart. City were quickly level through Vincent Kompany before Palacios cartwheeled high into the air to get a penalty, and although valid, it made me feel uncomfortable for the manner in which it had been "earned". Zaki despatched the spot kick and City returned empty handed from Wigan once again.

City ended September in eighth place with three wins and three defeats from their six games, while Wigan were a point worse off and two places lower in tenth.

October

Thursday 2nd October – Match 24
Manchester City v Omonoia Nicosia – UEFA Cup

The month opened with the second leg of City's UEFA Cup tie with Omonoia, which seemed like it should be straightforward enough, and perhaps one I could enjoy more, since the Blues had a 2-1 lead from the first leg.

People have asked me if I'd rather be sat watching the game from the stands now and again, rather than always working at matches, after all, I've never actually seen a City game from anywhere other than my seat in the press box at the City of Manchester Stadium. My answer is that I'd rather be commentating, because it focuses my mind on all the players for every minute of the game.

Just like most spectators, I'd lose my intense concentration if I wasn't working and would not be able to analyse the game in such depth. When I used to attend games regularly as a fan, I'd sit and quietly study the game, rather than get involved in the minutiae of refereeing decisions and crowd reactions. Perhaps my personality was suited to journalism from the start, although I still danced around with the rest when the goals went in!

I prepare for a commentary in different ways for different games. In the case of matches like this one, against a relatively unknown team from Cyprus, I research the opposition by using the contents of the excellent City programme, the internet and any appropriate leaflets or magazines I can find.

As I see it, and it's a very subjective job, I'm there to be the eyes of the listener who can't see the events that are unfolding and I believe there is always plenty to describe, even during a dull game. My summariser's job is to add expertise and analysis to my description. I wouldn't expect them to simply quote a long line of statistics but to supplement my words with something else, whether it be some comment on tactics, inside information, a personal experience, an observation I've missed or even a suitable humorous anecdote.

During games I tend to assume that most people listening will have a basic knowledge of both teams, particularly the local team, whether it be City, Wigan, Bury or Macclesfield, but each opposition deserves a different treatment.

Once the team sheets are distributed, I write out the formations on my sheet detailing the day's other fixtures and then transfer the "opposition team" onto my master sheet in number order, for quick reference during the game with any relevant statistics written underneath.

It's amazing how quickly I become familiar with the other team during a game, and within ten minutes I've usually stopped looking at my sheet, except for score updates from other games. Identification of players changes from spotting the number on their back or shorts to body shape and movement. By the end of a game I could probably identify all twenty two players if they were crossing the road twenty yards away in thick fog, just from the movement of their silhouette.

Those early minutes are more worrying for me, because the learning process hasn't been completed and my worst commentary moment came when Juventus scored against United at Old Trafford within the first few minutes.

I broke one of the golden rules of commentary by starting a sentence while not being certain I would be able to end it accurately with the name of the scorer.

The goal was scored by one of the best known players of his time, who wore white boots, which should have made by job easier! My sentence went along the lines of, "and the goal is scored by (still trying to identify him) ...... the man wearing the distinctive white boots (desperately waiting for him to turn his back to me, so I could read his shirt number) ......it can only be ......(on-air silence that seemed like forever) .....Alessandro Del Pierro!"

If there had been a big hole for me to jump into at that moment, I would have been in it. That taught me a lesson. These days I'd rather swallow my pride and describe the goal without identifying the scorer, if need be, than lead myself into a cul-de-sac of embarrassment.

For City's game against Omonoia the bigger problem would be saying long Greek names without getting tongue-tied – names like Charalambous, Georgallides and Ndikumana. I managed to get through it all successfully, just like City who won 2-1 again, thanks to goals from Elano and Wright-Phillips and City were through to the group stage of the UEFA Cup.

My ideal draw would be against my "second team" Schalke 04 – and the great thing being that that both clubs could progress, so I held my breath and hoped the balls would be drawn out in my favour.

Saturday 4th October – Match 25
Wigan Athletic v Middlesbrough – Premier League

Not exactly a free-flowing game but there's no doubt that Wigan were robbed, with Middlesbrough rarely pushing into the Latics half and never coming close to a goal until the last ten minutes or so. Jeremie Aliadiere, whose name trips off the tongue during commentary, scored the late goal that stole the points for Boro.

As well as the pleasure of watching Wigan, a real people's club, it's never dull commentating alongside Paul "statto" Rowley, who often reports on Latics games, despite being based in London as BBC local radio's Westminster correspondent. Paul is a very talented and experienced broadcaster who has an obsessive passion for Wigan Athletic.

He's spent his whole life in broadcasting and has a voice that makes you want to listen to the radio – colourful, expressive and fun, all at the same time. His broadcasting hero was Kenny Everett and Paul has the same kind of silly sense of humour.

His memory seems to be photographic and nothing gives him more pleasure than being able to recall a statistic about his favourite football club or many of the other things that clutter his mind. Occasionally he frustrates me.

"What did you think of that shot by Emile Heskey?", I might have asked him. "Well since making his England debut against Hungary in April 1999, he's had 57 shots and scored 23 of them – 17 with his right foot, 3 headers and 3 with the left foot", he might reply, "...but what did you think of the shot Paul!"

He's great fun though, and I love to tease him on air, which always produces a witty retort, and hopefully adds to the entertainment value of the commentary.

Sunday 5th October – Match 26
Manchester City v Liverpool – Premier League

This proved to be one of the best matches of the season. A sell out crowd created a passionate atmosphere and it was always open and entertaining. Stephen Ireland scored the first, from an assist by Robinho. Ireland has such natural ability, although sometimes I feel he needs to think about his play a bit more, rather than playing it all "off the cuff" – not that I'm complaining, he's a delight to watch and was proving to be City's best performer in the early stages of the season.

Javier Garrido got the second goal, with a stunning free-kick and it looked like being City's day. The fans I chatted to, as I headed down to the press room at half time, had grins like the Cheshire Cat and I must admit, my face was aching by the time I ordered my cup of tea from the ever-smiling Lucy behind the bar.

Within ten minutes of the restart, Liverpool were back in it, thanks to a goal by Fernando Torres – which prompted me into doing a terrible joke about him not hearing the drums – but it was City for whom the jungle warning signs should have been noticeable.

The turning point came on sixty six minutes when Pablo Zabaleta was sent off for a lunging challenge on Xabi Alonso – had it been Fernando Alonso he might have got out of the way! With City down to ten men, Mark Hughes brought on Gelson Fernandez and slotted him in at right back. I'm not sure I'd have made that change, but then I'm not paid a fortune to be a Premier League manager – which is probably just as well.

Within a couple of minutes Torres equalised and it started to look as if City would struggle to hold out for a point. The deciding goal was created down City's right back area and ended with Dirk Kuyt scoring the goal that gave Liverpool all three points.

It proved to be a "what if" game, but entertaining nonetheless, and a match that proved that the gap between the clubs wasn't as big as it had been in the last few seasons.

This was to be my last football match for over two weeks, as there was to be a break for internationals. I took a few days holiday, flying out to Austria with Irene and her sister. My mother-in-law, who was like a second mum to me, was Austrian – Irene's family are from the Vienna suburbs. I've loved Austria, since visiting there with my mum and dad, and some of our German family, when I was thirteen years old. My favourite place is the Zillertal Valley which is near to Innsbruck. It's unspoilt, picturesque and is the perfect escape from the hurley-burley of modern life.

On one family holiday there I was chatting to my younger son, Daniel, on the little steam train that runs along the valley, when a guy interrupted me to ask if I was Ian Cheeseman. It seemed a bit strange that he'd recognised me from my voice, as we holidayed in the middle of the Austrian mountains.

Our 2008 trip was to Gmunden, on the Traunsee, a beautiful lake surrounded by mountains. It was a musical weekend, spent admiring the scenery, enjoying good food and watching and listening to my favourite Austrian folk singers Sigrid and Marina.

On the Saturday, instead of commentating on football, we took the cable car to the top of the mountain, where we ate pork and dumplings, and wandered along the country trails being serenaded by "the girls". It was sunny enough to be shirt sleeve weather and I felt like I was in heaven.

The following day was a boat ride on the lake before a three hour concert and a lovely meal in the evening. I love football and 99% of the time I'd rather be at a game than doing just about anything else, but that weekend was the best of the year.

Listening to the music of Sigrid and Marina, Marc Pircher (another Austrian folk singer), Abba and many others) certainly lifts my spirits and guards against falling asleep at the wheel during those long journeys back from midweek games, especially when I'm travelling alone.

Monday 20th October – Match 27
Newcastle United v Manchester City – Premier League

Back to reality, and a visit to one of my favourite stadiums. Last time I sat in the "normal seats" at St James' Park, I'd almost thrown myself off the top tier, as I felt the vertigo of being so high, still at least my love of the Austrian mountains had prepared me for days like that.

The press box is much lower down, and it's quite easy to pop to pitch-side and grab a word with a City player or a member of the coaching staff, even if it's just to say hello.

Everyone's favourite person, in the Newcastle press room, is a lady called Kath. I'd never ask her age, of course, but I'll bet she remembers the days of Len Shackleton and Jackie Milburn. She's an old fashioned person, in the best sense of the expression. She always has time for everyone, never stops smiling and is everyone's friend.

City have someone similar at the City of Manchester Stadium called Rose, who looks after the press photographers in her own room down near the big service tunnel. Rose wears her hair in a "bee-hive" and bakes scones for the snappers to consume pre-match. I remember interviewing a nervous Rose during the last days of Maine Road, for the three hour documentary I put together to mark the closing of the old stadium.

Rose and Kath represent the heart and soul of a football club, though the fans don't know who they are and are unlikely to ever meet them – another reason for me to feel lucky to have my job.

Having enjoyed my pre-match chat and tea with Kath, I took my seat in the press box and watched Peter Beardsley and Malcolm Macdonald go about their business. Beardsley always seems to be pitch-side as part of the stadium tour, and Macdonald does work for one of the local radio stations.

Newcastle was a club in turmoil, Kevin Keegan had resigned a month earlier and some wanted the departure of owner Mike Ashley. The crowd was restless from the moment the game kicked off and it felt like a good time for City to be playing them – there was no Michael Owen in the line-up either.

Things went to plan, early on, Robinho scoring from the spot, sending Shay Given the wrong way, after being brought down by Beye, who was also sent off. A couple of weeks earlier, City had struggled with ten men against Liverpool, now surely they would take full advantage against the ten men of Newcastle.

Four decades of watching City has prepared me to expect the worst though, and just before half-time Shola Ameobi scored the equaliser, though surely Newcastle would tire in the second half? No – the next goal, though scored by Richard Dunne, put City behind. The blues got a point from a 2-2 draw thanks to Ireland's finish from Robinho's pass.

Tuesday 21st October – Match 28
MK Dons v Stockport County – League One

I went to primary school in Radcliffe, which is where my dad was born and brought up. He had a brother and two sisters. I therefore have several cousins, who I spent many happy hours with during my childhood. I used to play with Stephen and Andrew most but also enjoyed being with Olwyn, who I remember as being full of energy and always laughing.

I lost contact with my dad's family when we moved to Whitefield and they spread their wings and moved to other towns. My Aunty Rose had two more daughters, Katherine and Susan, who seemed much older than me – in reality perhaps only a year or two but it seemed a lot at the time.

Years later I visited several of my cousins in Milton Keynes, on the occasion of Bury playing at the National Hockey Stadium and had a great time reminiscing about the old days. One of the next generation was researching a family tree was so grateful to meet me.

Stockport's trip to the new MK Dons Stadium gave me another excuse to catch-up, so I had a lovely, lazy lunch with Susan, in a restaurant by a lake. Milton Keynes gets bad press for being a "new town" but I've always found it to be well organised and neatly set out, despite the record number of roundabouts in the town.

The ground, imaginatively named "stadiummk", is right next to a big retail park, like many of the new football venues, so it gave me a chance to do a bit of early Christmas Shopping (don't do much of that!) before getting ready for the game.

County fell behind in stoppage time at the end of the first half but fought back to win 2-1 thanks to a goal from Jason Taylor and an own goal.

Saturday 25th October – Match 29
Swindon Town v Oldham Athletic – League One

I knew it wouldn't be a great day when I arrived at the County Ground. The car park steward told me it would be £10 to leave my car just behind the town end. That's ridiculous by anybody's standards. I'll bet most supporters think that the press, especially those with loads of equipment to carry, always have a reserved parking spot. At Swindon it seems that's true – sort of – but at a price.

I could have just paid the money, but I feel it's my duty not to waste BBC money, so I turned around and left the car park and looked for somewhere else to leave the car, with, "You won't find anywhere else!", ringing in my ears.

I headed back to the "Magic Roundabout" as the locals call it, which is a junction made up of five mini-roundabouts in the centre of one huge roundabout. I don't know about Dougal and Dylan spinning around in circles, it certainly confused me.

Within a couple of minutes, and about half-a-mile away, I found a lay-by and parked there, before trudging back past the car park steward. I resisted the temptation of telling him I'd found somewhere else, despite his know-it-all attitude a few minutes earlier.

I expressed my views to Swindon's press steward, when he politely asked if I'd had a good journey down. He sympathised and told me it was part of a dispute between Swindon Town and the local council, who owned the car park.

The County Ground was where I made my Radio Manchester debut, back in October 1987. I'd been asked to do the game at the last minute, presumably due to a late change of plan, and I was doubling up, since I was already covering the game for Clubcall, an organisation that allowed fans to listen to match reports or commentaries via an 0898 number.

My years at Radio Cavell, in the hospital, had indirectly led to some occasional work for Clubcall. A guy called Mark Rooney had also been a hospital radio broadcaster but was then the sports editor at Clubcall. Unknown to me, he was listening to a cricket report I was doing, one summer Saturday, and found out I was a big City fan. That led to an invite to cover some games for them. My answer had been that I would do it, but only if he didn't ask me to miss a City game.

Once he offered me £50, a lot of money back then, to do a commentary on a game at Liverpool. On the same night City were at Torquay in the League Cup, so I went there, as a fan, instead. He thought I was mad, and I thought he might be right when I returned home on the football special at 3 o'clock in the morning, after seeing a terrible 0-0 draw.

On that BBC debut at Swindon, I was told I'd need to do an update on Clubcall and then Radio Manchester, every time there was a goal. Juggling the two forms of media, while dialling in on my old "reporter phone" would have been hard enough had it been a routine day, but I was nervous and the game proved to be a 4-3 win for City. Can you imagine the chaos in my head as I attempted to keep both plates spinning?

It certainly taught me the art of compromise. We all want to do everything in a perfect way, every word over the airwaves (or down the telephone line) being carefully crafted, but that day I simply did it all by instinct, using "bullet points" rather than a script. It was a great experience, though it didn't feel like it at the time.

Amazingly the press box I'd sat in, back in 1987 was largely unchanged, so the memories flooded back as I set up my equipment for the day's broadcasting. It was an easy day for me, just simple match reports into our main sports programme of the week.

The game seemed to start well for Oldham. They looked threatening every time they went forward and after twenty minutes or so I would have had a small bet that the Latics would go on to win the game, then defender Sean Morrison strolled through some weak defending to slot home and give

Swindon an undeserved lead.

Swindon added a second and the Latics never looked likely to get back into the game. By the time I was wiping away the crumbs of a lovely piece of cream cake I consumed in the press room, John Sheridan was marching in, with anger etched all over his face. The other local media seemed quite happy for me to ask my questions first, on this occasion, and he ripped into his players.

Sheridan was never one to use two words where one will do, but on this occasion he had plenty to say. I sent the interview back to Radio Manchester, packed up my equipment and carried it the half-mile back to the lay-by and headed home. At least the music on my i-pod was good for the return journey home.

Sunday 26th October – Match 30
Manchester City v Stoke City – Premier League

Along with City against Sunderland, this was probably the most anticipated fixture of the season for my "home" sidekick Nigel Gleghorn, who played more games for Stoke than any other league club. When City haven't got a home game, he works alongside the sports team at Radio Stoke and does many of their games, but he's always told them that he's fully committed to doing games with me at Eastlands.

I reckon it's probably got something to do with the fact that I always produce a Mars Bar at half-time.

If I'd been Jo, City's Brazilian striker, I'd have started to worry on this day, because he lost his place to Ched Evans. Don't misunderstand me, I've got nothing against Ched, but if you'd been replaced by a youngster, on considerably lower wages than you, so soon into your time at the "richest club in the world", I think you'd be worried too.

The "other" Brazilian, Robinho had a good day, bagging an impressive hattrick, on what proved to be another highly entertaining day, and a comfortable 3-0 win.

Before the game I'd been asked to give my views to an independent Stoke fans' website, which I was only to happy to do. Their reporter interviewed me on his mobile phone after the game. It was a bit strange standing outside the front of the stadium, trying to do a serious interview, into a guy's mobile phone. It's one thing to goof around doing silly home videos but I'd have to be mindful that this wasn't just a silly fan, but a fellow journalist. Always be careful what you say to a journalist!

Tuesday 28th October – Match 31
Bradford City v Bury – League Two

Winning away games is never easy – apparently. I have to admit, the reason why it's harder to win away games than homes games has always been a puzzle to me. It's still eleven versus eleven isn't it, and yet a club can win regularly at home and lose away games, playing against the same teams.

I'd been at Bradford City in October 1987, when Manchester City won 4-2, their first away win after 34 unsuccessful road trips, and I'd been at every one of those too. This was before my days as a full time journalist, and I remember that the Manchester Evening News ran a series of interviews with fans who'd attended all those fruitless away games. Charlie and I were two of the fans whose comments were printed.

To get into the stadium, I had to pass the memorial to those who lost their lives in the terrible fire of 1985, which is always a poignant moment. That day, 11th May 1985, was one of the great days of Maine Road, the 5-1 promotion winning game against Charlton Athletic. During that match I'd only heard a suggestion that there'd been a small fire at Valley Parade, and never realised the scale of the tragedy.

It was a cold October evening for this game against Bury, but a good game nonetheless. Bradford crowds are noisier than the average and I enjoy games in Yorkshire. There might be an ancient rivalry between Lancashire and Yorkshire but I think there are a lot of similarities between the people of those fine counties.

Granada TV seems to agree - half the cast of Coronation Street seem to have Yorkshire accents and no one down south seems to notice the difference.

Bradford's mascot, the City Gent, is the most unusual in the country, because he's a human being, which makes it extra puzzling that he doesn't win all the charity races that the mascots seem to do for charity.

The defining moment of the game came in the last five minutes when "Barry, Barry, Barry….." Conlon, came on as a substitute and scored the only goal of the game. Bury's good early season form had suffered a set-back.

I spoke to the Shakers boss Alan Knill and striker Andy Bishop, in the narrow corridor between the dressing room and the street, where the Bury coach was parked. Bishop's future was uncertain but he gave me the impression he wanted to succeed with Bury, which was nice to hear.

Back in the press box, I had a few words with Lindsay Sutton, a reporter from the Daily Mirror. Lindsay also spent some time working in the BBC press office, so I knew him quite well, and was aware of his passion for Bradford City.

We talked about the time he was being hunted by City fans at Maine Road and how the rest of us had protected him. There had been a picture story in the Daily Mirror, comparing the near empty City stadium for the Auto Windscreens Shield visit of Mansfield Town, to a sell out Old Trafford for Man United's European Cup game against Bayern Munich, the following night.

The article upset City fans who decided they would shout abuse at the Mirror reporter at the next home game against Bristol Rovers. Lindsay had nothing to do with the article, but they didn't know that or simply didn't care.

To get to his seat in the press box (which I always thought looked like a coconut shy), he had to walk among the supporters who congregated around the bars. Several fans had knocked on the press room door and demanded the Mirror reporter make himself known, the rest of us diverted them, while he slipped in and out. A good man like Lindsay certainly didn't deserve that kind of hassle.

Having talked about old times, Fred and I (Fred had travelled with me just to watch the game!) returned home.

Wednesday 29th October – Match 32
Middlesbrough v Manchester City – Premier League

Middlesbrough was where Paul Lake had played his last game for City. It had always seemed too early for his return from a serious knee injury but his trip there in August 1992 proved to be his saddest and he never played again.

That was at Ayresome Park, a ground I never really enjoyed visiting, if only for that reason. The one good reason to visit was that it had one of the best chippys I've ever discovered. So good that one year I bought an extra portion of chips to take home for Irene to try; warmed up first in the microwave of course.

My last visit to the Riverside Stadium had been on the final day of the 2007 – 2008 season, Sven Goran Eriksson's last in charge. By then, everyone knew that Sven had long since been sacked, not officially of course, that was to come after his farewell humiliation on a post-season trip to the Far East, for the pleasure of Thaksin Shinawatra.

The Riverside Stadium was, as usual, about ten degrees colder than the rest of the UK, and City were humiliatingly beaten 8-1. Here was a chance for the next generation to exert a little revenge, but sadly it wasn't to be.

This was a puzzler of a game – Micah Richards at left back??? As the game unfolded it was obvious that the experiment wasn't working. I'd also felt that this was a game that might have benefited from the experience and extra defensive abilities of Dietmar Hamann.

It was a poor performance, only brightened by the banter during our car journey to and from the game. We had our usual stop at the Little Chef on the A19 and Fred joked that they'd have reserved our usual table, by the window. Our most noteworthy visit came a few years ago when there were four of us in the car, Fred and me, Charlie and Chris Bailey, my trusted friend from the MEN.

At the end of our meal we asked if we could split the bill, which prompted our Liverpudlian waiter to become very agitated. He explained that he was out on licence from the local prison and was worried that if he split the bill, after it had been printed off on one receipt, it might be interpreted as fiddling, on his part. Since we wanted to play our part in rehabilitating this cheery man, we abided by his wishes – unless of course his cunning plan had actually worked, and we'd been had? We'll never know, but we've never seen him again!

November

Saturday 1st November – Match 33
Portsmouth v Wigan Athletic – Premier League

While it should be applauded that modern top flight clubs employ groundsmen, who with the aid of the latest technology, can produce perfect playing surfaces from August until May, I think it's a shame we don't occasionally see a less than perfect pitch.

I got my wish at this game. It rained incessantly from the moment I left home, just before 7 o'clock in the morning, until my arrival at Fratton Park. If there was a worry, it was that the game might not be played at all and I'd have made a long, fruitless journey; but the game went ahead.

Wigan needed a victory; they'd lost their four league games in October. Portsmouth's manager Harry Redknapp had left, as quickly as he'd arrived, to succeed Juande Ramos at Tottenham, so Tony Adams had stepped up at Pompey and was taking charge for the first time.

As the rain continued to bounce down, Wigan gritted their teeth and battled. Just before half time Amr Zaki scored from the penalty spot to give the Latics the lead.

In my opinion, Fratton Park is the worst stadium in the Premier League. It looks old and dilapidated. Until recently there was no roof over the visitors section. As far as the press facilities are concerned, they too are the worst in the top flight. Once I've squeezed into my seat, there's definitely no room to move my elbows. It's a good job I only have to talk and not play a violin.

I'm fairly certain that my preference for not wearing a coat, when I commentate, started at Portsmouth. After that, I started taking my coat off, just before kickoff, for all games, even when the temperatures are sub-zero.

I never notice the cold during the games, but within five minutes of the final whistle I have to put the coat back on, as the chill starts to affect me.

I feel less restricted without my coat on, and since I'm quite a physical commentator, who really gets involved in the game, I feel less confined – even verbally – when I've no coat on.

Portsmouth have very vociferous fans who create a great atmosphere, even if the Pompey Chimes gets on your nerves after a while. The home fans certainly got behind their team in the second half of this game, eventually culminating in a Portsmouth equaliser, through Niko Kranjcar.

Wigan's winner came in stoppage time, Lee Cattermole slipping the ball through to Emile Heskey who steered it in from a difficult angle, through the puddles, for his 100th league goal.

If the game had started an hour later, I'm sure it would never have been completed because so much rain was falling that huge puddles were forming. I've seen games abandoned because of waterlogging on several occasions, perhaps most memorably at Maine Road in December 2000. It was a game between Manchester City and Ipswich Town.

I was the on-pitch stadium PA man at that time, and so it was my duty to announce the abandonment to the crowd. It wasn't my decision, so therefore it wasn't my fault, but the crowd was unsympathetic when I told the 23, 000 disgruntled fans that day that the game was over. Still I suppose it could have been worse.

Can you imagine how upset Denis Law must have been when he'd scored all six goals as City led 6-2 at Luton in 1961, when the game was called off? He even scored during the re-scheduled match, when City lost 3-1. Six goals in a game and the record ripped from the record books thanks to that anonymous announcement from the PA – who'd want to be on the public address?

Sunday 2nd November – Match 34
Bolton Wanderers v Manchester City – Premier League

The Reebok Stadium is one of my favourite football grounds. It looks good and was well designed, although I'd have to say that the press box is one of the coldest. It's right at the back of the stand, high above the dual player tunnels, next to an air gap between the roof and the main structure of the stadium.

It's a place that I'm used to attending on a regular basis, as I do some hosting of the "Junior Whites", which is similar to Manchester City's Junior Blues. The JB's doesn't really exist as it once did. For many years there were monthly meetings featuring games, pancake races, fancy dress and things like that; these days they seem to concentrate on bigger events.

City have staged a Junior Blues pantomime for many years, right back to the involvement of legends like Francis Lee and Mike Summerbee in the social club, next to Maine Road. Down the years many local stars have appeared on stage as things as diverse as trees, (Nigel Gleghorn!), Morris Dancers and ghosts. Many of the stars of Coronation Street, local boxers, ex players and City staff have made guest appearances too.

I've played my part too, doing everything from acting as narrator, to singing an Elvis song dressed as a schoolboy and prancing about in a chicken costume. It's been great fun and the audience always seem to have had a good time. The real stars are the children who're just normal young fans. They rehearse each weekend for four or five months.

My memories of Bolton go back to their days at Burnden Park, but not as far as my dad's. He was at the old ground on 9th March 1946, the day of the disaster that claimed thirty three lives. He'd taken his sister, Rose, to see Stanley Matthews, who was playing for Stoke City in the FA Cup. Many other people had the same idea. It's been estimated that 85,000 turned up that day.

My dad and his sister stood at the back of the railway embankment but couldn't see a thing, though they could feel the crowd surging forward more than normal so concluded that there wasn't much point in staying. So they left and made their way home, disappointed. Later they found out about the disaster and how the dead and injured had been crushed by the numbers packed into Burnden Park that day. Dad felt that they'd had a lucky escape.

I was at Burnden Park on News Years Day 1979, when Peter Reid had a very unlucky day. It was snowing during the game and the conditions were becoming more dangerous by the minute. The Wanderers midfielder paid the penalty by suffering a terrible knee injury in a collision with the Everton goalkeeper George Wood.

The match was abandoned at half-time, but too late for Reid.

As far as this Bolton versus City match was concerned, I was amazed to see Micah Richards at left back again, I'd thought the team's failure at Middlesbrough, in the previous game, would mean we'd never see Micah in that position again.

It was a poor match, though Jussi Jaaskelainen, Bolton's wonderful goalkeeper, made two or three excellent saves. Ricardo Gardner had come on as a Wanderers' substitute, just before half-time, and his goal eventually broke the deadlock with just fifteen minutes to go. Bolton added a second, through a Richard Dunne own goal and City had slipped to another disappointing defeat.

Tuesday 4th November – Match 35
Darlington v Bury – Johnstone's Paint Trophy

I'd had to wait four years for my second appearance as a proper radio reporter, after my debut at Swindon in 1987. My second game was Darlington against Bury, at Feethams, in October 1991. I was a bit more experienced by now and of course four years older, but I was still very nervous.

I'd written out my introduction on an A4 sheet of paper, in plenty of time for my debut on Piccadilly Radio at two thirty. In fact I'd rewritten it several times, looking for perfection, but never quite finding it.

James H Reeve was the presenter, someone I'd listened to regularly and hugely admired, which made it even worse; I'd be speaking to one of my heroes. So much for the carefully scripted preview I'd eventually settled on, because James went into a long-winded introduction that meandered off into a comparison between my name and John Cleese, which he believed was a version of Cheeseman.

I can't remember how I reacted, but I do remember that he introduced me by asking me if I thought there was any connection between the two names.

It had the double effect of making me forget my nerves, which I think was his plan, but also throwing me off my carefully rehearsed script.

Whatever I said must have been ok, because during the months to come, I reported on quite a few games for Piccadilly Radio, usually when one of the local lower league teams was playing away from home on wet Tuesday evenings, when no one else wanted to go. They paid me, which was a bonus, but in truth I barely got enough to cover my petrol expenses. That hadn't been my motive though, because I had my foot on the ladder, not that I seriously expected to make a career of this job, but it was nice to be reporting on football on the radio.

These days, Darlington have a brand new stadium, much better than the old Feethams ground, which doubled up as a cricket ground. To get into the football stadium, you had to walk around the outfield of Darlington Cricket and Football Club.

Mike Brookes, the Rochdale press officer, and former Dale reporter for BBC Radio Manchester, had told me the previous season about the carvery at Darlington. At just £5 a head, it is an absolute must. I was really looking forward to this game, if only for the carvery!

I arrived early, too early really, and ended up talking to Darlington's press officer for almost an hour. What a lovely man. We put the world to rights, as we discussed the good and bad of modern football. I love speaking to people like him, another of the game's unsung heroes. He told me how Darlington had signed Franz Burgmeier, because the Chairman's teenage son had seen him play for Lichetenstein in a World Cup qualifier and become a fan. I was told he was a good player, so I gave him particular attention during the game.

Eventually the carvery opened and we enjoyed the mouth-watering meal together – he even signed me in as a member of staff, so I only had to pay £2!

Darlington's new arena is fit to grace the Championship, so it seemed a shame that just 1651 fans were in attendance. The stadium has a capacity of around 10,000.

On the pitch, things seemed to be going well for Bury when Ben Futcher headed them ahead, but it was ruled out for offside. Darlington scored their winner early in the second half through Alan White.

Thursday 6th November – Match 36
Manchester City v FC Twente – UEFA Cup

Back to European action and a visit from FC Twente of Holland, managed by Steve McClaren – or should that be "Shhteve" McClaren?

The former England boss had not had the best of exits from the national post when the tabloid journalists had labelled him the "Wally with the Brolly", after his rainy last game in charge at Wembley.

He was rebuilding his career with Twente, but had already set himself up for more mickey-taking. To try to fit in with the locals he had developed a fake Dutch accent.

"I sort of knew, er, when I came here, and erm Champions League, er Liverpool or Arsenal I thought maybe one of them we would draw and it is Arsenal, I think." What was that all about? I assume he thought that way of speaking would make it easier for the Dutch to understand him. At least he didn't shout, like most foreigners abroad.

I don't normally have time to attend the press conference staged by City's opponents, but this was one I didn't want to miss. I didn't expect the accent to be in evidence on this occasion though. He'd started off normally, but as the questions came, in English, but from the Dutch reporters, he started to slip back into his foreign accent, which became even funnier when Peter Slater (or should that be Schlater?), from BBC Five Live, asked him a couple of questions.

I couldn't help but snigger, when one English reporter, asked, with a straight face, if he was learning Dutch. He said he was and it was going well! This was one press conference that was well worth taking the trouble to attend.

The match was much better than the two previous league games had been, probably because Shaun Wright-Phillips had opened the scoring in the first five minutes. McClaren was clearly excited about being back in England and was extremely animated in his touchline technical area. I'm sure he felt he had a point to prove.

The game remained an open contest from the first minute until the last with City winning 3-2, but Twente's Stein Huysegems came very close to an equaliser, which many felt they'd deserved.

Saturday 8th November – Match 37
Wigan Athletic v Stoke City – Premier League

Given a choice, I'd always rather watch a game in a stadium than on TV. You can see the game much better. Watching a game on television is like looking at it through a letterbox. I do understand why TV directors use lots of close-ups of managers' and players' faces; I'd rather see the full picture.

In addition to being able to see things like off-the-ball movement and tactics better at a ground, there's also the noise, the smell, the interaction with other supporters, the debate and the banter.

Obviously there are exceptions. I sat on the front row, directly behind the goal, at Walsall once, and couldn't judge distances or angles properly. It did give me a chance to study, in great detail, what a goalkeeper does for the whole ninety minutes, when normally my eyes would be following the ball at the other end.

The other negative of watching football on television is that, no matter how good the game is, I do find myself nodding off from time to time. I don't know if it's the fact I'm so comfortable in my armchair or the rhythmic speaking of the commentator that prompts me to nap every now and again. I wake up, wondering if I've missed a shot or a goal. It is not a pleasant feeling.

Although I was never likely to catch forty winks as I commentated on Wigan against Stoke, it was not a great game. Wigan dominated possession and probably deserved to win, but they couldn't score a goal and when the final whistle went, Stoke City seemed delighted with a 0-0 draw. I still enjoyed the game, the banter with my summariser Paul Rowley, the half-time steak & kidney and the unique match day experience. Bring on the next game!

Sunday 9th November – Match 38
Manchester City v Tottenham Hotspur – Premier League

It seemed obvious, to me, that the new Spurs manager Harry Redknapp would be extra determined in this game, having already visited the City of Manchester Stadium with Portsmouth and been thrashed 6-0; and so it proved.

City took the lead with a great goal from Robinho, but Spurs, with Vedran Corluka facing City for the first time, fought back to win 2-1. It wasn't a terrible game, by any means, but disappointing nonetheless.

Games between City and Spurs have usually been open down the years, and naturally the 1981 FA Cup Final pops into my head when I think of fixtures between the teams. I'd thought that simply reaching a cup final would make it a great day, win or lose, but the experience of losing at Wembley, as a result of that oft-repeated Ricky Villa goal, was a heartbreaker.

I felt almost as bad as I'd felt when David Pleat danced on City's relegation day, or when the club was relegated to the third division, despite winning at Stoke. I can't explain why; perhaps something told me that it might be some time before City would get that close again.

Both matches, the 1-1 draw and the replay, were great games and Steve MacKenzie's goal on the Thursday was worth paying for on it's own, but I still felt very low as I travelled home on the football special on that Thursday evening.

The build-up had been good, if a little repetitive. I spent cup final eve at Howard Yeats' house, helping make cheese and ham sandwiches to be sold by the supporters club on the 12 special trains that had been organised to get fans down to Wembley. It was like working on a production line; I think I was spreading the margarine. We must have made over a thousand sandwiches before collecting the same number of pork pies and buying chocolate, crisps and drinks from the wholesalers.

On match day I arrived at Piccadilly Railway Station nice and early to help load up the trains and was then away on the first one. I was in charge of my own football special, with assistance from my then girlfriend, Irene, and several colleagues from the Co-op Bank, where I worked.

We got to Wembley early enough to enjoy the walk down Wembley Way, and to enjoy the pre-match build-up in the ground. I felt nervous throughout the game, even after Tommy Hutchison had given City the lead, and I can't really describe how it felt when he unintentionally headed home Tottenham's equaliser. Somehow, I had seen it coming.

The replay was an even better game, and I was on the ultimate high when City came from behind to lead 2-1. I suppose my eventual post-match depression had been made all the worse by the fact that City lost 3-2, after both sides had been ahead. I knew that this game would be remembered as one of the all-time great finals, but City had lost. Even if they went on to win the cup in the future, surely it would never be as good as it would have been winning that day.

All these years later I've concluded that I'd settle for a scruffy 1-0 win if it meant City had won the FA Cup.

Tuesday 11th November – Match 39
Arsenal v Wigan Athletic – League Cup

Sometimes the biggest treats happen when you least expect them. Don't get me wrong, I'd wanted Wigan to win and had travelled down to the Emirates Stadium full of hope, especially as Arsenal had a habit of playing a reserve team in the League Cup.

I should have known better, because I'd seen them win 2-1 at City in 2004 with a team that had an average age of just 19.

Arsenal's team against Wigan seemed disrespectful as I studied it prior to kick-off, while Wigan fielded virtually their first choice eleven; by the end of the game I only had admiration for the Arsenal youngsters.

The player who really caught my eye was 16-year-old Jack Wilshere. He looked to me like a superstar of the future. He controlled midfield and seemed to have perfect balance, good reading of the game and great vision. Carlos Vela and Jay Simpson scored the goals and also looked exciting prospects for the future.

It was nice too, to see the senior Arsenal players sitting behind the substitute's bench, watching the next generation breeze past a very good Wigan side, in fact goalkeeper Chris Kirkland had an excellent night, so the scoreline could have been even more emphatic, had it not been for his good work.

That said, I do have a bit of an issue with clubs fielding weakened sides in the Cup competitions. Speaking as a supporter, I'd rather see my team win a trophy than get three extra points in the league.

Slowly but surely the message from managers that survival in the Premier League, in particular, is more important than a run in the knock-out competitions is seeping into the public consciousness. What utter rubbish.

I understand the financial implications of being in the Premier League, but as a spectator I go to football matches dreaming of success. I want to be entertained and to occasionally have my breath taken away by some wonderful piece of skill from players who amaze me by their movement and wizardry.

Only on the last day of the season do I concern myself with the pleasure of staying in the division, but even then, when I reflect on great games and great moments, it is those other days that I remember and which keep me going back for more. Money is at the root of it all, of course, and that part of football is never going to go away, but surely we can still pretend that it's a sport. Sport is about trying to win, not trying to simply avoid defeat or failure.

Can you imagine watching a 5000m race at the Olympics where the sole objective, of most of the runners, is to avoid finishing last? Would tripping up one of their opponents be acceptable to achieve that goal?

Perhaps that's not the best analogy, because football is much more than just a race, at its best it's a ballet with a ball, a chess match between Bobby Fischer and Anatoly Karpov or the creative theatre of Shakespeare's greatest play. Sometimes it feels more like watching the East Germans building the Berlin Wall.

Saturday 15th November – Match 40
Bolton Wanderers v Liverpool – Premier League

The Build-up to my 40th match of the season, included an evening at the Chill Factor, near the Trafford Centre, where I took part in Children in Need, the annual Charity extravaganza. Ever since I joined the BBC in 1994, I've been involved in CIN, either as a presenter or contributor. I used to enjoy being the auctioneer on BBC GMR, as it was then known, taking bids on items as diverse as being the City mascot, to a day on a yacht or a rare piece of memorabilia or jewellery.

One year I co-hosted our radio programme from the studio and was suddenly told by the producer that I was speaking to Denise Welch, live from TV Centre in London and within five seconds she was speaking to me. I couldn't think who she was, so I tried every subtle trick in the book to work out who she was and listened very intensely to every answer she gave to my banal questions, in case there was a clue to who she was. She gave nothing away.

In the end I had to ask her outright, and the moment she told me she played Natalie in Coronation Street it clicked, but the disdain in her voice had given away that she felt I should have known who she was instantly. I felt about six inches tall, but carried on regardless. Later that evening we had the boy band "Take That" on the line, bidding for an auction item, I recognised their voices.

These days, I spend the evening of Children in Need, with my face out of view from the cameras, and yet I still play an active role and get to wave to all the people who come along with their cheques and donations. Even at the Chill Factor indoor skiing centre, I didn't need to worry about feeling the cold. I'm not going to spell it out, but it's always great fun.

Bolton Wanderers against Liverpool, the following day, seemed like a mouth-watering game, but not one I'd normally be covering. Jack Dearden is our Bolton reporter and has been for many years, so apart from their matches against City, I'm normally a spectator, or occasional touchline reporter. Jack couldn't do this game, so I deputised.

Jack is one of my best friends, we met before either of us became professionals. Jack was a gas fitter and I was a bank clerk when we met at Radio Cavell in Oldham. He'd come to the attention of the hospital radio station because he'd sold his car to fund a trip to Australia to cover the Rugby League version of the Ashes series.

We hit it off straight away and have always helped and advised each other throughout our careers. I helped Jack take his first steps into professional broadcasting when I introduced him to Clubcall, as they expanded into Rugby League. Before long we were discussing whether he should change careers when he was offered a fulltime job, based in their offices next to Boundary Park.

It was something I might have considered too, but I felt it was too much of a risk, with a wife and family to support and no trade to fall back on, if it all went wrong. Jack had a trade and no dependent family to worry about, so I urged him to take the chance, after all, "If you don't, you might regret this for the rest of your life", I told him.

Once he was working for Clubcall he helped me get more and more freelance work, which helped as I battled my way through some tough financial times. Irene had left the bank to have our first child and my wage, which wasn't exactly what Nick Leeson might have been making at his peak, wasn't extravagant.

One day Jack rang to ask me if I'd cover a Rugby League game – Dewsbury v Halifax at Crown Flatt. I'd only been to one Rugby League game in my life. Four years earlier I'd stood with Jack on the Chaddy End terracing at Boundary Park and he'd taught me the rules while watching Oldham against Halifax.

I liked the sport but didn't feel confident enough to do the coverage well. Jack convinced me that with his pre-match briefing I'd be ok, and since there wasn't a press box at the stadium, because the ground had been damaged by fire, all I had to do was a half-time and full-time report and a post-match interview. He also assured me he'd never ask me again, and that this would be a one-off.

During the next few years I was covering at least one game each weekend. Those experiences led to a chance to present unpaid half-time and full-time reports of a Challenge Cup tie between Leeds and Bradford Northern into Sunday Sport with Rodney May, for BBC GMR, which helped make them more aware of me there too.

I was continuing to work for the Bank, but spending more and more time at sporting events as a reporter. My main job, by now, was to drive a van around the north west branches delivering mail, so I listened to BBC GMR all day and loved it. My favourite presenter was Jeremy Dry, who did a very inventive afternoon show.

I contacted him with a request to record an interview with him, for my hospital radio show and he agreed. He presented on a Sunday morning too, his show finishing at 11am, the same time as mine. On that day I recorded my programme in advance and went down to the BBC and sat alongside him in his studio while he was broadcasting.

After he'd finished he asked me to play along with his introduction and then interview him. I couldn't understand why he was recording it too. When we'd finished he urged me to listen to his show during the following week, and promised that all would become clear.

During his Wednesday programme he used the interview "as live", something broadcasters did routinely at that time. The BBC doesn't do that anymore because of various issues about "listener trust" that have been highlighted in the media. What he did was funny and fun. He introduced me by saying the bosses had sent me in to interview him. I thought his use of my interview was very original.

He inspired me to do something original with my version of the interview and so I built a whole programme around it. I interviewed other presenters at GMR, including Jimmy Wagg, Andy Buckley and Sue McGarry, the wonderful, bubbly presenter of news programmes. I then told my hospital radio listeners that I was live at the BBC, in the next studio to Jeremy Dry, and that I had been asked by his bosses to burst into his studio, live, just before 11am to interview him. That's where I slotted in the piece we'd recorded a week earlier.

I sent a copy of the finished programme to Colin Philpott, BBC GMR's editor, who I'd also interviewed, and he seemed to like it. A few weeks later the station's head of sport, Andy Buckley, told me there was a job vacancy in the sports department, as a result of the temporary departure of David Oates to BBC 5live. Andy suggested I should apply for it.

I suppose my Rugby League coverage, the hospital radio programme and being seen by Andy at City, doing post-match interviews for the club video and working for Clubcall must have impressed him. I applied for the job and took lots of advice from Mike Sadler, who was part of the sports team. Mike spent loads of time chatting to me on the phone, for which I was very appreciative and, fully prepared, I went for the interview.

A couple of hours later, Andy rang me to offer me the job. It had been a great experience, but I hadn't expected to be offered the job, so I asked for some time to think it over. Did I want to lose my secure job at the bank, was I good enough to make the career switch and perhaps more significantly, did I want to miss any City games, because at that point I was on a run of 17 years without missing a game, home and away?

After discussing it with Irene, I decided to take the job, on the basis that if I was to become the Manchester City reporter, my dream job since being a teenager, I'd have to take this risk, and miss a few games, while I climbed the ladder at the BBC. The first to congratulate me was Jack, who came to my house with a bottle of champagne. He'd been interviewed for the job too, but despite his own disappointment was fulsome in his congratulations.

Once I was "in" at the BBC, I kept telling everyone how good Jack was and before long he was our regular Oldham Athletic reporter and when the next full-time staff job became available he was successful at the interview and I returned the compliment by taking champagne around to his house. My mate, and my son's godfather, was now working alongside me, which couldn't have been better.

Filling in for Jack, therefore, was an honour. I worked alongside Alan Gowling, our Bolton summariser and it proved to be a controversial game. Gary Cahill had a "goal" ruled out, just before half-time by referee Rob Styles, for a block on Liverpool keeper Pepe Reina, by Kevin Nolan; the score was 1-0 to Liverpool at that stage.

Jack and Alan don't like referees at the best of times, they'd have loved slaughtering the official, but it was me in the commentary chair, and I'm NOT Jack, so I left that to Alan. Liverpool scored a second goal near the end as the Wanderers fans left muttering obscenities, about the referee, under their breath.

Sunday 16th November – Match 41
Hull City v Manchester City – Premier League

This was my second trip to the KC Stadium of the season, so I was well prepared for the steep climb to the press box, high up above the pitch. I was presenting the afternoon's programme, as well as doing the commentary, and I decided it would be nice to indulge in a bit of nostalgia, inspired by City's brilliant "My First Game" initiative.

We spent two hours taking calls from supporters who told us about their first game as a fan. The time flew by very quickly and we were even joined by City's Executive Chairman Garry Cook for a few minutes who told us his first footballing experiences and more about City's idea to collect these types of memories on their website.

I added mine, a few days later, and it was selected, apparently totally on merit (!), to be made into a giant poster and put up on the mezzanine wall, behind the press box at the City of Manchester Stadium, forever. I'm extremely proud to have my words up alongside my fellow fans.

The game was full of mistakes and oddities. Goalkeeper Joe Hart went off injured after a collision with the scorer of Hull's first goal, Daniel Cousin. It need never have happened because Tal Ben Haim had lost concentration to gift Cousin the ball. A few minutes later Hull defender Kamil Zayatte returned the favour and Stephen Ireland made it 1-1.

A second from the mercurial Irishman made it 2-1 but, inevitably, a former City player, Geovanni, scored to level things again. Geovanni had been popular at City but was never really given a chance to play regularly by manager Sven Goran Eriksson. So it was back past the wonderful Humber Bridge with just a point and City were on a run of four Premier League games without a win.

Tuesday 18th November – Match 42
Droylsden v Darlington – FA Cup

My favourite FA Cup upset came in January 1981 at Moss Lane when Altrincham beat Sheffield United 3-0 in the FA Cup. Graham Heathcote was one of the scorers during a Monday night game witnessed by over 5000 spectators who packed inside the ground. I saw a few of Altrincham's big cup nights back then, including a 3-0 defeat to Spurs in 1979 at Maine Road.

Here's a statement I never thought I'd write, "I've played at Droylsden's "Butchers Arms" Stadium. It was a charity match a couple of years earlier, so this was the only place where I had a genuine player's perspective." That sounds so pretentious, but I'm fully aware that facing Michael Le Vell and Andrew Whyment (Coronation Street's Kevin Webster and Kirk Sutherland) is a bit different to facing Darlington's first team in the FA Cup.

The day before the game, I'd gone up to the Butchers Arms to interview Dave Pace and had also chatted to Stella Quinn, who runs the social club. What a fascinating woman. She'd taken charge of the team back in 2003 for the Manchester Premier Cup because Droylsden's colourful manager Dave Pace had fallen out with the authorities so he'd asked her to run the team, throughout the competition.

Stella is a determined woman, who suffers no fools and is a proud and passionate fan of the club. You just know, when you meet her, that she's hard working and full of determination. It was for people like her, that I wanted Droylsden to have a good night.

I decided to locate myself outside the conservatory-style press box, made from pvc, and sit on the adjacent benches in the open air, which meant a bit of cabling and the creative use of gaffer tape – an essential skill in local radio. Mike Pavasovic, our non-league expert, sat alongside me, as I presented our sports programme.

Hosting a three hour show from a ground, especially when you're not allowed to commentate is far more stressful and energy sapping than doing a commentary, because you end up having to think about so many different things all at the same time.

What are the scores in the other games taking place at the same time, what's the next interview (piece of audio) that I'm going to introduce, when is the next news or traffic update due etc? I love those nights, but they require a lot of concentration to keep all those "plates spinning".

Mike Pavasovic, or Pav as we call him, was my "presenter's friend" and because I've known him for quite a while, he is someone I can gently tease, but also I can tap into his extensive knowledge of non-league football.

It was a dramatic night, in more ways than one. The former Oldham striker Matthew Tipton scored a beautiful goal to win it for the Bloods, but the game was overshadowed by a lengthy delay, as the medics circled Darlington's Liam Hatch who'd fallen awkwardly on his neck.

I feared he'd broken his neck and would be paralysed or even die. I chatted to Mike while all this unfolded in front of us. He was brilliant, with just the right amount of gravitas in his voice. It can be a difficult situation to judge because overdoing it can lead to accusations of sensationalism, after the event, if it had proved to be a minor injury.

During the lengthy stoppage I grabbed one of the Darlington directors, who was walking past, for the latest news and former referee Jeff Winter, who was reporting on the game for a north east newspaper, also kept us up-to-the-minute as he got news from the touchline.

We feared for Liam Hatch, and less seriously we feared the game might not be concluded and would have to be replayed. The match did reach its conclusion but not before the fourth official had raised a board with a glowing red number 18 showing – which must be a record amount of added time.

Hatch was discharged from hospital the following morning. The long delay had been as a precaution because one of the players close to the incident had heard a crack as he hit the ground, and, as I understand it, the medics at the stadium didn't have the necessary equipment to safely move him onto a stretcher or the means to get him to hospital. Well done to the medics and thank goodness for a happy ending.

Happily, Hatch didn't suffer a broken neck, unlike the great City goalkeeper Bert Trautmann, who famously suffered that fate during the 1956 FA Cup Final; Bert never looked back after that.

Saturday 22nd November – Match 43
Manchester City v Arsenal – Premier League

Amazingly, this was City's first Saturday afternoon 3 o'clock kick-off of the season! A combination of fixtures being moved because of the UEFA Cup and

TV had meant games starting at every time and on every day possible. I'm a traditionalist, and I can remember how difficult I used to find juggling my working time and my football obsession, when I worked in a bank.

It must be very frustrating to have to plan around such uncertainties. Home games might be a little easier as they take less time, but trying to take advantage of cheap rail or bus fares for away trips is now nearly impossible. Is Sky TV to blame?

In Germany, the supporters mounted a nationwide campaign aimed at persuading the authorities to revert to the traditional Saturday 3.30pm kick-off time. They were fairly successful, with one game on Friday evening and two on Sunday at 5pm. The rest are at the traditional time.

It's a trade off – tradition and convenience for paying spectators or the TV money. It's a debate I've had with supporters at fans forums for many years.

City victories against Arsenal have been fairly thin on the ground, over the years, so I must admit I wasn't overflowing with confidence going into this game, but felt more optimistic when Joe Hart was named in goal. He'd seemed certain to miss out after the injury at Hull City.

It proved to be one of the best games of the season and a very impressive display from the Blues. Stephen Ireland gave City a half-time lead, though perhaps they had been fortunate at the other end a couple of times before that.

The second half belonged to City with Robinho adding a second with a sublime finish, clipping it over Almunia's head, all in one glorious movement. The third goal, in the 3-0 win, came right at the end of the game, via the penalty spot.

I think most people had expected Elano to take the penalty, but Daniel Sturridge picked up the ball and with no interference from the captain or the bench, he swaggered forward to score the goal. Elano didn't seem happy and the question on everyone's lips at the end was what if he'd missed?

Wednesday 26th November – Match 44
Schalke 04 (u18's) v Manchester City (reserves) – friendly

There was snow on the ground as my plane came in to land and a real nip in the air, but nothing much different, temperature-wise, to England as I flew into Germany on the Tuesday afternoon.

It seemed very strange to be spending the next leg of City's European adventure in Germany, especially because it's Schalke 04 - my other team. Arriving here, via Dusseldorf, was very familiar to me.

I didn't have to ask directions, it was like being at home. I've been there, watching Schalke, nearly 40 times, and that doesn't include the annual family holidays I spent there as a child. My mum, who died when I was just 17 years old, was from Gelsenkirchen.

I still miss my mum, I suppose in some ways it was the worst time in my life to lose her. If I'd been younger I might not have known her so well, if a little older I might have left home and had other relationships at the centre of my life.

It broke my heart to see this feisty, proud woman grow weaker during the months she suffered from cancer. She was a smoker, which can not have helped her health. Whether that was directly the cause of her premature passing, at just 49 years of age, I still don't know. I believe it was her drive and zest for life that has carried me through life, so she will always live on in me.

As I grew up, she was probably overprotective, since she'd had a couple of miscarriages and was also aware of the anti-German feeling among some people. I was born just fifteen years after the end of the Second World War. As well as Ian, I'm named after my German Uncle Karl and my English grandfather Ernest, meaning my initials would have spelt IKE, the nickname of General Eisenhower, then the US President.

Ike had played a significant part in the defeat of the Nazis. My mum didn't want me to be saddled with that nickname so she decided to change the spelling of Karl to Carl, which, in later years, I though was pretty cool.

After visiting Gelsenkirchen every summer since being born until my mid teens, I'd lost contact, in my own right, with the surviving members of my family. My life was full of growing up, studying, getting a job, courting, getting married and having a family, so I didn't think about Germany much, though I was always conscious that there was still resentment, from some, towards the country of my mother's birth, so I kept my roots fairly quiet.

As I turned 40 years old, I had an epiphany moment, and decided that I had to re-establish my connection with Gelsenkirchen, my mum's birthplace. Most of my relatives there had been women widowed by the war, so they had, one by one, passed away. I decided the best way to reconnect was through football, so I sent an Email to a Schalke fans' website, asking if anyone wanted to be a penfriend.

Andreas, Michael and Ben replied and within a few months I was on my way to meet them and to watch a Schalke game. Since then I've met many more Schalke fans and now have a network of good friends there. Many of them are now City fans too and have visited for several games here, including the last game at Maine Road and a couple of famous wins in the Manchester derby.

On my arrival in Gelsenkirchen, I usually satisfy my hunger with a few Reibekuchen (potato pancakes) and a Bratwurst, and this was no exception as I meandered through the Christmas market along the pedestrianised zone, which leads away from the train station. I made my way to the home of one of my Schalke friends Markus Rehse.

He, too, has developed a passion for City after I introduced him to the Bredbury Blues. Led by "Arnie", they came, en masse with me to a game at Schalke, inspired by my tales of how good it was there. A friendship has been growing between City and Schalke fans since.

Markus has, what looks like, a pub, in his huge spare room. It's full of Schalke memorabilia and quite a few City items too. He was busy laminating signs to help guide City fans to his fanzone, from the railway station. We chatted for a while, discussed the game and hoped there'd be no trouble between the fans, and agreed to meet up again the following day.

Next I caught the 302 tram, which took me past Schalke's stadium, until I was within walking distance of my auntie's house, where I was greeted with some delicious home cooking. With my remaining German family all around me, we enjoyed an evening looking at photographs from a bygone era. My auntie's cooking is very similar to what I'd been used to from my mum when growing up, and just as good.

As we chatted away, I received a phone-call from the TV station WDR, which is the regional version of ARD (the German BBC). They wanted to include an interview with me in their breakfast and tea-time previews of the City game. Despite working in the media I wasn't sure what they wanted from me so I agreed to be picked up by them the following morning and we carried on with our reminiscences.

Whenever I visit, I take with me a selection of goodies which the family enjoy, but which are not widely available in Germany, things like wine gums, liquorice allsorts and English toffees. On this occasion, with it being close to Christmas, I also took a box of mince pies. Have you ever tried to explain what mince pies are, especially in a foreign language?

I had to come up with a rational explanation, which sounds dafter the more you try to make it sound like a sensible thing to eat! I couldn't help thinking about Rachel, in "Friends" making a trifle which included custard, bananas, fruit, minced beef and peas and fresh cream. Her mistake didn't seem so silly at that moment.

The next morning, after breakfast, the WDR TV crew arrived. They told me they wanted to do a short interview, explaining my family connection to Schalke. I spent four hours acting out my arrival at my auntie's house and being filmed looking through old pictures before my auntie, who'd never done anything like this before, was also interviewed.

Then there were more "action shots" at my mum's final resting place, in the local cemetery, before we moved on to the press conference at the Veltins Arena, where I interviewed the Schalke midfielder Orlando Engelaar - and there's nothing Mickey Mouse about him. He's 1.97m tall, which is big and spoke perfect English, which actually came as no surprise.

Having felt like I'd spent the day in and out of make-up for the filming, and heaven knows I need it, I was glad to be back involved in the build-up to the game. Being the subject of this mini documentary, had felt like being filmed for the opening sequence of a James Bond film. I'm more Roger Moore than Daniel Craig by the way.

The Veltins Arena is fascinating. It has a closing roof, and the pitch rolls out underneath one of the stands on non-match days. The lush grass playing area had been moved inside the stadium, ready for City's evening training session and to allow final preparations for the game, with plenty of welding and last minute work still being done.

On Bundesliga days the stadium holds just over 61,000 fans, but when seats are bolted into the standing sections on European nights, the capacity is reduced to around 54,000. I knew it would be a great atmosphere for the game with over 2,500 City fans packed into one corner.

I met plenty of fans as I stood watching Schalke do their last minute preparations, on the training pitches near the stadium, before heading off to the nearby town of Bottrop for a game between a Schalke U19's and a City reserve side. I'm not sure why the game was played there, because I've previously seen games at one of their old stadiums in the town of Gelsenkirchen, but it was a neat little ground in Bottrop, with around 500 spectators in attendance.

I spotted a couple of City fans, but not many had made their way there. Paul Marshall scored the only goal to give City a much deserved 1-0 win.

To conclude my day, I met up with my BBC colleague Peter Slater, my friend Markus and Schalke's assistant press officer Thomas - another good friend. We spent the evening discussing, over a lovely Italian meal, the differences and many similarities between the two clubs and the two countries, a conversation I'd never been able to have in my younger days.

Thursday 27th November – Match 45
Schalke 04 v Manchester City – UEFA Cup

My normal UEFA Cup match day routine of going for a run was abandoned. I went to the zoo with the family! The biggest zoo in the Ruhr area was very close to the Schalke Arena and we were there by mid morning, as I'd already spent the early morning broadcasting the sports news on BBC Radio Manchester from inside the stadium, before being picked up by my auntie and her husband Harold and their grandson Philipp.

It was a very relaxing couple of hours, looking at the hippos and rhinos, although I did feel like I was looking in a mirror at times! I was frequently interrupted by phone calls from Manchester, before we returned home for the perfect lunch of homemade Rouladen (thinly sliced beef wrapped around onions and bacon and other stuff in a delicious gravy!), red cabbage and dumpling pieces.

The BBC has to pay for commentary rights to games, I'm sure many supporters think it's free, and the calls I'd been receiving were to inform me that Schalke insisted on adding an extra fee for this game. Fortunately this issue was eventually sorted out, because it would have been a heartbreaker for me if this game, of all games, had been the one I couldn't commentate on.

By early afternoon I was in the centre of town assessing the mood, now that the City fans were arriving in numbers. There seemed a good atmosphere, with groups of City and Schalke fans mixing together and exchanging scarves. Naturally, I met up with the Bredbury Blues at the fanzone, created by Markus. All seemed peaceful, though I was told the police had steered a group of undesirables away.

I headed off to the Veltins Arena to prepare for the game, only to be greeted with another request for an interview. This time it was the stadium broadcaster, who does an hour long countdown to kick off, to be shown on the video cube above the pitch and on the TV screens around the stadium.

They brought the camera and interviewer up to me in the press box and chatted to me, in German, in between my contributions into "Manchester Now", back home on Radio Manchester. This was another daunting experience, with my colleagues in the English media both laughing at me and applauding my efforts in equal proportions.

Once the long-awaited game got underway, I found it a very easy game to commentate, as I knew both sides so well. City won by 2-0 and in truth it was a comfortable victory, indeed with six points from the opening two games, City now seemed certain the progress to the knockout stage in 2009.

It was a bittersweet feeling for me though: on the one hand, I was delighted City had won, but at the same time disappointed that Schalke lost. I hoped they would win their last game against FC Twente in Holland and also progress to the knockout phase.

For me football had come full circle. My first game was City v Schalke, a 5-1 win at Maine Road in 1970, and I'd seen that special fixture again. In different ways, these were two of the best games I have ever seen, and this was a trip I'd never forget.

My biggest honour, was being able to write a column in the match day programme for the game, half in English half in German, welcoming the City fans and introducing City to the Schalke fans. There was even a picture of me and my Mum. I can't tell you how proud I was to honour her memory.

Saturday 29th November – Match 46
Chesterfield v Droylsden – FA Cup

As I arrived in Chesterfield on a sunny Saturday lunchtime, I could not have predicted the events that would unfold later in the afternoon. I had time to nip into the town centre to grab a bite to eat, as nothing was available at the ground. I pre-recorded my two o'clock scene-set for the programme and planned to be back by quarter past two for the team news.

As I strolled back up the hill to the ground I noticed a little bit of mist hanging around, but there didn't seem to be too much to worry about, at that stage. As I chatted to other members of the media and said hello to the Droylsden manager Dave Pace, down on the touchline, I started to notice that the mist was quickly becoming fog.

By kick-off time it must have been impossible for the supporters at one end of the ground to see the goal at the other end. The game should have been either delayed, to see if the fog cleared, or called off, at that point. From my position at the back of the stand, on the half-way line, I couldn't see the spectators in the stand opposite, but I could see both goals, though the players on the far side were unidentifiable, shadowy figures. This was one game I was happy to be reporting on rather than doing commentary.

Much to my surprise the game kicked off on time, and I realised this was going to be a tricky assignment. Whenever a goal looked possible I still had to burst into "off-air" commentary, and so when Neil Prince crossed from the Droylsden right wing for Carl Lamb to score, I simply described it as a ball appearing from the gloom was turned home by Lamb. Droylsden led 1-0 at half-time.

During the break I went for a cup of tea, out of sight of the pitch, returning just before the restart. It seemed slightly clearer to me, so I was astonished when there was then a long delay while the referee assessed the conditions. Eventually the game was called off, much to the disgust of the Bloods boss Dave Pace. I understood how he felt. Either the game should not have started or it should have been completed.

By the time I'd interviewed Pace and Lee Richardson, the Chesterfield boss, who not surprisingly had agreed with the half-time abandonment, it was nearly 5 o'clock. The fog was almost gone, but Droylsden would have to revisit Saltergate and the crooked spire, 10 days later.

Sunday 30th November – Match 47
Manchester City v Man United – Premier League

Derby days are either brilliant or terrible, depending on the result, which is all that matters to most people.

My favourite derbys include the 5-1 win in September 1989. I was up on the TV gantry that day and will never forget Andy Hinchcliffe's goal or Paul Lake telling me after the game that he'd eaten raw meat for breakfast.

The last derby at Maine Road, the first attended by my youngest son Daniel, and some of my German friends, was special too. Daniel had never seen City win against United and, as an eight year old, he'd suffered plenty of teasing from Reds fans, who outnumbered Blues by a ratio of 10 to 1 in his school. I'd wanted him, more than anyone else, to see them win. Shaun Goater's two goals had helped that happen.

From a practical point of view, I never enjoy sharing commentary as much as doing it all the way through. I can't deny that's partly because I simply love doing it all, but also because it feels more fragmented.

If City are at home I do the first twenty two and a half minutes and then our United reporter, Steve Wyeth, takes it up to half-time. We have different personalities and our own way of doing things. As a listener I prefer a continuous ball-by-ball commentary, and have never understood why 5live use two commentators in this way, for all their games.

On local radio we do this to appease the fans of the two clubs who might otherwise feel there might be a lack of objectivity. I don't believe that would be the case, but I understand the argument, particularly in a Manchester derby, where passions run high.

Having beat United home and away during the previous season, I feared the worst for City, and so it proved. Wayne Rooney scored the only goal of the game, which was also noteworthy for the dismissal of Cristiano Ronaldo for deliberate handball. At least the City fans had something to enjoy, on an otherwise disappointing day for the Blues.

December

Tuesday 2nd December – Match 48
Swansea City (u18's) v Manchester City (u18's) – FA Youth Cup

Manchester City's Youth Academy has consistently outperformed their equivalents throughout English football. There has been a steady stream of boys who have progressed through the various age groups before making their professional debuts in the first team. The one thing missing, until 2008, was the FA Youth Cup in the trophy cabinet.

Daniel Sturridge was the stand-out player from that winning team, but was too old to play in the team that was defending the trophy, along with several others, so this was a chance to look at the next generation. My passion for football, and City in particular, is boundless, I've been obsessed since being a boy myself, so rather than protesting against a long trip to Swansea for this game, I was the driving force behind it.

Fred Eyre is just like me – or should it be that I'm just like him, sometimes the edges blur – so he was just as keen to travel to South Wales, as I was. The added bonus was that I'd never visited the Liberty Stadium, so this would be a new ground for me.

I joined the "92 club" back in 1984, and their rules had insisted that a ground can only be counted if you see a competitive first team match there. I respect their rules, but for my own purposes, and satisfaction, this would still count.

As far as the Youth Cup is concerned, I travelled far and wide to see games long before I became the City reporter and I'm sure I once saw the former president of FIFA, Sir Stanley Rous, at a Youth Cup game at Watford, so I was in good company.

The team of 1986, which won the trophy by beating Man United in the final, was a special group. Almost all of them went on to have impressive careers, many of them in City's first team. In case you've forgotten, that City side included Ian Brightwell, Andy Hinchcliffe, Steve Redmond, David White, Paul Moulden, Paul Lake and my favourite at that time, Ian Scott.

Of this latest group of young City stars, I was interested to see how Alex Nimely, Andrew Tutte, Robbie Mak, Ahmad Benali and Kieran Trippier would progress. I have to say, though, that I've picked out the wrong ones in the past. During that 1986 season I wasn't sure Paul Lake would make it, I thought he was a bit gangly to have a career in the first team. How wrong was I, though in my defence he was a centre forward at the time?

Finding the Liberty Stadium proved a little trickier than it should have been, I think Fred must have been navigating, but eventually, without the floodlights to aim for – I used to love the old stadiums for that reason alone – we found our way to a parking spot outside the main entrance, a rare luxury, never enjoyed at first team games.

My coverage of this match was based on regular reports, so Fred was just there as an observer. Knowing this, I decided I'd only need one pair of headphones and one microphone. Usually I have spares of everything, in fact I usually carry far too much equipment with me, which is why I've got muscles in my spit! This was to be the night I regretted not having back-ups because as I settled down for the game, the wire that leads from the headphones to the bit I plug into my ISDN kit gently fell out, for no apparent reason.

I asked around for a spare, maybe Swansea City had headphones, perhaps in their PA box; but they didn't.

My microphone worked, but how would I hear my cue to do a report. I wouldn't say I panicked, but it focussed my mind for a few minutes. I eventually concluded that I'd have to dial up the studio on my mobile phone and listen to the station that way. It was a little disconcerting and meant extra work for the programme presenter Matt White, who showed great patience with me and superb professionalism throughout.

I was happy to report on an impressive 3-0 win for the Blues thanks to two goals from Alex Nimely and one from Robbie Mak.

Wednesday 3rd December – Match 49
Manchester City v Paris St.Germain – UEFA Cup

What a pity it wasn't Paris in the Springtime – instead it was Manchester in December! This was not a night of European glory. I had been told that the Paris fans had one of the worst reputations in Europe. My friends in Germany had told me the Parisians had been strip-searched for their visit to Schalke, so it was with a little trepidation that I went to the game, not that any trouble was likely to affect me.

Until this season, City had only played once in European competition since they last truly qualified, through their league position, back in 1978. Unlike many of the club's younger fans, I'm old enough to have seen some of those great European nights from the 1970's with the games against Juventus, Widzew Lodz, Standard Liege and AC Milan still sticking in the memory.

I remember Zbigniew Boniek scoring a free-kick for Lodz at Maine Road, when City were still lining up the wall, in a 2-2 draw, Brian Kidd scoring the only goal in a 1-0 win against Juventus and a comfortable 3-0 win against AC Milan after the first leg had been put back until Thursday afternoon because of fog.

I've been told about the fans who had to leave the San Siro at half-time in that game to catch their flight back to England, not knowing what the final score was until they arrived back in Manchester. I didn't go to Milan, the last City game I've missed through choice, to this very day. I was a student at Manchester Polytechnic, studying social science, and I couldn't afford to go to Italy, so I sat in Piccadilly Gardens listening to commentary on my transistor radio.

I used to enjoy listening to Ian Frame's commentaries, although the "eureka moment", when I knew that was the job I wanted to do, came when listening to commentary of the derby in November 1975. City won 4-0 and Colin Bell suffered his career-ending knee injury. What a fateful day that proved to be. While my hero, whose autobiography I later wrote, was in pain and trying to come to terms with the consequences of Martin Buchan's tackle, I started to dream that I would some day be the City commentator on the radio.

I seem to recall that "The Baron" was the presenter that evening, with Ian

Frame the commentator. I remember, distinctly, the words he delivered as the final whistle blew. "....and City go marching through to the quarter finals of the League Cup". On the couple of occasions when I've had the privilege of describing the action when City have gone through to the last eight of a cup competition I've repeated those words, apart from the League Cup bit, of course, as my homage to that evening of inspiration.

I've been asked a few times, by fellow supporters, to name my all-time favourite City players, and I always mention Nicolas Anelka, who I loved to watch during his time with the Blues. Like all the top creative players, because they're the ones who polarize views, Anelka had plenty of critics, but I wasn't one of them.

At his best he was a classic continental counter-attacking striker, though never a hard working, tackling back type. I'm happy to have one or two players like that in my team, the "wow" players I call them, and Anelka fell into that category. He was nick-named "Le Sulk", unfairly I thought. I can't claim to know him, though I interviewed him a few times and have heard many off-the-record stories.

I've come to the conclusion that he was intensely shy and quite private and found it difficult to deal with the English "alpha-male" dressing rooms and associated horse play.

I was told that on one trip to a training camp, aimed at creating team-bonding, Anelka didn't want to go clay pigeon shooting with the rest, preferring to relax and read a book. It didn't go down well with his team mates, but is that sulking, being a loner, not wanting to mix or something else? I understand both sides of the argument.

Anelka started his career at Paris St.Germain. He clearly loves that club and it was no surprise to see him in the crowd.

It wasn't the best of games though. I'd looked forward to it so much, with Claude Makelele and Mateja Kezman playing for the visitors, but the match proved to be an anti-climax and certainly not a patch on those wonderful European nights of the 1970's.

Saturday 6th December – Match 50
Fulham v Manchester City – Premier League

It's always nice having Chris Bailey with us for this trip, because he talks and talks about his affection for the area, while Fred reminds us exactly where the murdered TV personality Jill Dando's house was and how he once parked his car outside her front door in Gowan Avenue, which is just around the corner from Craven Cottage.

We usually drive to the ground and park somewhere nearby, while at Chelsea and Arsenal we park at a convenient tube station and complete the journey on public transport. The journey to Fulham is very familiar, down the M6 and M40, turn right at the BBC, close to Loftus Road, round Shepherds Bush Green, though Hammersmith, past the Charing Cross Hospital, to the accompaniment of Fred saying, "that's where George Best died", before we find somewhere to leave the car, on a parking meter near the ground.

It's a great experience driving up and down the country to games in the company of Fred, Chris and Charlie with other occasional travelling companions. Each of us, me more than most, take it in turns to be victims of their banter and of course the mood switches from happy to grumpy (in equal measure), as we put the world to rights.

Everything from political correctness to politics and of course the world of football is scrutinised with Chris chatting constantly from the moment of our early departure to our late arrival home. There have been many occasions where supporters have expressed surprise that I drive down to London or Portsmouth on the morning of the game and back again in the evening, having done the commentary in the middle of the day. People have a strange perception of what it's like doing this job for real.

I don't have a chauffeur, nor do I stop in a hotel, except on European trips or for the occasional early match, far from home. To be honest I love driving and prefer to be behind the wheel than travelling as a passenger, and I'd rather have a long day which ends with sleeping in my own bed, rather than in some soulless hotel.

Fred is very committed to everything he does, and often has very little sleep the night before a long journey, because he'll have been speaking at a sportsman's dinner and not got home until two o'clock in the morning. On those occasions I don't blame him for being less than enthusiastic, when I've informed him I'd be picking him up at seven thirty.

Fred loves his coffee, but it has to be Costa, the others won't do, so we have memorised which motorway service stations serve his favourite brew and which don't. I've got a reputation for enjoying a cooked breakfast en route to away games, but I should explain that away games are the only time I eat them.

I feel that I need a break once the journey is two thirds completed, to de-stress ahead of the match and to make sure I can eat peacefully, because despite the impressive spread usually offered up by Premier League Clubs these days, I'm often too busy at the ground to enjoy more than a drink and biscuit.

On arrival at Fulham we took a stroll along the Thames before this game, as unusually we had stopped at a modest hotel near Putney Bridge because of the 12.45 kick-off. Joining us for breakfast was a Romanian friend of mine called Val, who was in England for a couple of days with his company.

I first came into contact with Val in the mid 1980's, when he wrote a letter to the supporters club asking for penfriends. I started to write to him and later found out that his letters, to and from England, had made him come under the scrutiny of the communist party. Sometimes I would write to him, about football, and he'd not receive my letter. Presumably it had been intercepted by the secret police who had not approved of some comment I'd made. He had to be cautious about what he wrote to me.

After the fall of President Nicolae Ceaueşcu in December 1989, Val suddenly started to write much more open letters and I really got to know him. He was well educated and highly qualified and yet earned approximately £25 per month.

Within a few months he was planning a trip to England to see his adopted team City. He chose the Blues because of his admiration for the supporters in bad times and identified with their loyalty. I picked Val up from Heathrow Airport, his father had financed his flight by selling his car. I took Val to the local supermarket and his eyes were out on stalks as he surveyed the goodies that we take so much for granted.

He told me he'd had to queue for hours, each week, to buy milk for his young son Eddi. In England he could have filled his trolley with as much milk as he'd wanted in a variety of flavours and colours. He'd arrived in England with eleven US dollars in his pocket and not much more than the clothes he'd travelled in.

He sat with me in the press box at Old Trafford for a derby, I think it was the one City lost 1-0 in 1991, but he still enjoyed the experience. After a week with me, and an appearance on my hospital radio programme, he moved onto another of his penfriends. I dedicated a song to him on the radio, by Susanna Hoffs, former lead singer of the Bangles.

The words of "Unconditional Love" summed him up, not just because of his illogical affection for City, such an underperforming club, but also because there was no doubt that he would return to his life in Romania, to be with his wife Lori, when I could have understood if he'd been tempted to seek a better life in England.

After breakfast with Val in the hotel at Putney Bridge, we strolled through the park, along the Thames, to Craven Cottage, where, as usual, it was warm and sunny. The ground is older than most in the Premier League, but unlike Portsmouth, its age adds character. The press box is surrounded by vociferous Fulham fans, who are funny and passionate in equal measure.

It's always a pleasure watching games at the Cottage, and it seemed like it would be the perfect day, in so many ways, when Benjani headed home a Pablo Zabaleta cross, to give City the lead inside the first ten minutes. Val must have had a perfect view as he sat behind that goal, with his fellow City fans.

Fulham's equaliser came from Jimmy Bullard, after half an hour. I found it shocking that I couldn't use my annual Moritz Volz pun, because he'd left to join Ipswich, but it's always fun to see their PA announcer "Diddy" David Hamilton, who did continuity links on the TV when I was a child, and Mohammed Al Fayed, doing his walk around the pitch waving to the supporters. There's nowhere else like Fulham!

Tuesday 9th December – Match 51
Chesterfield v Droylsden – FA Cup

Back to Chesterfield, a ground I'd first visited for a League Cup tie in 1977 when Brian Kidd's goal had helped City win 1-0. This time it was the FA Cup and the second attempt to settle the tie that had been abandoned with Droylsden leading, in the fog. This tie was never destined to be "normal".

Mike Pavasovic was with me again, having just been made redundant from his job with the Oldham Evening Chronicle, so understandably he was a little more subdued and our conversation to and from the game was very philosophical. Pav is a good man and I could empathise with the turmoil he was facing in is his private life. Once we were in position, squeezed into the press box, he was his usual self, as I wondered what could possibly be more dramatic than the fogged-off first game.

When Chesterfield took a 1-0 lead I suspect, like me, Pav was assuming that Droylsden's chance had disappeared in the fog, but Alex Brown levelled things and the dream of an upset was back on. Then came something I'd never seen before.

There was an injury to a Droylsden player, so his team-mates knocked the ball into touch to allow treatment from the medical staff. From the restart, Chesterfield's Jamie Ward threw the ball to their star striker Jack Lester who, without thinking, lobbed the ball towards the Droylsden goal, over the head of the keeper and into the net.

Bedlam ensued with Dave Pace, the Bloods boss and his Spireites counterpart Lee Richardson involved in some verbal earbashing on the touchline. I spotted the Chesterfield defender Kevin Austin suggesting to his team-mates that something had to be done to correct this mistake. After the game everyone else wanted to take the credit for this very sporting action, but I believe Austin was the instigator of what happened next.

From the kick-off Droylsden's Steve Halford was allowed to walk towards the Chesterfield goal, unchallenged, and tap in an equaliser. It was only right that the game finished all square at 2-2 and so there'd be a replay back at the Butchers Arms a week later.

I was really getting involved in Droylsden's cup run, by now, and was disappointed to realise that I'd be in Spain with City in the UEFA Cup, when this tie would be completed, but I could hardly complain. Travelling to Spain was hardly going to be an inconvenience as I knew the rain would stay mainly on the plane.

On the way home, I treated Pav to some fish & chips, after all it had been another dramatic day, both on and off the pitch.

Friday 12th December – Match 52
Chesterfield v Macclesfield Town – League Two

This was a journey I was becoming very familiar with, as I headed back to Chesterfield for the third time in a fortnight. At least I knew that if I timed my arrival right I'd be able to park on the town hall car park for just £1.20.

The tight little press box at Saltergate is so antiquated that having gaffer tape is essential, but I'd left mine in the car. Fortunately Geoff Mitchell, Radio Derby's Chesterfield reporter, found a bit of previously used tape, which had just enough stickiness left to hold my ISDN mixer in place.

The main stand at Chesterfield is old and wooden, and reminds me of how dangerous football grounds used to be when smoking was allowed; Bradford being the tragic example that springs to mind. Old doesn't necessarily mean bad though, and one of the most endearing things about a visit to Chesterfield is the tiny little press room below stairs. The teas and coffees are handmade, not from those disgusting foil-packed instant mixes, and the sausage rolls and cakes are homemade, just as lovingly made as Rose's scones at City.

I can recommend the fruit cake, each piece wrapped in cling film, to keep it fresh.

This was the first time I'd seen Macclesfield Town in action during this season, and I was very impressed by the way they played and in particular with the contribution of striker Martin Gritton, who must have also impressed the Chesterfield hierarchy because they signed him later in the season.

It was also the first time I'd met the Macclesfield boss Keith Alexander, who impressed me even more than Gritton. What a down-to-earth sensible manager. His answers to my questions were well thought out. He was in a good mood because the Silkmen had won 4-2, with two goals from Martin Gritton.

Saturday 13th December – Match 53
Manchester City v Everton – Premier League

One of the proudest moments of my life was was being managed by David Moyes, in the David Eyres' testimonial at Boundary Park. I've been lucky enough to have played football at Maine Road and the City of Manchester Stadium too, in games organised by the charity "Football Aid". I've also played at Boundary Park, on the plastic pitch, for the Co-op Bank, at Macclesfield as a guest for City Old Boys (yes I've played for City!) and at Droylsden, for BBC Radio Manchester.

All these were not games I would ever count as "real games", though I'm tempted in the case of the old boys game, but the fact that there were paying spectators and I played against professional footballers meant that the David Eyres match counts as a "real" game.

I have kept meticulous records of every match I've attended, since that first one back in 1970. I can tell you exactly how many matches I've seen, how many goals; anything you want. I've seen over 1600 competitive City games, friendlies, reserves and youth games come into a different category. I've also seen another 800 games that didn't involve City, which is a lot of football!

The only match in my record books, which I've played in, was the "Celebrity XI" v Oldham Athletic Legends in May 2006. I'd hosted David's testimonial dinner a few weeks earlier and I guess he'd asked me to play in the game as a thank-you, not realising how hopeless I am at playing.

I'd been ill on the day of his dinner, which is very unusual for me, so it had been very hard work to get through the evening.

What do you think the odds would be that I'd also be feeling terrible on the day of the game too? I don't think I've ever felt as ill as I did on that match day, but, as the old cliché goes, I'd have walked over broken glass to play.

As I slowly made my way over Clayton Playing Fields, towards Boundary Park, I wondered if I'd even make it to the ground, let alone play. In the dressing room with me was Graham Lambert from the "Inspiral Carpets" and the comedian Paddy McGuinness. In walked our manager for the day, David Moyes. What a lovely guy. He knew most of us were hopeless. I knew he was humouring us with his team talk, but I loved every minute. To my astonishment, I was in from the start. I must have looked better than I felt.

I was exhausted by the end of the warm up, but managed to run about, a bit, for twenty minutes or so, before being taken off, with Moyes praising my efforts, as I took my seat on the bench. I didn't deserve any praise and he knew it, I'm sure his reaction would have been different if I'd been a professional. I got another 20 minute run out in the second half. For the record we lost 11-4!

Seeing David Moyes, a more grumpy looking David Moyes, stood in front of the away dugout at the City of Manchester Stadium, is different to seeing other managers, I feel as if I know him, he was my manager after all!

How he'd cope with not having a fit striker to name in his team was a puzzle, perhaps I should have brought my boots? I expected City to win, under the circumstances, but feared a "typical City" scenario. If it could it would; surely City wouldn't lose at home to a team without a striker?

Everton won 1-0, with a goal in the last minute from Tim Cahill, so often City's nemesis.

Thursday 18th December – Match 54
Real Racing Club (reserves) v Manchester City (reserves) – Friendly

The only direct flights from the UK to Santander were from London Stansted, an airport I was becoming more and more familiar with. I couldn't travel on Wednesday because the daily flight wouldn't arrive until late that evening, which would mean missing City's arrival, and the subsequent press conference.

As a result I had the pleasure of listening to Jack covering the Droylsden v Chesterfield game, via my laptop in my hotel room. I couldn't believe it when I heard that the floodlights had failed, with the Bloods losing 2-0. I can't deny that, rather selfishly, I was quite pleased, because I might now be able to go to the next attempt to conclude the tie. Somehow it didn't surprise me that there'd been another twist in the tale of this FA Cup tie.

There were conspiracy theories suggesting that someone sabotaged the floodlights at the Butchers Arms, but despite my desire to be at that game, I can assure you I was completely innocent.

Back in Spain, it seemed odd to see Christmas Tree-shaped lights on the beach and a tree in the reception to my hotel. I'd visited Spain many times with my family on holiday, but always at the height of the summer season. It didn't seem right to be in sunny Spain in the winter. Father Christmas must surely wear swimming trunks when visiting Santander!

I'd always travelled in shorts and a T-shirt when travelling so far south, quickly putting my sunglasses on, once safely outside the terminal building, but on this occasion I was wearing a coat, hat and gloves. There was a certain irony too, that City's UEFA Cup campaign had returned to the seaside, having started at the heart of the summer in the far-flung Faroes.

The temperature was actually warmer than back home, at about 14C.

My first problem, on arrival at my hotel, overlooking the Sardinaro beach, was that I'd left my suitcase key in England, so the hotel handyman had to pick the lock so I could access my PJs and toothbrush, which proved highly embarrassing when my underwear spilled out on the floor in front of him. It's a good job they were clean. It worried me that it was so easy to break into my belongings, and there was me thinking my little lock had made everything secure.

Naturally, I was ravenous by this point so I headed towards the hotel restaurant to peruse the menu, which was written in Spanish, with an English translation underneath. An American voice piped up, "I wouldn't trust the translation, we ordered lamb with salad and got lamb stew." The Spanish word for salad and stew are apparently very similar.

That American voice belonged to Nick Perera, a 22-year-old striker, who was in Santander to have a trial with Racing. He was hoping to play in Thursday's reserve friendly between Racing and City.

We talked for a while and he told me about his life in California and his hopes of impressing the scouts who'd be at his game. He told me that the weather had been terrible during the previous few days with a thunderstorm on Monday. Apparently things improved about the time I got there.

On the Wednesday morning I, 'Woke up this morning feeling fine..' as the song goes, so after breakfast I put on my running shoes and went for a four mile run along the beach, to get the blood flowing.

I'd tried to go jogging in all the countries I'd visited - I'm a regular in my local gym (hard to believe if you've seen me!) and try to make sure I keep fit while away. It's an interesting process too, because you see the local people going about their daily business. That said, I didn't see many locals on the beach, just a couple of fellow joggers and one or two dog walkers.

It was a lovely beach, and with the waves crashing in, the air was refreshing. It was raining that morning and the clouds were very low, so it was just like being at home. After a quick shower, I assessed the local shopping scene before reporting back on my exploits for BBC Radio Manchester.

There was a Christmas market, of sorts, with small wooden stalls selling delicate ornaments and lovely toys. The shops seemed more varied than in England, where the same high street chains dominate every town centre. Here the shopping seemed more varied.

The receptionist at my hotel, Fernando, was a Racing fan, so he was delighted to hear the rumour that Robinho, Shaun Wright-Phillips and Stephen Ireland might start the game on the bench.

I watched the early part of City's training session inside the stadium, which was just a couple of hundred yards from the beach. The pitch looked a bit patchy but the ball seemed to run true and after all the rain we'd had, there was a fair bit of spray coming off the ball.

The day finished with a visit to the local pizza place and a stroll along the prom. The City fans I bumped into seemed happy enough, so I headed back to the hotel ready for an early night, ahead of the double-header on Thursday - the reserve team friendly in the morning followed by the UEFA Cup game in the evening.

It drizzled as I stood on the touchline to watch City's reserves play their

Racing counterparts, at their training ground. The game was played on an all-weather surface surrounded by high-rise blocks. I noticed just one spectator taking advantage of the view from the flats, though there were around 150 spectators around the pitch, several being from Manchester.

It was great to chat with City's director of football Mike Rigg for a few moments, good relationships with the coaching staff never does any harm.

I was particularly interested to see how Nick Perera would perform, and after a nervy looking start, he seemed to be getting better when taken off in the second half. He'd told me the day before, over a coffee with his dad, that there'd been some resistance from the Spanish players to his inclusion in the team. Some had refused to pass the ball to him during the training sessions.

Mike Rigg asked me about him, when he discovered I knew a little about him. When I revealed his age, his interest waned. It seems that by 22 years of age, if you're not in a first team somewhere, you're not going to make it. City took the lead early on, thanks to a goal by James Poole, but Racing went on to win 2-1.

Thursday 18th December – Match 55
Real Racing Club v Manchester City – UEFA Cup

Back at the seaside I walked out to the Palacio La Magdalena, which was formerly the summer residence of the King of Spain. On the approach to the Palacio there was a display of seagoing vessels. The three old sailing ships might have been intended for the Armada, but clearly didn't make it. I met up with Chris and we exchanged opinions about Santander, as we explored the area around the Palace.

The waves were huge, much bigger than I'd experienced when I visited Santander with my family, a couple of years earlier, on the ferry from Plymouth. The waves we were watching in December were impressive enough to surf on, with the heroic types swimming out through the (presumably) freezing water before spending ten seconds up on their board riding the crest of a roller, falling in spectacularly and then swimming back out to do it all over again.

Chris and I eventually opted for the much more comfortable seafood restaurant next to the beach. I'm usually on a see-food diet, so this suited me. We had excellent views, including some of City's backroom staff out jogging. English wasn't as readily spoken in Santander, as it had been at all the other foreign locations I'd visited, so it was with some trepidation that we asked the waiter to explain what the options were. Chris recognised the word for chicken and our, very patient, waiter helped us pick out something delicious to eat.

I arrived at the Stadio de Sardinero early, to discover that I was sat in the corner of the stand behind the goal line, at the opposite end to the City fans. That wasn't the only problem. The plug sockets weren't working either, so I asked the club's press officer if an electrician could help me. I should have guessed, at that point, that it wasn't going to be my night.

At least my new friend Nick Perera didn't let me down. He fulfilled his role as match summariser very well and had some very interesting, objective things to say about the game.

He clearly wasn't impressed by the general lack of commitment shown by the City players. Still, at least PSG's win against FC Twente meant the Blues won the group anyway, despite the disappointing 3-1 defeat in Santander. The next morning I spoke to a few City fans who expressed their disgust at the attitude shown by the players. City were already guaranteed to progress to the knock-out stage of the competition and it seemed like they didn't care about this game.

Having been a paying spectator, for many years, I totally sympathised with their views. It had cost one family I met, well over a thousand pounds to watch the City players go through the motions. I didn't enjoy the game either. I also felt some sympathy for Racing because at one stage they thought they'd done enough to go through too, but a late goal in the game between PSG and FC Twente had seen them just fall short.

The net result was that City had won the group, by default, which would mean, in theory, an easier game, when the competition resumed in the new year. I spent most of the next day hanging around in Santander before an early evening flight back to Stansted, and the late evening drive back home, listening to my ipod. It felt like a very long journey home.

Saturday 20th December – Match 56
Oldham Athletic v Leyton Orient – League One

After sleeping off my long trip back from Spain, I awoke to be wished "Happy Birthday" by Irene, Steven and Daniel. I don't mind having my birthday near Christmas. As a child it meant that I got a couple of presents before everyone else and that there were decorations and parties all the time, as if they were celebrating my special day too.

At least the match I was covering, was just a short walk away, so I didn't leave home until just before one o'clock. Boundary Park was the venue for the first interview I ever carried out. The interviewee was the Oldham Athletic secretary Tom Finn; the subject was the club's plastic pitch.

I'd written all my questions down on an A4 sheet of paper. He seemed as nervous as me. I can't remember much about my questions or his answers, though I've probably got a recording of that interview on a cassette somewhere, because I've kept quite a lot of the early stuff I did.

I think it is very useful, when you start out in broadcasting, to record yourself and listen back. It quickly gets you past the, "I don't sound like that do I", stage and onto the, "why did I say that, why do I say erm so much, why am I repeating myself, I said why am I repeating myself", stage. I learnt a lot from listening back to those recordings. The interview with Tom Finn would have sounded very stilted and I now advise students, who're learning their trade, not to write questions down.

Have key subjects prepared, in your head, but listen to the answers and adapt your line of questioning and phraseology as you go along. The interview will be much better. End of lesson!

The plastic pitch, which wrecked so many knees, has long since been ripped up, so Oldham against Leyton Orient was played on a natural grass surface which was in pretty good condition for the time of year.

Latics had a bigger than average crowd for this game. I'd like to think they were there to share my birthday celebrations, but it was actually because of a reduced ticket price offer, as it was the last shopping Saturday before Christmas. I'd always prefer to be at a match than fighting through the

From 35°C in Cyprus to -5°C in Copenhagen

This is how close I got to Paul McCartney, Yoko Ono, Olivia Harrison and Ringo Starr in Las Vegas - I think I got a ticket to ride!

h my soul mate since the football specials, Charlie

The music I listen to:
Austrian singers "Singrid and Marina" and with my all-time hero Benny Andersson from Abba in 1980

Sipping champagne on the private jet to Tenerife

EB's spectacular ground in the Faroes

About to comment on my dream match, Shalke v City

y's greatest German Bert Trautmann

pal and travelling companion (and brilliant
rnalist) Chris Bailey, in Herning, Denmark

I loved working with Stuart Pearce - he was totally genuine

My Romanian friend Val during his first visit to England at Maine Road

I'm the young guy on the right, with my team of stewards going to Wembley in 1981 for the football special

29th April 1990, commentating at Wembley for Radio Cavell on the day Steven was born

ity and Oldham legend Bobby Johnstone,
ne of my video summarisers, on the TV
antry at Maine Road

Interviewing Rodney Marsh in
Tampa, Florida

Ricky Hatton, as down to earth
as ever, next to a roulette table
in Ceasars Palace, Las Vegas

)ne of my favourite
ictures, with Norman
Visdom at Maine Road

One of my modern day heroes, Robinho

Posing with the City mascot Moonchester at a Junior Blues pyjama party

A special moment, City legend Tony Book and the FA Cup

Signing copies of 'Reluctant Hero' with Colin Bell

y Mum and me, aged 14, at a
edding in Germany (wearing my
and Grammar School blazer)

: the City 'shop' in Beijing with
e only City shirt they had on sale

amera-shy Liz Douglas, who runs City's
nior fan-club - a real unsung hero

Irene's family, with her sister
Andrea (left) and her Mum and Dad

Jack Dearden and Radio Cavell Chairman
David McGealy wishing me well as I say
farewell to Hospital Radio after ten years

This is the man who taught me to
dance to Star Trekkin, Squirrel

The bus I broadcasted from in Lokeren

The Faroes in July, one of my first meetings with Mark Hughes

I help Jim Cassell show off the FA Youth Cup

In China with Stockport County

He's funny, highly knowledgeable and sits alongside me for City's home games - he's Nigel Gleghorn

Singing an Elvis song in the City panto

I felt a bit of a clown as I stood with Sun Jihai, Sylvain Distin and City's head of communications Vicky Kloss at a Junior Blues event

My son Steven starring as Aladdin in the City Panto

My first City panto as Prince Charzan with Ian Brightwell, Scott Hiley and the young City fans

One of my proudest days, my son Daniel, as mascot, leading out the team, with Richard Dunne at Chelsea

That's me in a dress, with Micah Richards in the annual City pantomime

The family:
Irene, Daniel and Steven after Kevin Keegan's promotion season

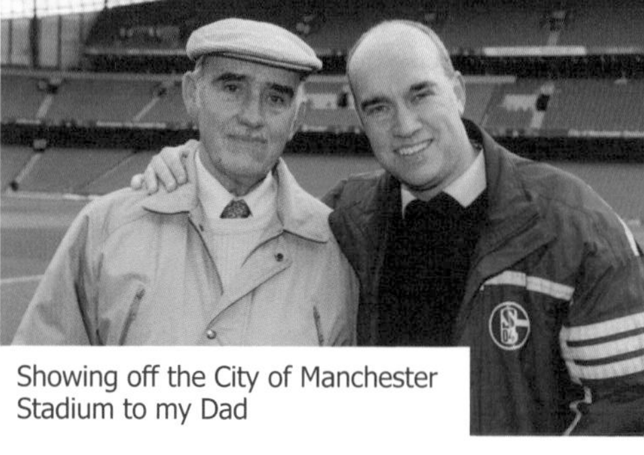

Showing off the City of Manchester Stadium to my Dad

Three generations of Cheeseman's at Eastlands

My inspiration, my friend and my sidekick, Fred Eyre

Collecting for Radio Cavell with Jack Dearden - equally embarrassing for us both!

A gentleman called Sven

I'm 19 years old in Germany, about to attend my first City away game in Europe

The irrepressible Kevin Keegan

Kickoff on the muddy, but playable Home Park pitch - my 92nd league ground

Andy Hitchcliffe and David White at Radio Cavell, the morning after promotion at Bradford

Christmas shoppers, so I've never needed that kind of incentive, but it clearly worked because nearly 7,000 were inside the ground at kick-off.

As always seems to happen when a club attracts a bigger than average crowd, the game ended in disappointment. Latics led through an Andy Liddell penalty only for the London club to get a late equaliser from a tap-in, following a saved penalty that should never have been. At least I had my birthday cake to look forward to!

Sunday 21st December – Match 57
West Bromich Albion v Manchester City – Premier League

City hadn't had great results in December, but this one seemed the ideal opportunity to return to winning ways, after all West Brom were bottom and the Blues hadn't won away from home since August, and it was the day after my birthday! During my forty years watching City, I'd learnt to expect the unexpected, but surely this game would go as expected!

Trips to the Hawthorns always remind me of Cyrille Regis and Laurie Cunningham. Regis was a powerful centre forward who had a touch that belied his massive physique.

In the late 1980's I was commentating regularly on City's club video and the company who did the filming decided to make a documentary, which seemed quite revolutionary at the time. The film crew took me to the away game at West Brom in November 1987 and asked me to do commentary from the TV gantry plus a couple of interviews. I'm not sure much of it was used, although I do remember interviewing David White after the League Cup win against Watford. We both looked like little boys, as I remember.

After the game at West Brom I was told the cameraman and his soundman would go straight back to their Sheffield HQ but , "you needn't worry, because we've arranged for you to go back on the team coach." Fantastic, I thought! I'll be travelling back on the team bus, how can it get any better. Surely that's every supporter's dream; I'd be a guest in the inner sanctum.

It proved to be a nightmare. Travelling with the players is never what it seems. They don't know you, they don't want you there, but it wasn't the players that were the problem, it was the manager, Mel Machin. He should have been in a reasonable mood because City had drawn the game 1-1, off the back of four straight wins, including the 10-1 against Huddersfield.

For some reason he was furious, whether it was because he arrived at the team bus to find me sat in the front seat, quietly looking out of the window, or because of something that had just been said in the dressing room, I'll never know. As he stepped onto the front step of the coach, he asked me who I was, clearly holding his temper back to a manageable level.

I told him and explained that arrangements had been made for me to travel back on the team bus as I'd been involved in filming an official club video. He stormed off to argue with either the film crew, who'd gone by now, or anyone else he could find, with the aim of having me kicked off.

Jimmy Frizzell, now in the role of General Manager stepped in as peacemaker. He knew me, and made it clear to Machin that I was the innocent party in all this and that I'd be stranded in Birmingham without a lift home. I was reluctantly allowed to stay, but I spent the whole journey staring out of the window, making no eye contact with anyone. It was one of the most uncomfortable journeys I've ever endured.

As I recall, Machin got off the coach somewhere on Bucklow Hill, between the M6 and the M56. As soon as he got off "Frizz" started to talk to me, sympathising with my situation and trying to assure me that there would be no ongoing problems with Mel Machin. At the "Posthouse", near the airport, everyone got off the coach; my car was parked outside Maine Road. Without hesitation Frizz offered me a lift back to the ground, and by the time I was being dropped off on the forecourt I was feeling a bit less stressed.

For this trip to the Hawthorns it was our usual happy group, and we all felt optimistic, except Charlie who reminded us that City never produce what you expect. After a bright start, and with the star names like Ireland, Hart, Dunne, Wright-Phillips and Kompany back in the start line-up, though Robinho had missed out through injury, things went downhill.

When West Brom took the lead through Luke Moore there seemed no way back, but an inventive backheel from Felipe Caicedo produced a deflected equaliser, with just four minutes to go. A point wasn't a great return from a fixture like this, but better than nothing, then up stepped Roman Bednar to head past Hart for the winner.

At least the journey home was not as difficult as the one years ago, though I had to try to get away quickly as I was hosting the Christmas party for young City fans back at the City of Manchester Stadium. If I referred to it as the Junior Blues you'd know what it was, but the name was changed to "Live4City", which doesn't have quite the same identity.

It was a great event, though I missed the first few minutes. As usual Liz Douglas had put her heart and soul into organising the fun-filled extravaganza, and there was plenty for the families in attendance to watch and do. I'm so proud to be involved with City at events like these and get a thrill from seeing the faces of the youngsters when they have a good time.

My party piece is dancing to "Star Trekkin'" the song recorded by the Firm in 1987. I learnt the dance when on a family holiday to Ibiza. A bouncy Birmingham lad, who went by the nickname of "Squirrel", performed it brilliantly and I've copied it ever since. It's the sort of thing most adults would be embarrassed to do, and maybe I should be, but as long as the children are having a good time I don't mind making a spectacle of myself. There are too many "precious" people in this world.

Tuesday 23rd December – Match 58
Droylsden v Chesterfield – FA Cup

I'd wanted to see this tie through to its conclusion, and I'd got my wish. Seated alongside me again was Pav, and the big question was, what could possibly be the twist to this game?

It was a cracking match, with Droylsden living the dream as they went 2-0 up, both goals being scored by Sean Newton. This was exactly what I'd hoped to see and both Pav and I were loving every minute of it, despite co-hosting a three hour programme, during which we couldn't commentate again. I'd had limited time to prepare the programme, so much of it consisted of us talking about everything and nothing, and introducing a few general interviews, the sports team had conjured up.

Despite a late goal back from Jack Lester, the Bloods won the tie 2-1 and would face Ipswich in the third round. I wouldn't be able to do that game, as much as it appealed to me, because City faced Nottingham Forest at the City of Manchester Stadium on the same day.

The scenes at the Butchers Arms were brilliant, fans running on the pitch, players being chair-lifted off, and manager Dave Pace was bubbling with joy when he came up to talk to us live, just before the end of the programme. It was an evening that had drama to spare, classic local radio stuff and I was so proud to be there to take our listeners through it.

After the fans had gone and the place had calmed down, I packed up my equipment and headed for the exit, only to bump into Dave Pace. He thanked me for coming and told me it hadn't felt right when I wasn't there for the game that had been abandoned due to floodlight failure. I felt ten feet tall, even though I knew it was a throw away line by Pacey. It had been a non-controversial fairytale at last, or so it seemed.

The following day it emerged that Sean Newton shouldn't have played in the game. Chesterfield lodged their complaint after the final whistle, claiming that Newton should have been serving a suspension.

Droylsden had informed the FA that he would serve his ban against Vauxhall Motors on Boxing Day, at a stage when the aborted replay had yet to be arranged. Just reading this has probably confused you, so is it any wonder that the whole thing became the fiasco that eventually led to Droylsden being kicked out of the FA Cup and Chesterfield being handed their place in the third round.

Perhaps if Newton had come on as a late substitute rather than scored both goals the story might have ended differently, but after all the controversy and drama, Droylsden's FA Cup run was over.

Friday 26th December (Boxing Day) – Match 59
Manchester City v Hull City – Premier League

I've heard many people moan about Christmas, but not me, I love it. Not the commercialism, but the family aspect and spending time together. I'm not a particularly religious person, but the story of Christmas has a great message, so I take my lead from that.

Because my mum was German, and Irene's was Austrian, we start our celebrations on Christmas Eve and after going to the Bridgewater Hall's carol sing-a-long, we drink a toast to our friends and open our presents in the evening, as is done in the rest of Europe.

As a child there were a couple of years when I opened mine on Christmas morning, as my parents tried to make sure I didn't get teased for being different, but even as a child we were more often in step with the family traditions of our parents. Christmas Day is still special, of course, with a traditional Christmas dinner, at home with family and close friends, before falling asleep in front of the TV with a paper hat on my head.

Then, there's Boxing Day; the best football day of the year. I can't imagine not having a game on Boxing Day and more often than not City seem to have a home game, which is perfect.

Years ago, while covering a City game for Clubcall, I sat next to Brian Clark at Hull City's Boothferry Park, while he covered the game for radio. He had my dream job and I remember chatting to him. He asked me about myself. He was very friendly and generous with his time, as he still is. I do remember telling him quite pointedly, that I wanted to do his job. I was determined but not aggressive as I explained that he had my dream job.

All these years later, I often flash back to that day at Boothferry Park - it was a Full Members Cup game in November 1985 - when I hand over to Brian for an update from a Stockport game on a Saturday afternoon.

After starting the season really well, Phil Brown's Hull City were starting to falter, and with Robinho fit again, this was the perfect opportunity for City to bounce back from the embarrassment of West Brom. Very quickly it became apparent that this would be City's day. Within half an hour the Blues were 3-0 up and the Christmas celebrations were definitely stretching to a third day. At half-time City led 4-0, a score-line that always prompted it's own song back in the '70's, when it happened more frequently. "Four nil, four nil, four nil, four nil......" (to the tune of Amazing Grace!)

The perma-tanned Hull manager, kept his players on the pitch during the interval, sitting them down in front of their large contingent of travelling supporters for the team talk. Some saw it as the right thing to do, others questioned if he was being an exhibitionist, simply doing it to distance himself from their poor performance.

It had the effect of making the second half more even, or perhaps City just took their "foot off the pedal". Whatever the reason, there were just two more goals, one each, with the scoring finishing at 5-1, then it was off home for a turkey butty or turkey soup, I can't remember which.

Sunday 28th December – Match 60
Blackburn Rovers v Manchester City – Premier League

The last game of the year and a first return to Ewood Park for Mark Hughes, though that was probably more significant for the media and even the fans than the City boss, who didn't seem to be the slightest bit bothered. He claimed it was just another game. It seemed like a bad time to be going there, with Sam Allardyce newly installed as Rovers manager.

There were no City fans stood on the hill, overlooking the ground, as there had been on that May promotion day back in 2000. There was no Shaun Goater or Paul Dickov either, or Mark Kennedy leaping into Joe Royle's arms on the touchline down below my vantage point in the main stand. Great memories, though everyone will remember Blackburn hitting the frame of the goal, several times, before things started to go right, but it all added to the drama didn't it?

I suppose that one of the consolations of being a bit of a yo-yo team, for a few years, was that at least there were some promotions, which in truth, at that moment, probably didn't feel much different to winning the league or winning a cup, although I haven't had much to compare it to!

Blackburn started this game as the bottom team in the Premier League, just as West Brom had done a week earlier, so maybe this would finally be City's long awaited away win. By half-time, City were trailing 1-0 as Benni McCarthy scored, just as the referee had prepared to end the first period.

Despite City's determined efforts to get back into the game, a second Rovers goal went in with just six minutes left, so it looked like another lacklustre defeat. Suddenly Daniel Sturridge, on as substitute, changed things.

Helped out by Robinho, he scored the first, before returning the compliment by beautifully setting up Robinho for the equaliser, and heartbreak for Big Sam; but the City fans didn't care, from the jaws of a humiliating defeat, their team had regrouped and come away with a hard-fought point. The year had ended on a positive note.

January

Saturday 3rd January 2009 – Match 61
Manchester City v Nottingham Forest – FA Cup

Football is about winning, few people would argue with that statement, and certainly not those who work in the game, as a player or a coach. As a spectator, I have a slightly different opinion, although of course I want my team to win every game, every week and therefore win every trophy.

Let me try to explain my point of view. Every team fails, except the one that wins each competition, but they fail in differing degrees. The team that loses in the first round, to a team from a lower division, especially when playing at home, has failed, of that there can be no doubt. To some though, reaching a semi-final, doing better than last season or reaching Wembley might be seen as success.

I know my team can't win every game or every trophy, so I go to games to be entertained. Entertainment, just like winning, means different things to different people. To some it means fast flowing team play with slick passing; to others it means watching a player do something special or a great goal.

During the early 1990's, City finished fifth in successive seasons and yet I can remember many supporters being very unhappy with the way the team played. Niall Quinn was the focus of City's attack during those seasons and the long ball tactic became commonplace. These were the club's most "successful" seasons since the late 1970's.

Many of the younger generation of City fans look back at the play-off final of 1999 against Gillingham, at Wembley, as one of the club's great games. Is that because it was a win? Yes, undoubtedly it was, but was that success? I suppose it was, because City achieved their pre-season goal of promotion, but it was from the third division to the second. Success must, therefore, be more than just winning.

I enjoyed the Kevin Keegan era, some of the football played during his promotion season, and the early days back in the Premier League, was sublime. Watching Ali Benarbia, Eyal Berkovic and Shaun Wright-Phillips was a pleasure - win, lose or draw. I understand the need for a winning mentality and work rate but I can't deny a fondness for flamboyance.

During my time watching City, it started with Rodney Marsh and Mike Summerbee and includes Peter Barnes, Dennis Tueart, Kaziu Deyna, Dave Bennett, Barry Silkman (yes honestly), Tommy Hutchison, Paul Lake, Paul Walsh, Uwe Rosler, Gio Kinkladze, Peter Beagrie, Shaun Wright-Phillips, Nicolas Anelka, Elano and Robinho. Those have been the players I've been excited by, and they're also the most debated members of the team.

Do they try hard enough, do they run enough, have they been worth the money? I'd suggest that without some of those players doing the unexpected every now and again, football would not be as pleasurable. I'm not saying those were necessarily the best players to have represented City, it's my list of the "unpredictables", those who'd do things that, on occasions, have, quite literally taken my breath away. Colin Bell was my hero, but he was rarely flamboyant.

Losing at home to Nottingham Forest, in the third round of the FA Cup, would be a miserable result, whatever you're football philosophy. Watching a cup upset is generally exciting, unless you support the big team. The worst feeling I've had, in a cup competition, was back in January 1980, at the Shay, in Halifax.

The only consolation coming from City's ignominious exit from the FA Cup was that they must have learnt a lesson that day as they reached the final the following season. Maybe City would respond to losing 3-0 at home to Nottingham Forest by reaching the final during the 2009-2010 season, making it worth the humiliation of losing to a Championship team that had won just five league games all season.

Billy Davies had just been appointed as their new manager, but made a big deal of saying he'd just watch from the stands rather than take charge. Whatever he said publicly, it seemed to do the trick and City, who'd rested

Robinho, Stephen Ireland and Nedum Onuoha, were out. Don't even get me started on resting players in the FA Cup.

Saturday 10th January – Match 62
Bury v Barnet – League Two

Everyone expects bad weather in January, but Portsmouth is one of those places that always seems to be milder than the rest of the country, so I was fairly confident City's game at Fratton Park would go ahead, even though other fixtures were being called off on Friday.

The deep frosts had been at their worst in the middle of the week, but the forecast was for milder conditions over the weekend. I suppose I'm stating the obvious when I say that games usually went ahead on frozen pitches when I was younger, as long as the surface was deemed to be flat.

As a long standing supporter, who has spent his whole life travelling the length and breadth of the country to watch matches, I'm a great believer in getting games played if at all possible. Fans plan their trips months in advance and it can be expensive to watch their team and there's nothing more frustrating than the game being called off, meaning more time off work for the rearranged fixture.

City had a game at Plymouth one Tuesday night, in the League Cup, back in 1988, which was postponed, due to a waterlogged pitch, as the coach I was travelling on was passing Taunton. We turned around and arrived back at Maine Road at midnight to be welcomed by Howard Yeats, the travel club organiser, who told us the team had stayed down in Plymouth and they'd try and play the game the following evening.

That could have been a logistical nightmare, had I not already booked the Wednesday off, to recover from the anticipated late night on the Tuesday. I'm sure some of the fans couldn't make it the next day, unless they took a sicky. For the record City played the following night, I was there, and they won 6-3.

City's trip to Portsmouth was looking decidedly dodgy though when I found out that Fratton Park didn't have undersoil heating. What a ridiculous state of affairs in 2009. Millions of pounds are spent on transfer fees and players' wages and yet Portsmouth wouldn't spend the money on protecting their playing surface from the extremes of the winter. I'd assumed that there was a Premier League rule that enforced undersoil heating. It seems not.

If I had any say in it, I would withhold the appropriate amount from the TV money unless pitch protection was installed.

With that information, I now feared the game might not go ahead, but I still had to set off for the game as normal, early on Saturday morning. Normally there's plenty of chat, among my travelling companions, as we drive along, but on this occasion we were on edge because we had to have an ear on 5live, especially during its sports bulletins.

By eight o'clock we'd been on the road, from Fred's house, for half an hour, and we were told that a decision would be made after a nine o'clock pitch inspection. We headed on down the M6 fully aware that the overnight temperature in Portsmouth had been about six degrees below freezing, BUT they'd had covers on, which wouldn't be removed for another hour.

By nine o'clock we were near Birmingham. I was driving slower than normal, never really going much above 55mph. The voice on the radio told us that they were still trying to sort out one section of the playing surface, near the main stand, but that most of the pitch was fine. Another pitch inspection would apparently be conducted in half an hour.

We continued onto the M42 heading for the M40. It seemed a long thirty minutes before the next update suggested that the decision had been delayed a little longer and we were assured we'd be the first to know the outcome, as soon as a decision was made. I couldn't drive too slowly, because if the game WAS on, we might struggle to get there on time. I was driving slower and slower and was now averaging less than 50mph, as I followed the lorries, in the inside lane.

By ten o'clock there was still no decision, so I was beginning to assume that the game would be on, after all the trouble they were clearly going to, to make sure it went ahead. At fifteen minutes past ten my phone, Fred's phone and Chris's phone started to buzz with texts just as the radio announced the game was off. We were on the A34 approaching Oxford and we'd been on the road for three hours.

Frustrated, I came off at the next exit, turned around and started the journey back to Manchester. We were hungry, thirsty and fed up and pulled in at the first Little Chef we found, to enjoy its famous Olympic Breakfast, the best it had ever tasted. As frustrating as we were feeling, there's a perverse sense of satisfaction when you find out that there's someone worse off than you.

As I munched on my succulent sausage, Dave Wallace, editor of the City fanzine "King of the Kippax" texted me to reveal he'd travelled down to Portsmouth on the Friday and had spent the morning strolling through the City, oblivious of any doubt over whether the game would go ahead. I couldn't help sniggering a little as I read it, which was unforgivable really.

I dropped Fred off at his house at ten past two nearly seven hours after we'd set out on our fruitless journey, weary and without reward. I decided I would get my football fix by going to Bury v Barnet, one of the few surviving games. I wasn't covering the game, of course, so I sat and watched as a spectator, next to my colleague Bill Rice who had been assigned to do the game.

The pitch was hard but flat and although not the best match I'd ever seen, I enjoyed it. I looked at the Barnet fans and wondered what their long trip had been like. Had they been uncertain about whether the game would be played? By the end I'm certain they did, as Bury won 1-0, thanks to a goal by Michael Jones, just before half-time.

Sunday 11th January – Match 63
Wigan Athletic v Tottenham Hotspur – Premier League

There are many reasons to admire Wigan Athletic, who've shown the football world that with some support from a passionate and wealthy owner, it's still possible to live the dream. Here were the Latics, who'd played non-league football during my lifetime, beating Tottenham Hotspur, in the magnificent JJB Stadium.

On the day, they had much better players too, though the domination of Wilson Palacios in midfield didn't go unnoticed by the Spurs hierarchy who signed him later in the month. Palacios controlled midfield, despite being up against Modric, Lennon, Zokora and O'Hara.

It took almost the full ninety minutes to get their winner, with Maynor Figueroa scoring in the final minute. Spurs had shown a swagger, right from the start, and believed they should take all three points but the Latics outfought them and outplayed them for a deserved victory.

As a child I'd always liked Tottenham, they seemed a friendly club who played skilful football. My first trip to Wembley had been to see Norwich City against Spurs in the 1973 League Cup Final. My family lived in Norwich at that time, as my dad gained promotion as a railway traffic controller. I can't say I was ever keen to move down there, but I was twelve years old and had little choice but to accept the decision of my parents.

I found it hard to cope with making new friends with people who had such strange accents. They took the mickey out of mine all the time and I remember hitting out at one lad, called Bird, in a woodwork class, when he kept teasing me about my northern accent. As I turned to go for him I forgot I had a tool in my hand, which I'd been using to thin down a piece of wood. "Is it a bird or is it a plane", I thought as I struck him in the face, leaving him with a thick lip. We were both told to sit in the hallway while further action was considered.

Half an hour later some important visitors were being shown around the school, Wymondham College, so we were allowed to go back into class, so that our misbehaviour didn't need to be explained. I got away with my instinctive, if crude, form of self-defence, in more ways than one.

It was a strange school, especially having spent the first two terms of senior school, before moving south, at Canon Slade School in Bolton. I'd gone there because my parents thought I'd get a better education at a church school and my best mate, Graham Mason, had decided to go there too.

Wymondham College was also a grammar school but most of its buildings were Nissan huts, left over from a hospital used during World War Two. They looked like baked bean tins, with the label taken off, cut down the middle, length ways, and laid down on the flat side. The roof, therefore, was made of corrugated steel. On the other hand, the buildings where the boarders slept, were more modern, and doubled up as the canteen and meeting rooms.

We lived in Norwich for a year, during which time I went to a few games at Carrow Road with my next door neighbour, Mr Fox, who was a turnstile operator. City's visit was the highlight of the season, with Tony Towers scoring in a 1-1 draw. At school they were trying to convince me to be a Norwich City fan, which was never going to happen!

Toward the end of that season Norwich City, with Graham Paddon, a Manchester lad, their big star, reached the League Cup Final. My dad's work colleague Mr Wilson took me to the game and after spending the morning in London, feeding the pigeons in Trafalgar Square, we got in early so we could stand next to the wall behind the goal.

I remember Mr Wilson distributing sausage rolls to me and his two sons and daughter, as we enjoyed the pre-match atmosphere ahead of kick-off. Norwich lost 1-0 with Ralph Coates, complete with comb-over hairstyle, scoring the only goal, at our end. Although I was supposed to be supporting Norwich, I really wanted Tottenham to win, probably just to spite my mates at school, who were so determined to turn me into a Norwich fan.

We returned to live in Manchester, Whitefield to be precise, at Easter, just a few weeks after that League Cup Final. My mum and dad had put a deposit on a new house at Easton, a small village just off the A47, but the building company went bust. There was some doubt that my dad's office might have to move to London and both my Mum and I were homesick for Manchester.

We took it as a sign and left Hethersett, where we'd lived for exactly one year, to return home. Even though my mum wasn't English by birth, she missed her friends in the north and the friendliness of the neighbours and work colleagues.

I was happy to be back and spent the rest of my time at senior school at Stand Grammar School in Whitefield. Within weeks of returning, my dad bought two season tickets for Maine Road in "H" centre and I've hardly missed a City game since.

Monday 12th January – Match 64
Oldham Athletic v Hartlepool United – League One

By now, the thaw had set in and there was never any danger that this game wouldn't go ahead. It should have been played on the previous Saturday, the day City's game at Portsmouth had been called off, so it was a bonus fixture for me. It was the debut of loan signing Dean Windass.

Oldham's administrators deserve a big pat on the back, in my opinion, for their quick thinking and swift rearrangement of this game, although I realise it might not have suited everyone. I can understand the practical reasons they did it. It avoided any sort of fixture backlog, they didn't have to reprint the programmes and as for the pies – well I assume they got new ones!

Latics were very much in the hunt for automatic promotion or at least a place in the play-offs and started the game in third place, so I can't deny I was excited as I walked across Clayton Playing Fields, to take my position in the press box.

Before I got married in 1984, I had no affinity with Oldham. I'd seen one game there, a 2-1 win against Burnley in March 1980. Once I met, and was courting Irene (an old-fashioned word, but I like it), I started to go to Boundary Park whenever I could and have probably seen more games there than any other stadium except City. Now that I've lived in Oldham for over twenty five years, I consider myself to be a part-time Latics fan.

The Latics boss, John Sheridan, had signed Dean Windass to add firepower and although he wasn't particularly mobile, his experience and clever touches made a noticeable difference. He played just behind the normal striking positions, acting as a link between midfield and Lee Hughes.

It wasn't long before Hughes scored and during the second half Dean Smalley added a second. Latics won 2-1 and everything was heading in the right direction. I spoke to Windass after the game, though he had to be persuaded to do the interview. He was passionate and spoke a lot of common sense. He told me he'd joined Oldham to help his old mate John Sheridan and to play first team football. He claimed money hadn't motivated him.

I left Boundary Park in high spirits. Despite the cold weather, I'd seen three games in three days, and the three sides I'd wanted to win had all taken the three points. Does it get any better?

Tuesday 13th January – Match 65
Swindon Town v Stockport County – League One

This was another game that had been swiftly rearranged, when called off the previous weekend. It's not often that I stay in a hotel, but it made no sense to head back north from Swindon, after the game, as I would be back in Portsmouth the following evening for City's youth cup tie. Fred and I booked into a bed and breakfast in Portsmouth, which would mean a late night arrival, but no need for a long journey on the Wednesday.

City's 3-1 victory at Swindon, in February 1998, turned out to be a pivotal game for me. I'd been miserable that season, having been told I'd have to be the studio producer on Saturday afternoons because Steve Chisholm, one of my colleagues in the sports team, was going to take six months leave to travel the world. He and I had covered all the Saturday production shifts and early sports bulletins for a couple of years and his flexibility, and reluctance to do earlies had meant I hardly ever missed a City game, home and away.

The news that I was to studio produce on Saturday afternoons was like a dagger through my heart. During my whole adult life I had always watched football, and City in particular, on Saturday afternoons. I didn't want to be studio bound, and my boss, Andy Buckley, knew it. He told me he had no alternative, as I was the best man for the job. The other person who'd been considered was my mate Jack Dearden, but Andy wasn't convinced that Jack would be a good producer.

I felt I was being punished for being too much of an all rounder and was very unhappy. I spent several months directing Jimmy Wagg, listening to City fans going past the BBC building, from one o'clock on Saturdays, as they went to the game and then saw them coming back happy, or perhaps more often, sad, after five o'clock. I wanted to be with them and felt like I was in a prison.

During the week I could go to City games and found myself in the bizarre situation of attending midweek games like Queens Park Rangers away on a Wednesday night but missing home games against Bury and Wolves. I'd been prepared to go to great lengths to follow my obsession, like working an early shift from 5am to 2pm, driving to London or the south coast for an away game, returning at 2am, dining in the kebab shop opposite the BBC, and then doing another early shift from 5am to 2pm before going home to sleep. On the weekends either side I'd be studio bound and it was driving me crazy.

I'd asked Andy if I could go to the game at Swindon and he asked me who would cover for me in the studio, I suggested Jack, who reluctantly filled in for me. When it came time to broadcast the full time results he'd dropped his papers, with the scores on, and Andy was furious, blaming me for wanting to take the day off.

When Steve Chisholm returned from his six month trip, I requested I be taken off Saturdays. Everyone knew how miserable I'd become. The station editor at that time, Karen Hannah, talked to me about a possible solution and offered me the chance to leave the sports team and work on another project. I leapt at the chance, even though most people thought I was mad for leaving the sports team. I even questioned my own sanity, but I knew I couldn't cope with missing City games.

The new project was to revamp the "What's On" listings, which none of the presenters enjoyed reading out. I took the chance with both hands and worked long hours pre-recording 35 items per week. I invited amateur actors, singers, flower arrangers and basket weavers aplenty to come to our studios and I interviewed them for inclusion in the "Events Diary".

I usually had a student placement working with me and I used their individual personalities to create original ways of creating the recordings about predictable items, in a more entertaining way. My favourite was my introduction to a UFO exhibition in Blackpool, which started with a thirty second comic recreation of War of the Worlds. My efforts didn't go unnoticed, and before long I was doing fill-in presentation for Phil Trow, Phil Wood and Allan Beswick.

I still had a connection to the sports team, as I was presenting two weekly programmes. On Mondays I hosted a sporting "Desert Island Discs" style show, which allowed me to uncover the personalities and family histories of our local sports stars. I loved doing that show as much as anything I've ever done. I'm not a big fan of "soundbite" broadcasting which has become more and more prevalent as the years go by.

This format allowed the person to speak, and I'd rather listen to them than the presenter, or in this case, me. I've always been a fan of Michael Parkinson, who never said more than he needed to, during interviews. There are times, of course, when the interviewer has to coax the interviewee out of their shell, and so I understand the need to ask long questions or show some personality in those situations, but only when needed.

When you've got Joe Royle, Kenneth Wolstenholme or Joey Barton as your guest, you just direct the conversation and sit back and listen, and I'm a good listener. I did that programme for nearly two years, and was never happier. I also presented a Thursday night sports quiz, into which I put hours of preparation. Anyone can set questions, but I wanted them to be interesting, local questions that would provide the chance for humour and entertainment to those not directly involved in the quiz.

As I was no longer working at weekends, I was asked by City to become involved in their match day public address and, of course, this wouldn't interfere with my desire to watch City, home and away. I did that job for a couple of years.

Then one day, out of the blue, Andy Buckley asked me to rejoin his sports team. My immediate response was no, but Andy had anticipated this and told me he was prepared to let me have City match days as my days off. This seemed too good to be true, but he convinced me that he meant it.

I was both flattered and delighted that I could watch City and go back into the sports team. I accepted. Within weeks Andy shocked me again. He'd known that my burning ambition and lifelong goal was to be the City reporter. He was the City reporter, but he told me he was planning to step aside. He was applying for a job in TV, which would initially last six months. He promised me that if he was successful, I'd get the City job. "What if you come back in six months", I wondered. "If that happens", he told me, "I won't return to the role because I've done it long enough and want a change".

I'd dreamt of this day for years, and yet when it arrived I took it all very calmly, like I'd been expecting it, even though I'd wondered if I'd ever get the chance.

The decision had to be ratified by Steve Taylor, the new station editor. He told me the job was mine on October 17th 2001 and my first match as City correspondent was at Portsmouth on November 17th 2001. My lucky number is 17! I'd thought my chance had gone after the "behind the scenes" incidents of that trip to Swindon back in 1998.

This trip to Swindon, with Stockport, was to be less significant in the story of my life, with a late goal from the impressive Anthony Pilkington earning Stockport a 1-1 draw which was followed by our late night drive to Portsmouth and checking in at the Duke of Buckingham for a good nights sleep.

Wednesday 14th January – Match 66
Portsmouth (u18's) v Manchester City (u18's) – FA Youth Cup

Fred and I woke up to a pleasant Portsmouth morning and a delicious cooked breakfast in the bar of the pub downstairs, in front of a warming coal fire from an old fashioned fireplace. We were located close to the docks, so we decided to head in that direction and see what we found.

As we strolled along the road that led to the historic boatyard, we noticed some footballers training and crossed the road to get a better view. Amazingly, it was City's youth team being put through their paces by Jim Cassell, Alex Gibson and the other coaches. What were the chances that they'd be doing their final session before that night's big match on pitches so close to our bed and breakfast?

Jim Cassell came over to say hello. I'd known Jim since his days at Oldham Athletic and Fred knew everyone in the academy very well, as his son Steve is one of their coaches. After a couple of minutes Alex Gibson came over too and we became conscious that we were distracting the lads, unintentionally, so we said our goodbyes and continued towards the historic dockyard.

I don't know what I expected to find there but I was impressed when we walked through the gates to see the HMS Warrior, the first iron-clad, armoured warship in the world. It was moored next to the "Costa Coffee", Fred's favourite, so I left him sipping a cappuccino while I went on board to explore.

On my return we headed off to see the rest of the dockyard, where we saw modern naval vessels and HMS Victory, a ship I've always been fascinated by.

I'd wanted to build the Airfix model of Victory when I was a boy but my dad thought it would be too complicated for me. He insisted that I start by building a few model planes but I quickly lost patience and never went onto the Victory. I've read about the ship and its place in history, but here it was, right in front of me, in all its glory.

I wanted to go onboard and asked Fred if he felt the same. He was less enthusiastic but we booked on a tour and waited for our appointment while watching the navy cadets marching up and down. We also visited the Mary Rose, which was indoors, and was gently being sprinkled by special jets of a preserving resin.

The guided tour of HMS Victory was fascinating. As we heard about the terrible conditions the ordinary sailors faced, I felt a chill, and the place where those who misbehaved were lashed with whips, was awful. Fred was tiring, so we headed for cover and had a warm meal.

I had received several calls from the office throughout the day as the breaking story was that City were close to signing Kaka from AC Milan for £100 million. I'd had a few months to get used to the concept that City could bid for anyone, and were now the richest club in the world, so maybe I was a bit blasé as this story broke.

It certainly prompted plenty of opinion and column inches in the tabloids. Was it morally acceptable to offer such an amount of money for one footballer? Of course not, but was it any less moral than Trevor Francis becoming the first £1 million footballer, or Real Madrid apparently considering a £75 million bid for Ronaldo from Man United?

But this was Manchester City, so the headlines were damning, and even the politicians and football administrators were condemning the club for what they described as inappropriate activities. Perhaps it was more to do with jealously or a threat to the so-called "big four" and their domination of the Premier League.

For years, City had stumbled along, never threatening to disturb the equilibrium, never offending anyone and being "everyone's second favourite team". Alex Ferguson and his players have claimed the Manchester derby is less important than their games against Liverpool, Arsenal, Chelsea and others. Suddenly City were flexing their muscles; what was wrong with that?

Now, you can make an argument that modern football isn't played on a level playing field, metaphorically speaking, and I wouldn't argue with that. How can it be right that a small group of the best supported and wealthiest clubs dominate the game, but then again isn't that what happens in all forms of business?

Football is a professional sport, with those at the top of the tree using their financial muscle to build themselves up in such a way that if ever bad times come, on the field, they can buy their way back to the top. Isn't it just like the closing stages of a game of Monopoly, when one player has hotels positioned on half the properties on the board? Nothing can be done about who's going to win, the only objective for the other players being to spend as much time avoiding their inevitable demise as possible.

They've tried to "level the playing field" in motor racing, after complaints that Formula One was dominated by the richest teams, which of course is generally true. A1 was to be the sports saviour. The cars are all the same, so the racing is much fairer, but it's still F1 that pulls in the crowds, the sponsorship and the TV viewers. It seems to me that most people prefer the glamour.

I have mixed views on this subject. The old-fashioned, more traditional clubs are in the lower divisions these days; clubs like Bury, Stockport, Rochdale and Oldham. Their supporters watch a much more evenly balanced competition, though there are still clubs with money and those who're struggling.

Whatever the rights and wrongs of the Premier League, my club, Manchester City, for the first time in years, was dreaming of winning trophies again, so why should I complain. That sounds very selfish doesn't it, but I can't change things, so I'm happy to enjoy the ride, after all, it's still twenty two men kicking a bag of wind around, isn't it?

Youth team football is probably as pure as it comes, albeit the big clubs can usually still attract the best youngsters, but generally it's more about good scouting and coaching and City have one of the best youth set-ups in the world.

Dedryck Boyata scored the only goal of the game at Fratton Park and it was back on the road for the long journey home. This time we drove past the

Little Chef, we'd frequented on the previous Saturday, when our journey to Portsmouth had been aborted.

We called at a motorway service station, briefly, where I asked for a double-entendre, and the woman gave me one.

Saturday 17th January – Match 67
Manchester City v Wigan Athletic – Premier League

This was a game between two teams that I know really well, making it very easy to commentate on, as I could identify all the players instantly. Normally I'd prepare for a game by writing out both teams in formation and then transferring the "other" team onto my "master" sheet, in number order.

People ask me how it's possible to identify players so quickly during a game and the truth is that there is not one answer to that question. I can identify the City players purely from the way they run, in fact I'm sure I could tell who is who in silhouette. Sometimes that applies to some of the players on the other team too, but a quick reference to the number on their back or on their shorts can help and it's also possible to make an accurate guess from their position.

Keeping your mind slightly ahead of the play also helps; in other words spotting runs into the penalty area before a cross is made, ready for instant recognition in the heat of the moment. No one is perfect, not even me, so I have a cunning plan, to buy a couple of seconds, if I can't tell who's scored. I keep describing the general action until I can spot a shirt number. It's probably best to stop this technique, if you've still not done it five minutes after the goal!

I believe a commentary should include serious up-tempo description of the action mixed with analysis from your expert, some humour and additional stats and info to enhance the descriptive content. Too many stats can spoil things though, and my emphasis is always on description, after all, it is radio, not TV.

With this game being City against Wigan, I try to make a point of being even handed in my commentary to avoid being criticised for being biased, as both teams are from the Radio Manchester area. Having two experts, one who follows each club, is a big help. I try to be honest in my commentary style, and will call a spade a spade.

Naturally the Kaka story was very much the talk of the press room ahead of the game and all the fans I bumped into were talking about it too. The word was that City's Executive Chairman, Garry Cook, was going to fly out to Milan the following day, to try to negotiate a deal. Opinions were split, as they had been throughout City's attempt to sign the Brazilian.

The game was a good one and well fought, with Wayne Bridge making an impressive debut at left-back and I felt this was one of City's best performances of the season. That might seem a strange statement given some of the results achieved in other games, but Wigan were a very well organised team, who'd only lost narrowly at Old Trafford during midweek, and they'd never been beaten at the City of Manchester Stadium. City's goal came from Pablo Zabaletta.

That evening I heard the stories of Milan fans pleading with Kaka to stay, as he played a league game against Fiorentina at the San Siro and I feared that the deal might collapse before the negotiations had even taken place. I'd seen a similar situation happen when City tried to recruit Joe Royle as manager from Oldham Athletic. Royle had stayed at Boundary Park after desperate pleas from the Oldham fans to stay.

By Monday, the headlines were screaming out that City had missed out on Kaka and by early Tuesday morning I was interviewing Garry Cook in his office where he told me, in great detail, what had happened. This was where he used the expression, which was later widely reported on all media outlets, that Milan had "bottled it". I understood his frustration, especially as he'd told me, and Chris Bailey, what his negotiating position would be before he'd travelled out to Italy.

Naturally both Chris and I kept that private conversation confidential, as he'd asked us to, but many of the details came into the public domain during the analysis of what had gone wrong.

It seemed that City had wanted to do things morally, with the deal structured in quite a complicated way, designed to help Kaka distribute much of his income to charities. His father, and advisor, had seemed to be in agreement but then the emotion of the Fiorentina game and the worries about loss of popularity from Milan's owner, and Italian Prime Minister, Silvio Berlusconi, had seen a change of mind, hence Cook's "bottled it" expression.

It was open season for the media to criticise City for ever believing they could sign Kaka or that so much money should be spent on one player.

I'd been looking forward to having Wednesday as my midweek day off, because my son Daniel was setting out on media career. It was his first day as a paperboy. I'd promised to go round with him, pulling his cart along, as he popped the local Advertiser through the letterboxes.

As we set out, I received a call from City asking if I was free to fly to Tenerife that evening. To say that phone call came out of the blue is a massive understatement. "When do I need to be there?", I asked as I continued to drag the papers behind me. It was half past three in the afternoon, and the answer was, "Be there by six o'clock." I told Daniel what was happening and he thought I was going to leave him immediately, to complete his round alone.

I stayed with him, of course, until every paper had been delivered and we returned home together. I then told Irene I thought I'd be back by late Thursday evening, threw a few overnight items in a bag, plus my broadcasting equipment and set off for the airport.

There were six passengers on the flight, including Chris, new signing Nigel De Jong and City's head of communications Vicky Kloss. I'd never flown in a private jet and didn't know what to expect, but it all sounded very glamorous. By half past six we were taxiing down the runway and I was preparing for a takeoff facing backwards, which worried me slightly because the only experience like that I'd ever had, was on the Revolution at Blackpool and I'd nearly thrown up after that!

It wasn't as bad as I'd expected, as we hurtled along. All the usual landmarks, like Concorde and the terminal buildings, whizzed past in the wrong direction. Once we were up above the clouds the co-pilot told us to help ourselves to any food we could find and any of the liquid refreshments, including champagne. Wow, this was the high life.

All too quickly, it felt like any other flight; boring and never-ending but with extra leg room! We touched down late, at a deserted Tenerife airport, with just a camera crew and passport control to greet us, and a mini-bus for transfer to the hotel. We'd interviewed Nigel De Jong in Manchester, before takeoff, and since small talk for four and a half hours with a Premier League footballer doesn't last more than two or three minutes, I was glad to finally get to the hotel at three o'clock in the morning, and go to bed. Four hours later I was up and about again, reporting on the trip during Radio Manchester's breakfast programme. Things are never quite as glamorous as they seem.

City had invited me along to talk to De Jong, Mark Hughes and the other new signing, Craig Bellamy. The following morning, after a quick breakfast on the warm and sunny terrace of the impressive Abama Hotel, the group who'd flown out interviewed Hughes in the reception area and were promised Bellamy after training.

Having sent the interviews back to Radio Manchester, I did some filming on my camcorder for a TV piece into North West Tonight, which would be broadcast on my return. By the time the players returned from training, we'd got word that Bellamy didn't want to talk but Richard Dunne would, so we gathered again in reception to chat to the City skipper.

Although it was obvious that we'd been invited to Tenerife for PR purposes, in an attempt to repair some of the criticism that followed the collapse of the Kaka deal, there was no attempt to control our questions, nor did the answers seem orchestrated. I would have been very unhappy, had that been the case, because I value my journalistic independence very highly.

By the time all the interviews, filming and reporting back to Radio Manchester had been completed, there was three hours left until we were being picked up by taxi to start the return journey, via a normal holiday airline.

I'm not a sun worshipper, but I was shattered from lack of sleep and fancied spending this valuable time lying next to the hotel pool. City's legendary kit man, Les Chapman, gave me a pair of shorts and I was poolside quicker than a whippet up a yorkshireman's leg.

We landed back in Manchester in the early hours of Friday morning and despite asking a taxi to take me back to the private jet area, neither he nor I knew how to get there, so I got out to prevent the trip becoming too expensive and spent the next forty five minutes wandering around in the rain, trying to find my car (while also desperate to find a toilet!).

Saturday 24th January – Match 68
Dagenham & Redbridge v Rochdale – League Two

I suppose it would have been much easier, and I'd have had a much shorter working day, if I'd opted for a game at Gigg Lane, but when I saw that we needed someone to cover this game, I was keen to do it, as it would take me back within touching distance of having visited all ninety two league grounds.

I didn't travel alone, as a friend of a friend had asked me if her son, Kyle, could spend some time "shadowing" me, as he was keen to get into sports journalism, so I suggested he make the journey with me. It would provide me with company and also meant I could talk to him for longer and offer proper advice.

It's a good way to judge a media student too. If he'd only wanted to join me at a more glamorous game, I'd have assumed he was more interested in the game than learning anything about the media.

Charlie Lambert, once of North West Tonight Sport, asked me to spend the morning at the University of Central Lancashire, earlier in the year, speaking to the students he was teaching, so I ended up coaching them on how to write and read sports bulletins. They were split into two groups, and after I had given the first group some feedback, they started to pick up their bags and coats to leave the classroom.

I was amazed, and asked a lad from the second group why they had left so promptly, since the session was supposed to finish at one o'clock and there was still twenty minutes to go. "Because they want to get a seat in the canteen and have a bit of extra time for their lunch", came the answer.

"Wouldn't they want to stay and hear my comments on the second group?" I asked. "If I were in their position I'd want to absorb as much information as possible from a professional who does the job I want to."

"I wouldn't have left", continued his quick witted reply. "So why was the first thing you did, when you entered the room, to look at the clock?" He had no answer. When we finished the session, the second group headed off for lunch, except one lad who stayed to ask me a few questions. I'd be prepared to bet he's the one most likely to succeed.

To give him his credit, my passenger to Dagenham & Redbridge was keen and attentive and I enjoyed his company throughout the trip and I hoped he would make it, but I'm well aware that there are hundreds of people who'd love to do my job, and there are thousands of students taking media courses who want to become professionals. The few that succeed will probably be the ones whose passion for their career exceeds their desire for a seat in the canteen at lunchtime.

The game was a lower division classic. The Daggers were ahead within ten minutes but Dale fought back to take a 2-1 lead thanks to a superb Tom Kennedy freekick and a Nicky Adams tap in, after great team play in the build-up. Dagenham & Redbridge came stronger in the second half and won 3-2.

Keith Hill, the Dale manager, who is always emotional after games, was highly critical of his team and virtually wrote off their chances of promotion, which may have been simply how he felt in the heat of the moment or a double bluff to motivate his players. Time would tell.

Tuesday 27th January – Match 69
Scunthorpe United v Oldham Athletic – League One

This had been such a dramatic season for me, so far, that I'd wondered if I was ever going to go to a routine game, where nothing much happened. I'd been to Glanford Park before, so there was nothing new about the stadium, and I was travelling alone, so I was listening to the radio and then some Austrian folk music during the journey, so nothing much to report there either.

My view of the game wasn't the best, but I could see enough to know that the Latics didn't have a good evening. They lost 2-0. It was a match that wouldn't live long in the memory; in fact I think I've already forgotten about it.

The big bonus of the trip, was that while I was waiting to interview John

Sheridan, all the unsold pies were returned, and I was told that I could help myself. I wasn't going to say no and enjoyed a Balti Pie while formulating my questions.

I got away from the stadium quickly, despite my slow waddle back to the car with an extra pie inside me. There was one thing that was slightly troubling me though. I was in a hire car and had been called by the rental company a few hours before delivery, to ask if I'd accept a smaller car, which I accepted.

I can't remember what model or make it was but it was very basic. "As long as it gets me there and back in one piece...." I thought, but from the moment I set off something felt wrong. I stopped and inspected the car on the outside and everything seemed okay but the steering was pulling slightly to the left. The tyres seemed fine, so I carried on with the journey.

Every time I switched from lane to lane on the motorway I could feel the cats eyes like I was riding over cobbles. I tried not to switch lanes too much. As I prepared for the return journey, I gave the car another external inspection and again checked that the tyres were fully inflated; all seemed well, but it still felt wrong as I drove along.

I instinctively felt I should not listen to music during the journey as singing along to Sigrid and Marina might distract me, so I switched on the radio but set the sound level quite low. As I turned onto the M62 from the M18 I decided to stay in the middle lane, even though there was hardly any traffic on the motorway. I accelerated to about 60mph, a little slower than normal and then suddenly I was fighting the steering wheel and had to stop as quickly and as safely as possible. The front right tyre had burst catastrophically and I was hanging on like it was a white knuckle rollercoaster.

Eventually I pulled onto the hard shoulder and got out to inspect the car. There was hardly anything left of the tyre, the tread had separated from the tyre walls that were now left in shreds.

It was pitch black and it was eleven o'clock, I knew this was now going to be another late night. I called the recovery services and was told I'd be a priority case and they'd be there within the hour. The usual advice is to stand away from the car, behind the crash barrier.

It was bitterly cold and it was starting to rain. I climbed over the barrier to find there was a steep downwards grassy slope leading into a small stream. I stood there for forty five minutes, though it felt like hours, shivering and getting more perished by the minute. Had the incident not been on a dark motorway, in a strange car and been on a normal roadside, I might have changed the wheel myself but with huge house-sized juggernauts pounding along within inches of the car, every minute or so, I decided to let an expert sort it out.

I'd given my precise location to the call centre; within 1 mile of the M18 on the west bound M62, even including the number written on the board on the side of the road. After an hour I called back and asked how close I was to receiving some help. "They've gone past you on the other side, be there in two minutes", came the cheery reply. An hour later the helpful man from the local garage, who'd been subcontracted to change my wheel, was explaining that he'd been given the wrong location. At least I think that's what he said in his broad Yorkshire accent.

With the remnants of the wheel and tyre in the boot, and my wet feet now permanently angled like Donald Duck's, I was finally on my way. It was one o'clock in the morning and I was driving along with one of those temporary wheels now fitted which meant I had to drive home at no more than 50mph, which felt like slow motion on an empty motorway.

That incident could have driven me to drink, and as I'd stood there waiting, I'd almost been tempted to take a drink from the cars brake fluid, something I have to admit I've done in the past. It was a terrible addiction, but I'd always had the consolation of knowing that I could stop at any time!

Wednesday 28th January – Match 70
Manchester City v Newcastle United – Premier League

I never bet, well very rarely, but this was a game I was certain City would win. Newcastle were in turmoil and Craig Bellamy and Nigel De Jong were making their City debuts. I don't think I've ever bet more than £5 on anything, even the Grand National, but I went crazy and put £10 on a City win.

The truth, perhaps a little unusually for City, is that I was always on a winner with Shaun Wright-Phillips confirming City's early dominance and Bellamy scoring deep into the second half. Newcastle did get a late consolation goal, but never threatened to get back into it.

Joey Barton started the game in midfield for Newcastle and received a suitably cool reaction from the City fans. He was always a difficult person to weigh up. He didn't stand out as a player when coming through City's junior ranks but always had passion aplenty and a terrific will to win, which can often take a person further than just natural talent. That's something I can relate to. I'm sure I'm not the best at what I do, but I'd always been determined to fulfil my ambition of being the City reporter and I certainly don't lack passion.

I first met Joey at one of City's travelling roadshows, which were instigated by Chris Bird, who was working hard on the PR side of the club at that time. This one was staged at British Aerospace in Chadderton and I was the host, as I'd been at them all, throughout the Manchester area.

Joey was a kid, a cheeky Scouser, who could take a joke and get you back as well, which all added to the fun and informality of the evening. I really enjoyed hosting those events, just to be involved with the club.

He was the star of the show and I don't think anyone left without singing his praises. I was proud to see him break into the first team and on those rare occasions when it's possible to chat informally to players, he was always gregarious and funny.

Something started to go wrong as he hit the big time. There was the famous Jamie Tandy "cigar" incident and his troubles in Bangkok, and although I still wanted to like him, it was becoming more difficult. I'd wanted to believe his apparent heartfelt apology in the press conference room at the City of Manchester Stadium, but more troubles quickly followed, including the Ousmane Dabo training ground spat and the McDonalds CCTV incident. The excuses started to sound more and more hollow and Joey's honeymoon period was over; and yet he could still be charming.

One day, I was helping Susan Bookbinder, the former 5live newsreader, train some of the younger players how to deal with the media, when Joey offered to join us and pass on his wisdom. We sat there, in the old press room at Carrington, which was later replaced by a small portakabin in the car park (another story!), with Micah Richards, Ishmail Miller and Daniel Sturridge;

Joey joined in.

I can't remember what he said but it was mature, sensible and sincerely delivered, then he departed as quickly as he'd appeared. That was the Joey Barton I liked. His antics away from the club were enough to persuade me that it would be best for everyone if he left City. It wouldn't matter to me if he were the world's most talented footballer, I wouldn't want such a person at the club I love so much.

Joey's parting shot was his infamous rant after the 1-1 draw at Watford in April 2007. He told us that he wouldn't blame the supporters if they didn't renew their season tickets.

I can't imagine that Stuart Pearce would have known much about the contents of the twenty minute interview and very strangely, Paul Tyrrell, the press officer, didn't monitor this interview, as he usually did, despite organising it.

It was hot stuff and ended up being broadcast everywhere and reported in all the tabloids. What was the purpose of his outburst? Was it his farewell speech or was it politically motivated? I guess we'll never know for sure, but I have my theories.

Saturday 31st January – Match 71
Stoke City v Manchester City – Premier League

I didn't expect this game to be a classic, nor did I expect City to lose, but James Beattie's goal proved decisive. I have many happy memories of Stoke's old Victoria Ground, particularly the scoring debut of Trevor Francis there in September 1981 and the boxing day fancy dress, two years earlier.

As I arrived at the Britannia Stadium, my mind immediately went back to the lowest point of my time as a City fan, the 5-2 win in May 1998 that couldn't prevent relegation to the third division. It was a heartbreaking match, followed by the worst kind of football violence, which I'd thought had long since disappeared into the history books. I can remember the Stoke fans throwing stones and City fans mounting a counter-offensive; it was like a scene out of Saving Private Ryan!

Joe Royle had succeeded Frank Clark, my least favourite manager (and I have quite a few to select from!), and I wanted to see Joe be a huge success, which ultimately he was, guiding the club through successive promotions, for very little financial outlay. He was one of the best people in football. A man's man, who trusts journalists, loves the game and rarely has a smile off his face.

I had one fundamental issue with him, though, as a manager. He rarely selected Gio Kinkladze during the fifteen games he'd had to try to undo the damage done by Alan Ball and Frank Clark. He picked Kinkladze as a starter just four times and brought him on as a sub at Stoke.

City got 7 points from the five games he played in, 11 points from the ten he didn't. Stats don't always tell the whole story, but I felt dropping City's best player, even though there have been many arguments down the years about his overall contribution to the team, was a bad mistake. One more point that season, perhaps one more Kinkladze goal, might have kept City up; but then again, we wouldn't then have had the play-off final against Gillingham!

February

Tuesday 3rd February – Match 72
Stockport County v MK Dons – League One

The cheery face of Stockport County, during the previous few years, has been Norman Beverley. He's basically a supporter and I've found him to be a true gentleman who has put his heart and soul into the football club. County's former Chairman rose through the ranks as part of the supporters' trust, which became the driving force, and perhaps saviour of this proud club.

The theory of supporters' trusts is one that appeals to me, but in practise I'm not sure they work, because football has become so dominated by money. If the "sport" was like any other business and had to live within its means, then trusts would be ideal, but as we know, to get the competitive edge, money can make the crucial difference. Rich owners can either inject cash directly, use their private wealth to guarantee loans or simply pull some strings when required.

There's a refreshing enthusiasm and honesty about having fan ownership, but County were in danger of illustrating why it doesn't work. During January they'd been forced to sell two of their best players, Anthony Pilkington and Jim McNulty, and there were mutterings of discontent behind the scenes.

The County manager, Jim Gannon, a deep thinker and proud man, who'd always been willing to share his concerns, had expressed his worry about their departures. Managing Director Mark Maguire talked about balancing the financial realities of the club, in his match day programme notes and it was becoming more and more apparent that there was a growing tension, behind the scenes, that would develop further as the season unfolded.

Stockport started this game one point behind Leeds United, just outside the play-off places, but the momentum they'd had after promotion the previous season, was beginning to falter.

The deterioration of the playing surface at Edgeley Park was becoming more and more noticeable. Wear and tear was clearly the reason, and another contributing factor to the uneasy relationship between County and their ground sharers Sale Sharks.

My arrival at the ground started with a visit to the press room, which doubled up as the office of Des Hinks, their press officer, programme editor, former GMR Stockport reporter, fan, and anything else you can think of. Every lower division football club needs and has someone like Des; a jack of all trades. At Bury it is Gordon Sorfleet, at Oldham it is Gordon Lawton etc etc.

I've always enjoyed meeting up with fellow broadcaster Jon Keighren. During my early days, Jon used some of my interviews on his Friday night programme on Signal Cheshire, and he asked me to deputise for him a couple of times, when he was unavailable. I guess he took a bit of a risk by allowing me onto the airwaves, so I owe him a debt of gratitude.

MK Dons won the game 1-0 thanks to a predictable goal scorer, because it always happens doesn't it, the former County striker Aaron Wilbraham.

Wednesday 4th February – Match 73
Manchester City (u18's) v Newcastle United (u18's) – FA Youth Cup

The usual dedicated group of die-hard City fans were there for this one, just under a thousand fans in total, to see City's youngsters impress with a 4-2 win, thanks to goals by Greg Cunningham, Robbie Mak, Alex Nimely and another from Robbie Mak.

I am used to seeing Brian Hince at many of the City games I attend because he's as dedicated a fan as I've ever seen, especially considering the extra problems he suffers as a wheelchair-bound supporter. I remember seeing Brian, who's the nephew of former City player and journalist, Paul Hince, outside Loftus Road, a few years ago, and he told me something that still amazes me to this day. He told me that he would only be able to see one half of the game.

"Have you got to leave early?" I innocently queried. "No, I've got to share my ticket with another supporter, as there aren't enough spaces to accommodate the disabled City fans, so we're going to watch half the match each." To say I was stunned by that response is a bit of an understatement.

I understand that there might be times when there are not enough tickets to meet demand, and that can apply to anyone, but you would have thought a solution could have been found, wouldn't you? The match was not a sell-out, so there must have been a way of making sure both City fans could see the whole game.

Brian was as obsessed as me, going to all the club's games, home and away, including reserves and youth team, despite his physical problems. That takes some determination and great support from his family and other helpers. I'm sure he enjoyed the Youth Cup win against Newcastle as much as I did, and was just as satisfied to see the boy blues progress to the last eight of the youth cup, again. At least Brian got to see the whole of this game.

Saturday 7th February – Match 74
Manchester City v Middlesbrough – Premier League

On the one hand, I was delighted that there had been an increase in the number of games shown live on TV, because it allowed fans who hadn't the resources or opportunity to go to games to follow their team. I benefit from this by being able to watch my "other" team Schalke, every week, sometimes the full ninety minutes and sometimes through highlights.

On the other hand, kick-off times are all over the place and quite frankly there's too much football on TV, which means that special games like the FA Cup final have become "just another game". I'd prefer fewer televised games, which would mean fewer kick-off times being switched.

In Germany, a footballing country I know well, there's a live game on a Friday night and two on Sunday, which kick-off simultaneously; the rest play in parallel from 3.30pm on Saturday afternoon. Half our fixtures are moved for TV coverage, with others moved due to police concerns or a club's involvement in European competition, which, if you think about it, is also because of Thursday night TV coverage.

As a commentator, I can't deny that the moving of fixtures is less of a problem for me, after all my working week is organised around the games, so it wouldn't matter when they were played, but I do have a family and it affects them.

When I used to work in a bank, I'd be constantly trying to work out if a game day might be changed and I'd be trying to book full days or half day holidays before anyone else got the same day. Booking cheaper train tickets becomes more problematical too, so I'm very sympathetic to the situation.

If a game is on TV, it's usually the only one being played, which gives me the chance to construct a more polished commentary, since games at a busier time include score updates and reports from other games, but then again, fewer people are likely to be listening.

Whatever time the game starts, and this was a 12.45 kick-off, I try to pop up to the second level of the Colin Bell stand, as a matter of routine, to deliver a team sheet to my son Daniel, and say hello to him. It only takes a couple of minutes and doesn't spoil my pre-match preparations. There are occasions when I'm presenting the programme as well commentating. On those occasions I have to give it a miss, but more often than not I can fill him in with the team changes.

It was debut day for Shay Given, as I'd told Daniel a few minutes before kick-off, and he impressed everyone with his sharp reflexes and his apparent ability to change direction in mid-flight when keeping out a shot from Afonso Alves.

Craig Bellamy scored the decisive goal to help earn City their 1-0 win.

Saturday 14th February – Match 75
Portsmouth v Manchester City – Premier League

The blank Saturday, due to City's early exit from the FA Cup, at least allowed the re-scheduling of this game at 3 o'clock on a Saturday. No one likes driving back from Portsmouth after a night game, which had been the case after the recent Youth Cup tie there, so I was happy the way things worked out; although I'd rather have been seeing City in an FA Cup tie.

Fred and I had chatted with Paul Hart, son of former City manager Johnny

Hart, after the recent Youth Cup tie, as that was his job at the time. Hart was now the first team manager, following the departure of Tony Adams. At the time of the postponement of the original fixture, it had been assumed it would suit City, as they were busy recruiting new players, who might have been integrated by the time the game was re-scheduled. That all sounded fine until the switch in managers.

It's a well known footballing fact that all new managers get a "honeymoon period" and City would be playing them, according to that theory, on the worst possible day; and so it proved to be.

I'd relocated myself into the overspill section of the Fratton Park press box, one of the advantages of arriving early, so that I wasn't squashed in between Radio Solent and other local journalists and broadcasters. This involved lots of cabling under desks, across gangways and up behind the old slatted wooden seats. I had plenty of gaffer tape and don't mind getting down on my hands and knees. It proved worthwhile as we had a bit more leg room, which is always appreciated by Fred. It also meant less verbal competition from our colleagues.

My switch of seats was the only success of the day. City lost 2-0. I was a bit surprised by the decision to bring young Shaleum Logan straight into the team at rightback. It seemed far more logical to move Pablo Zabaleta into that position; but what do I know?

The long drive home always seemed far more tiring after a defeat, but on this occasion we'd all been looking forward to the return journey, because we were to afford ourselves a rare treat by making a small diversion. We wanted to test out the new-look Little Chef, at Popham.

There'd been a Channel 4 documentary about the roadside eatery wanting to improve its image and its menu. I've always found their restaurants to be consistent and provide a decent quality meal, but the TV chef Heston Blumenthal had been asked to offer improvements. One of his suggestions had apparently been to create an ice-cream that sat in a bowl surrounded by dry ice. They decided not to use that idea but there were other things we'd heard about and wanted to sample.

Fred was the least enthusiastic, fearing we'd get lost trying to find the place, but he was won over by the experience, once we were in the right location. My first impression was that the restaurant was packed out with younger clientele than usual, some sitting on stools, one couple playing cards, as if they were on a social night out, rather than the usual pit-stop. We found an American style booth, complete with a leatherette bench, and started people watching and studying the menu.

There was the "All New Olympic Breakfast" which included Wiltshire-cured back bacon and a slice of Ramsay of Carluke black pudding, but I wanted to try something different. Would it be Braised Ox Cheeks or Hereford Steak and Abbot Ale Pie? I fancied the, slightly more conventional, Chicken Tikka Masala, with a sideorder of Chunky Chips.

Our waitress seemed really nice but her enthusiastic approach, something we don't see that often in this country, reminded me of an older version of Catherine Tate's comedy character "Amanda", perhaps best remembered for her occasional catchphrase "I'm a fiery Taurean with my moon in Uranus - careful, I'll do the jokes".

As we awaited our selection of new-look Little Chef fayre, we observed the delivery of fish and chips on the next table, complete with "crushed peas and the smell of the chippy", which involved the waitress spraying something around the customer from a small bottle, as if it were an exotic perfume.

The woman giggled as the chippy smell was dispensed and I suddenly felt a little jealous and hoped for an Indian takeaway scent to be brought out with my meal.

The food was excellent, the toilets, which we took turns to sample after a recommendation by another diner, were spotless, bright and with food facts written on the wall to distract you while peeing. For example, did you know that, "To tell how fresh an egg is, put it in a glass of cold water. If it sinks but stays in an upright position, it is fresh; if it sinks but falls into a semi-horizontal position, it is probably a week or so old; if it floats, then it is stale and should not be used." I could have stayed in their, peeing, all evening.

Sunday 15th February
Leigh Centurians v London Skolars – Northern Rail Cup

Although this book is about a season reporting on football, I thought I'd throw this Rugby League match into the mix, just to make a point. I get asked all the time, "What do you do when City aren't playing, or during the summer?"

I think it's fair to say that commentating on City games is what most people know me for, but I work five days a week for the BBC, whether it's winter or summer. Much of my time is spent travelling to and from games, attending press conferences or commentating and reporting, but I also prepare, write and present sports bulletins. I present and produce radio programmes, write stories, blogs and articles on the internet and create "packages" (short audio illustrations of stories).

There's also the archiving of the most crucial interviews and all the goals, forward planning, answering emails and letters, networking, attending meetings, answering the phone and covering other non-football related sports, like Rugby League.

In our area we have Lancashire County Cricket Club, Manchester Phoenix Ice-Hockey club, Belle Vue Aces and plenty of other sports to cover, including boxing, and athletics. I love Rugby League, and this was a chance to visit the new Leigh Sports Village Stadium.

The stadium impressed me from the moment I arrived, but was still a work-in-progress on the inside, especially the press box, which had been taped off, like a police crime scene, because they'd installed indoor electric plug sockets rather than their weatherproof counterparts.

I'd been sent to this game because we were aware of this problem and so the ISDN facilities we require to broadcast might not be accessible. One of the stewards allowed me to run a cable to a seat outside the exclusion zone and I used batteries rather than the mains as my power supply, so I was ready to go, just before kick-off.

I hadn't had much time to research the two teams, but I had the two line-ups written down in front of me, which was all I thought I would need as the plan was that I would do short reports during Phil Kinsella's commentary from Rochdale Hornets.

Five minutes into the game Phil's ISDN line had a problem and Jack asked me to go into commentary. I had no choice, and did the best I could, though I'd be the first to admit it wasn't up to my usual standards. What made it worse was that there was no atmosphere with such a small crowd in attendance, I didn't have an expert with me, I didn't know how long I'd be commentating for and it was a very one-sided game. Phil's technical problems went on for a long time and I commentated from Leigh for most of the first half. For once I was relieved when the time came to switch back to Rochdale.

Normally I love commentating, but not on this occasion. Leigh won the game 74-6, so at least everyone else seemed happy enough and the after match interviews were straightforward.

Thursday 19th February – Match 76
FC Kobenhavn v Manchester City – UEFA Cup

I'd flown direct from Manchester to Copenhagen, for the game at FC Midtjylland, so that would have been the obvious thing to do for this game, but it was cheaper to fly out of Birmingham, so I booked myself on the Tuesday evening flight and arrived at my hotel in darkness, ready for sleep. It was strange landing at an airport where the runway doesn't run alongside the airport buildings. Once the plane had landed, we carried on in a straight line to the terminals. It was hard to tell in the dark, but there was snow on the ground.

I awoke the next morning, ready to explore, and decided I'd spend the morning and early afternoon in neighbouring Sweden. I couldn't resist the chance to cross between the countries on the Øresund Bridge, which hadn't existed when I visited Copenhagen as a young man, back in 1980.

In those days, the only way to cross was by ferry. My trip had started in Gothenburg and then onto Stockholm, where I'd met my heroes Abba! I'd watched a documentary about the construction of the bridge on one of the Discovery channels on TV and it had fascinated me. Here I was taking the train across, starting with the tunnel, onto the man-made island and eventually across the bridge.

It took about 35 minutes to make the journey from Copenhagen to Malmö. There's no need to show a passport during the switch in countries, there wasn't back in 1980 either, as there is a strong bond between the Scandinavian countries, a sort of love/hate relationship sometimes, just like in the UK, between England and the other home nations.

I started by calling in at the tourist information office, in the railway station and was given the low-down on where to go by Lisa Gustafsson, who was wearing a feather boa to celebrate the upcoming visit of the heats of the Eurovision Song Contest.

She told me that "most things worth seeing are within walking distance. We are called the 'Town of Parks' and we are more laid-back than Copenhagen. You can relax here and have fun too. The bridge means we visit each other quite often and it's quite a bit cheaper here."

She also revealed that Malmö once belonged to Denmark - which explained a lot, because I could hardly tell I was in a different country.

Making use of Lisa's advice, I caught the Number 3 bus to Malmo's football stadium, which proved to be two-in-one, the old Malmö Stadium and, next door, the almost completed Swedbank Stadium, due to open in April 2009.

I had a look around both and bumped into Jan Möller, the goalkeeper beaten by a Trevor Francis header in Munich in the 1979 European Cup Final. After joking that he didn't want to talk about it, the keeper, who also had a spell with Bristol City, told me about, what was still, the biggest day in Malmö's history.

He went on to give me his views on City's chances against FC Copenhagen, and his was an opinion worth noting – after all, as he explained, Malmö "play training games against Copenhagen regularly."

"They beat us 4-1 in a friendly a couple of weeks ago," he offered, "and they played well in that game. Despite that, I think a draw would be a good result for FCK."

The other thing, I just had to do, was walk to the coastline and see the country-linking bridge from the Swedish side. It was a long walk and included a close up view of an impressive skyscraper called "the Turning Torso", which had a unique twisted frame.

Soon it was time to head back to Denmark, so I walked through the historic old town, past the statues, open air ice-rink and afternoon shoppers, as snow gently fell around me. The temperature was hovering around -3 degrees celcius.

Back across the bridge, I headed for the Parken Stadium, where City had just arrived for their evening training session. I hadn't realised the stadium had a roof, so there seemed no danger of the weather affecting the game, but the pitch looked a bit like a patch-work quilt which was less of a surprise when I discovered it was freshly laid by a company from Scunthorpe, under the supervision of their Preston-born groundsman on Monday evening. You couldn't make that sort of thing up, could you?

And it gets better - it had been relaid because a show, presenting all that's new in the world of that well known children's educational toy, Lego, had been staged there for four days and the boarding used underfoot had ruined large sections of the grass.

It snowed all day as I explored Copenhagen on match day, but it was a fine snow, almost too fine to be real, like it was little flecks of polystyrene. The temperatures didn't rise above freezing all day, so it stayed on the ground and slowly, almost unnoticed, built up as the hours passed.

After doing a couple of reports into Radio Manchester's breakfast programme, I went for my usual match day run. I normally criticise the footballers who wear gloves, but on this occasion I had gloves, woolly hat and jogging pants and even considered taking a hot water bottle. I ran twice around the nearby frozen lake and you'd be amazed at how many fellow joggers I passed; I assumed there must be a runners' convention taking place nearby.

Now feeling re-energised and fresh, I headed into the City centre, past a playground full of laughing teenagers, enjoying their break in the snow. I'm sure it would have been far too dangerous for youngsters to be allowed to "play out" in safety conscious England; someone might have sued.

I got my bearings at the tourist information centre, which was efficient but less friendly than its Swedish counterpart, and walked off for a wander, past the 'closed for the winter' Tivoli Gardens and Funfair, and into the main square.

Copenhagen's favourite son is the children's storyteller Hans Christian Andersen, and I'd wished he was still alive to write a few more pages of City's fairytale, hopefully with a happy ending in Istanbul in May.

I posed for a picture with Andersen's statue, while I waited to meet up with Ulrika Martensson from the City's press office. She recommended I take the harbour and canal cruise later in the afternoon, but first I just had to see the 'Little Mermaid', one of Andersen's most famous creations.

It was a long walk and I wondered if I'd ever get there. Along the way, I saw a guy salting the footpaths and was fascinated by the fact that he wasn't using the gritty rock salt we use back home, but what looked to be, to my untrained eye, sea salt - it was certainly white in colour. The gritting lorries, I saw three of them working in front of one public building, which I can't imagine seeing in England, also use the white salt, which doesn't leave a residue but seems very effective.

Eventually, after passing many City fans returning from the statue, I reached the 'Little Mermaid'. I posed for a picture, after watching one over-enthusiastic and balance-challenged City fan go head over heels, as he clambered down alongside the city's most famous landmark.

After that, it was onto the boat trip, which was a delight, thanks to our guide, Lars. We went out past the 'Little Mermaid' again, through the old naval dockyards, and back along the narrow, picturesque canals. An hour very well spent. By now, Copenhagen was filling up with good natured City fans, some moaning about the high prices, with which I couldn't argue. I think I paid £9 for a Big Mac meal.

Finally it was time for the match, and to my surprise the roof of the Parken Stadium was open when I got there, so the light snow fell onto the pitch throughout the game. It must have looked much worse than it really was on TV or to the spectators looking up at the snow falling against the bright lights of the floodlights. Someone told me they'd heard that six inches fell during the day - I'd say there might have been up to an inch.

The game was full of bizarre goals, with Nedum Onuoha being gifted the first, as their keeper let his weak shot slip into the net. City should have taken full advantage, and though a 2-2 draw would have been seen as a good result before the match, I was left feeling a bit disappointed. There was still work to be done in the second leg.

I couldn't find the tube station after the game, or a bus stop or a taxi, so with my broadcast equipment making my rucksack feel very heavy, I jogged the two miles back to the hotel as quickly as possible because I still had to write my BBC blog, pack my equipment and travel bag carefully and get as much sleep as possible before an early start for the flight home.

I got to sleep at 2am, was up again at 7am, and quickly on my way to the airport. I'd looked on their webcams the morning before, to check if the snow would delay the arrival of the City fans, but despite apparently being snowbound, by British standards, public transport and planes were running to time. It must have been the "right type of snow".

I have to admit I felt a little jealous as I waited for my flight back to Birmingham, as I watched plenty of City fans, and one or two journalists, boarding the Manchester bound direct flight at the next gate; I was still home by teatime though!

Saturday 21st February – Match 77
Middlesbrough v Wigan Athletic – Premier League

The easy option, during a post-match interview or a football phone-in, is to blame the referee for all the woes of the game, but I think it's an excuse to hide behind. It's true that in any one game, a single decision can make a difference but since I believe that referees are fair, conscientious and honest for ninety nine percent of the time, their decisions are based on their best assessment of a situation, at that time.

Try sitting among the home fans, at a game where you support neither team, and you will usually walk away feeling that the referee had a good game, even though everyone around you feels he was against their team. Go to the away end and the other supporters will tell you the match official was against them. Who'd be a referee?

I still hear City fans talking about the City "goal" ruled out by Alf Grey during the League Cup semi-final against Liverpool in 1981. Isn't it the case though, that great teams, winning teams, make their own luck? If City had been mentally strong enough that day, wouldn't they have let that decision pass by and go and score another goal? I feel the same way about managers and players who use a bad decision as an excuse for their failings or the new belief that players can't play two games a week; it's all in the head.

When Michael Schumacher had a flat tyre or was hit by another car, he channelled his frustration into getting the best he could still achieve that day; that's because he was the best F1 driver of his generation. That's what made him a winner.

Mike Dean was the referee for this game at the Riverside Stadium and I thought he was excellent, in fact it was one of the best refereeing displays I've seen. There was one moment that particularly impressed me, when he spotted a dive inside the penalty area and as fans all around me vented their fury, I leaned over to former referee Jeff Winter, who was sat alongside me. He explained exactly what had happened from his perspective in the stand and with the added accuracy of TV replays.

Mr Dean had got the decision spot on, though very few of the 24,000 in the ground would have agreed. It was a poor game, defences dominated, as they say, and it finished 0-0.

Once again, after a relatively routine trip and match, the drama was reserved for the journey home. As I descended from the highest point of the M62 I suddenly saw debris all over the road ahead me and had to swerve around it to avoid an accident. As I picked my way around the shards of metal and rubber I could see one vehicle had leapt the central barrier and was on the Yorkshire bound side; the other was in the middle lane on my side.

It must have been a horrendous accident but it wasn't possible or appropriate to try to work out the severity of the injuries, which might have been sustained by those who were involved. I was a little shocked by what I'd seen and relieved that my journey was almost over.

Sunday 22nd February – Match 78
Liverpool v Manchester City – Premier League

This was one of City's best away performances of the season, though it owed a lot to negativity, with three defensive midfielders playing in front of a back four and goalkeeper.

Slightly against the run of play, City took the lead through a deflected shot from Craig Bellamy, though once they'd taken the lead, City looked stronger and stronger. Liverpool have always had a winning mentality though and it was obvious that they would come back into the game. A late goal from Dirk Kuyt meant City had to settle for a 1-1 draw.

I remember sitting at Anfield, during the best years of Robbie Fowler, as a Liverpool player, and seeing City take the lead. With about ten minutes to go I wondered who'd get Liverpool's equaliser rather than expecting City to win. Robbie Fowler scored a couple of minutes later.

I've seen City win at Anfield twice, the first being on boxing day 1981 when Kevin Bond, Kevin Reeves and Asa Hartford had scored in a 3-1 win. At that time Liverpool were virtually unbeatable at Anfield and I couldn't quite believe it was happening. Almost a year to the day later, City lost 5-2 there, on the way to the first relegation I witnessed, David Pleat's silly dance and all.

The second win at Anfield came on the penultimate day of the 2002-2003 season with Peter Schmeichel performing heroics in goal and Nicolas Anelka scoring both goals in a 2-1 win. I love Anfield and the fans at that stadium, they've always had a terrific sense of humour and I love the intimacy of the ground. It will be shame if they move to a new stadium, but I suppose it's bound to happen.

I've stood on the Kop too, for a Merseyside derby. It was on a day when City didn't have a game, and I was at a bit of a loose end. I turned up without a ticket and hoped to buy a ticket from a tout, but soon discovered the price was beyond my means. I got talking to a steward at the Kop end and he took pity on me and sneaked me in, not wanting any financial reward in return. I wish I could remember what I'd said to him, I could try it again!

What astounded me most, once I was inside, was that there were Everton fans on the Kop too, wearing their colours and stood side by side with the Liverpool fans. There was no aggravation, no threat of violence but plenty of good natured banter. I came away from the game wondering why it couldn't be like that in the Manchester Derby too; and this was well before the tragic events at Hillsborough in 1989, after which those huge standing terraces had been closed.

After City's 1-1 draw of 2009, I was taken outside the ground, with the other local journalists and brought back in through the players' entrance, ready to do the post-match interviews. For quite a while Robinho and Elano stood close by, waiting for a car to arrive that was to take them to a function they were attending that evening.

I was tempted to try to talk to them or perhaps get my programme signed for Daniel, but I was told by my fellow journalists, that this was not the "done thing". I didn't see what the problem was but accepted their views and just said a polite hello before turning away and ignoring them.

Our player interview was with Craig Bellamy, who always spoke well, despite his reputation for being a hot-head. He certainly hasn't seemed that way when I've been in his company, in fact he seems like a very polite and articulate person, and very much a family man.

He took the opportunity to tell us how well he got on with Robinho, after reports in the tabloids had suggested the two hated each other. On the field there certainly seemed no evidence to back up those newspaper claims, and I (perhaps naively) had no reason to disbelieve what he was telling us.

Tuesday 24th February – Match 79
Colchester United v Stockport County – League One

This was a special day, for more than one reason. Firstly I was visiting my 92nd ground, again, and I'd get to visit my dad, who lives near Norwich.

I joined the 92 club, for supporters and professionals who've seen a game at all 92 league grounds, back in 1985. As a meticulous record keeper, I soon spotted that I was well over halfway to that goal in the early 80's and decided I would try to complete the task as quickly as possible, as I was getting married in 1984, which might mean travelling to games might become more difficult!

I'd wanted to complete my original 92 at a bigger ground or somewhere special. I'd visited all the top flight grounds with city, so I decided I'd target Plymouth, it being the furthest away and an historic City (of Sir Francis Drake, bowls and the Armada fame). Since there was a fixture over Easter that would be perfect, and City played the following day, I had to complete the others before then.

I used to travel long distances for midweek games, alone, to visit the grounds I was missing. It was tiring and time consuming. I met up with Bristol Rovers fan Gordon Pearce, the founder of the 92 club, when I visited Eastville and slowly counted down to the last two; Aldershot and Plymouth.

Aldershot wasn't meant to be my penultimate ground, but everytime I targeted one of their home games, it was postponed. I got to know the lady who answered the phone there very well and by the time I finally visited for a game, three days before my Easter trip to Plymouth, I was well known to them. As I sat in my seat in the main stand, much to my astonishment, the PA asked me to make myself known to a steward who then escorted me to the boardroom to be a guest of the Chairman.

Everyone seemed interested in my adventures and I was offered all the luxuries of being in the directors' box, like warm tea and a piece of fruit cake. Their kindness made it all the sadder for me, years later, when Aldershot went bust. I was so happy for them when the newly established Aldershot Town were promoted back into the football league.

Later that week I drove down, in torrential rain, with my bride-to-be Irene, for the final game. The big question was; would it be called off due to waterlogging? We'd decided to treat ourselves to an overnight stay in a bed and breakfast, to allow for some sightseeing and relaxation, but I couldn't really relax knowing that the game might be off. We called in at Home Park, when we arrived, to see huge puddles on the pitch, which didn't help my state of mind.

Our landlady assured us that the wind would dry the pitch, once the rain stopped and although it was muddy the following day, the game went ahead. I saw home victories during those visits to my last two grounds. Aldershot beat Halifax Town 2-0 on the Tuesday and Plymouth were 1-0 victors against Bristol City, on Good Friday, 5th April 1985.

I think the worst ground I saw on my travels was The Shay (Halifax) and, apart from Maine Road, the best was Anfield. I sent off my list of first matches attended, at each ground, and got my tie, and an enamel badge to show I'd done it. I could have cheated, but that would be like missing part of a marathon, or the B of the Bang; what would be the point?

Since then I've been ticking off all the new stadiums, one by one, but I'd never quite got back to a full and current 92, until this season, when the trip to Colchester would get me back to the full complement.

The 92 club rules state that you need to see a first team competitive game on each ground. If I'm honest, the game I attended at Newport County (against Frank McLintock's Brentford) was abandoned, due to fog after an hour, so I've never been sure if that broke the rules the first time around, and my trip to Swansea's new Liberty Stadium in 2009 was for a Youth Cup tie, so does that make me a fraud?

En Route to Colchester I made a slight detour to Norwich, where my dad lives, just around the corner from the bungalow we'd lived in for 12 months when I was a boy. After my mum died in 1977, my dad had a terrible time coping but kept in touch with his friend Ivor Wilson. On one trip to visit him, he met Sadie, whom he later married. After a spell in Merstham in Surrey, they moved back to Hethersett, near Norwich and have lived there, very happily, ever since.

They play short mat indoor bowls on a Tuesday, so the only way I could spend time with them was by going along as well. I didn't expect to play, but they had an odd number of players, so I ended up playing against my dad. I hadn't played any sort of bowls since lunchtimes on the crown green near Whitefield train station, a short walk away from Stand Grammar School.

Marianne, Don, Roger, Norman Alan, Olive and the rest all made me very welcome and were very patient in explaining the subtleties of the short mat rules. My team was the winning team in both games I played. You never lose it do you?

In my excitement at seeing my dad and winning at bowls, my arrival in Colchester was a little later than it should have been, and I was starting to panic a little when I couldn't find the ground, with just an hour to go to kick-off. I hadn't realised, but I'd driven very close to the new stadium on the main road from Norwich, but I was on Layer Road, where the old ground used to be, before I'd realised it, and the adrenalin was flowing.

I pulled over and asked a man for directions, he'd been the third I'd asked, none of them even knew Colchester United had a new ground! I finally got some luck, as the kind gentleman, trying to give me directions though my lowered window, was going to the game, so I offered him a lift and he got into the passenger seat and navigated me to the Weston Homes Community Stadium.

What a charming man he was, a Good Samaritan, in my hour of need. I rushed into the ground to find it wasn't quite complete, so I needed a steward to guide me to my seat. As I walked in, I received a call from the office telling me that Jim Gannon, the County manager, was going for a job interview at Brighton, the following day.

I headed for the directors' lounge and persuaded Martin Reid, the County Chairman, to speak to us live. Five minutes later he was on Radio Manchester expressing his hopes that Gannon would stay. The game flew by, with former Oldham player Marc Tierney scoring the only goal in a 1-0 win for Colchester.

After the match I was desperate to get Gannon on the programme live, and with five minutes to go I thought my chance had gone, as I saw him heading down the tunnel as I was speaking on air. I couldn't chase after him, so I made a split second decision to shout to Des Hinks, asking him to ask Gannon if he'd come up to speak to me immediately.

It must have sounded a bit amateurish to the listener, but I decided that a slight compromise on-air was worth the possibility of hearing the man all County fans wanted to hear from. It worked, Des heard me, went and got him and within seconds he was telling us his views.

He also promised me, that whatever happened at Brighton, the following day, he would travel back in the afternoon, by plane or train, and would fulfil his promise to be my studio guest for an hour, to talk about his life and career and to play a few of his favourite songs, like the old "desert island discs" show I used to enjoy presenting.

I even joked that he might want to select "Should I stay or should I go" by the Clash.

As good as his word, he turned up the following evening and we enjoyed a fascinating hour together. He'd turned down the Brighton job, preferring to stay loyal to Stockport, although it was apparent that his patience with the club was starting to wear thin.

My return journey from Colchester had not been without incident. As I headed north, singing along with my i-pod, to keep me awake, I saw something on fire ahead of me. As I slowed I could see huge flames coming from a lorry parked under a bridge with, what I assumed to be, the driver stood on the hard shoulder, just behind the vehicle. I moved to the outside lane, there were no other vehicles around, and drove past, as far away from the burning lorry as possible.

Within seconds I saw a fire engine join the motorway, just ahead of me and I followed it to the next junction where it came off and headed back the other way. I knew it was going to the incident and I was also aware that if I'd been ten minutes further back down the road, I might have spent an hour at a standstill while the fire was extinguished.

I got home at 3 o'clock in the morning, and when I switched on the national news, the next morning, I heard about how the damage from the fire had meant the M1 was still down to two lanes.

Thursday 26th February - Match 80
Manchester City v FC Kobenhavn – UEFA Cup

The first leg had been more open than it should have been, but I never doubted that City would win through this tie. On the evidence of what I'd seen, Copehagen were about the same standard as an English Championship team, not that Nottingham Forest had worried about that in the FA Cup.

It was to be Craig Bellamy's day, he scored twice, his second being set up by Robinho, which provided more evidence that the pair were the best of mates both on and off the pitch.

The Danes got a late consolation, but City were through to the last sixteen of the UEFA Cup.

Saturday 28th February – Match 81
Chelsea v Wigan Athletic – Premier League

This was to be a football weekend in London, as Fred and I would be doing commentary on two games in the Capital in two days. I booked us into the Ibis at Barking, as the Sunday game was an early kick-off for City at West Ham.

I'd been at the Chelsea v Wigan fixture with Paul Rowley a year earlier when Emile Heskey's late equaliser in a 1-1 draw had all but handed the title to Man United. Wigan's record against the "big four" since they'd been promoted to the top flight, wasn't good, but I fancied them to push Chelsea again, as they were playing consistently well and under the management of Steve Bruce had become a very hard team to beat. Paul Scharner went close to giving the Latics a lead they would have fully deserved, and Titus Bramble had a header cleared off the line before Chelsea's John Terry scored a scrappy goal.

Eight minutes from time Olivier Kapa looked to have made it déjà vu for Chelsea with a much-deserved equalizer, but that never-say-die attitude that Chelsea possessed kept them going until the end and I could feel the pain of everyone at Wigan when Frank Lampard scored a last gasp winner for the Pensioners.

As I waited to speak to Steve Bruce, the former Chelsea player Gus Poyet said hello and Shaun Wright-Phillips visited the changing room area. When he was still at City, I'd hosted a function at which Antoine Sibierski had been a guest, and he'd promised to give me one of his match-worn shirts. This was the day he fulfilled that promise, so I was now the owner of the number 6 shirt he wore as a brief substitute that day.

We'd parked close to Chelsea's ground, and I didn't know whether to go back up the A40 to the M25 to take the long route around to Barking, or to head through central London. As Barking is not much more than 10 miles away from Chelsea, as the crow flies, Fred suggested the shorter route.

An hour later we were crawling past Fortnum and Masons, Harrods, Eros, through Trafalgar Square and around by the London Eye. We were moving that slowly that Fred could have got out, sat down in a Costa Coffee, enjoyed a cappuccino and slowly caught me up again at no more than strolling pace.

It took us two hours to make the journey; oh how I'd hate to live in London.

Fred had threatened to bring his new birthday gift, a sat nav, but decided against it, so we then spent ten minutes trying to find the hotel, when both extremely tired. After something to eat in the hotel restaurant, served by a very efficient Lithuanian waitress of Ukrainian decent – my father-in-law would have been proud – we went to our rooms.

I fell asleep almost as soon as my head hit the pillow, as I tried to watch Match of the Day, which I'd turned off halfway through. I switched on the TV as soon as I awoke the next morning, with the repeat of Match of the Day at exactly the point I'd left it the previous night. Perhaps that's why they repeat it.

March

Sunday 1st March – Match 82
West Ham United v Manchester City – Premier League

Starting the day so close to Upton Park meant that both Fred and I were unusually fresh for a game being played so far from home and after a leisurely breakfast we drove nearer to the ground and looked for a suitable side street on which we could leave the car.

I generally prefer to park near a tube station in the capital; the previous evening's journey from Chelsea demonstrating why. This was a Sunday morning, though, so being parked somewhere close by, would allow for a quicker getaway. Kick-off was at the ridiculously early time of 12.30 because of TV, naturally, and because the League Cup Final was taking place that afternoon.

London City Airport isn't too far away from Upton Park, and I once flew into there for a game at Millwall. It was at the time when I wasn't working full-time in the sports department at Radio Manchester. I'd been asked to host a touring roadshow around the shopping centres of Greater Manchester and on this particular day I was in Wigan.

When I say it was a roadshow, it was more of a "meet the public" exercise, with a small studio in the centre of a display of pictures and presenter photocards. I had to encourage passers by to have a go at reading a news or a sports bulletin and as a reward they would be able to take away a cassette recording, as a keepsake.

I enjoyed meeting our listeners and it gave me a real insight into who I was speaking to when I was on air. Once the schools finished for the day, the shopping centres were quickly taken over by swarms of giggling youngsters who saw our studio as a chance to have a play. I was encouraged to shut the "experience" at about 3.45pm.

On this day, Tuesday 29th September 1998, I'd booked a flight from Manchester to London City Airport at 5.15pm, which meant I would have approximately ninety minutes to get from Wigan to Manchester Airport.

Never has the sound of a fire alarm been so pleasant as when one went off that day in the Grand Arcade shopping centre at just after half past three. I was told to get out fast and that it would be at least thirty minutes before I could return. I threw everything inside the studio, locked the door and headed for the airport. Very quickly I was in the air and, an hour after take off, I was in the centre of London catching the Docklands Light Railway to the New Den.

Three years later I was back at Millwall, but this time as the City reporter. Away fans had been banned because of problems in the previous encounter between the two clubs in the New Den; the visitors section was completely empty. Before the game I interviewed one of the Millwall security staff and wondered what they would have to do, since there were no away fans to consider. "We're here to look after the press", was his rather unsettling reply.

Unusually, there was no reserved seating in the press box, so I quickly made sure I sat close to our broadcast line, but noticed the socket was on the exterior wooden wall of the press area. Something in my head told me not to sit there, because I would be very close to the supporters, so I used a longer cable than normal and positioned myself over an access tunnel, which itself led into an area reserved for corporate guests.

Just to be doubly sure I sat Peter Barnes, who was my summariser at the time, nearer to the supporters than me, as a sort of safety barrier.

Once the game got underway I carried on as normal, though it was a strange atmosphere with no vocal support for City. The match was being shown on a giant screen back at Maine Road. More than ever before, I started imagining who would be listening. I knew some of those at Maine Road would, and there'd be plenty more at home and in their cars. Although it sounds soppy, I felt like I was there representing all those who would normally have made the trip. I felt privileged to be their representative; their eyes.

When City took the lead thanks to a goal from Shaun Goater, set up by Shaun Wright-Phillips, I reacted in my usual ecstatic way, but very quickly became aware that the ground was silent apart from me yelling at the top of my voice. There was a commentator there from Century Radio too, but he was much more reserved and went largely unnoticed. I'd been identified by all the Millwall fans around me, who were now giving me the evil eye.

Millwall equalised just before half-time, but City were still the better side and their fans knew it. During the break a few home supporters turned to face me and glared and grimaced; well I think they were grimacing, I couldn't really tell, particularly the bloke wearing a surgical mask. These days I would have assumed he was simply frightened of catching bird flu, but I think he was just pig sick.

Even the woman sat directly below me in the corporate area seemed intent on staring at me. When Darren Huckerby added a second goal I commentated as normal but was more aware of the threat around me, as even more angry faces turned towards me, including the previous suspects. Millwall again drew level, much to their glee.

With seven minutes left Shaun Wright-Phillips, who'd never scored for City before, hit a screaming winner. I went ballistic and (perhaps foolishly) didn't care about the reaction around me, though I did keep my eyes very firmly on the crowd, rather than the pitch. I feared they might throw things at me, like I was a coconut at the funfair.

Because my eyes were focussed on the fans, I never noticed Darren Huckerby, Kevin Horlock and the rest of the City players running to the away end to thank the empty terraces for their support. Fortunately Peter, who was less concerned about the hooligans than me, kept our listeners fully informed, as I sank lower into my seat.

I believe that's where City's "invisible man" song started, as a tribute to the absent City fans. To say I felt intimidated, that day, is an understatement, although it was a day I'll never forget and one I wouldn't have wanted to miss. I was never more glad to leave a football stadium though.

Down the years West Ham fans have also had a bad reputation, so for many years I was a little intimidated when travelling to Upton Park; their reputation, though, has improved immeasurably in recent years.

I love hearing the West Ham fans sing "I'm forever blowing bubbles", especially when they sing unaccompanied by music from the PA just before kick-off. It's a throw back to the old days. The game itself was a bit flat but included the return of Valeri Bojonov to first team action, which was a highlight in itself. City lost 1-0, so despite not travelling there and back in a day, it would again seem like a long journey home.

This was made even worse by one major oversight by Fred and me. We couldn't remember exactly where we'd left the car and certainly hadn't memorised the street name. Just to make it more embarrassing, as we trudged up and down the streets that led off Barking Road, I'd agreed to give a lift home to Ged, a groundsman for City's Academy at Platt Lane, and we must have seemed like idiots as we spent twenty minutes looking for the car. Eventually we found it, though I'm sure we'd already walked the length of that street three times and passed the car without seeing it.

Monday 2nd March – Match 83
Oldham Athletic v Leeds United – League One

This was an exciting week for me with five games in five days; it doesn't get much better than that.

I'd known for weeks that Oldham would be wearing a pink kit, which I was looking forward to seeing. Many of the Latics fans had also taken the opportunity to wear pink too, so it became like a huge fancy dress party.

The pink theme was to support "Think4Pink" a charity set up to help raise funds for the Victoria Unit at the Royal Oldham Hospital, which helped people with breast-related diseases. The teams came out to the Pink Panther theme music, It later transpired that the Oldham manager John Sheridan wasn't best pleased with many of the events on the night. I'm sure he was happy enough to support the charity but felt the off-field antics had distracted his players.

The match was shown on Sky Sports and was a good game that ended all square, after Lee Hughes had scored a very precise goal, that I'm sure could have threaded the eye of a needle from an acute angle. Fred came to the game, just for the fun of it, perhaps he couldn't bear being separated from me after our weekend in London! Another famous face sat close by was the former Salford City Reds Rugby League coach Karl Harrison, who was a big Leeds fan.

I'm not a stranger to fund raising for Charity myself, and down there years I've had lots of fun. While at Radio Cavell, Jack Dearden and I dressed up as Panto Dames and shook our collecting tins in Oldham town centre. I got a few funny looks but for some reason Jack didn't. I assumed the people of Oldham had seen him out and about, dressed like that, before.

The most enjoyable fund-raising day was the time I set myself the task of travelling by as many different forms of transport as I could, in one day. I was not alone in my challenge, my Sunday morning co-presenter, Carolynne Jones was also being sponsored. I can't remember the number we achieved but I can remember that we started by skiing down the artificial ski slope at Rossendale and during the course of the day we went canoeing along the canal, hopped on pogo sticks, rode horses and flew in a light aircraft before ending up on a train home from Blackpool where we'd done lots of different rides on the Pleasure Beach.

Since I joined the BBC in 1994, I've always been involved in Children in Need. I reported from Manchester's Arndale Centre, interviewing Jason Orange's dad, who had a hand-pushed sales cart at the time. I've hosted the on-air auction and jointly presented our main Children in Need programme. Occasionally we got to speak to the big stars who were at television centre in London for the main TV show, but of course we couldn't see them, so I didn't always know who they were.

In March 2008, I offered to do something sporty for Sport Relief and ran from the City of Manchester Stadium to the JJB Stadium in Wigan via Old Trafford and Bolton's Reebok Stadium. I started at breakfast time and finished during our drivetime programme, with a few stops and interviews along the way. I covered about 30 miles that day, the charity marathon running I'd done in my younger days, certainly helped me keep going for such a long time.

I consider it a privilege to get involved in these types of events; I've also been a committee member of the children's charity the Variety Club of Great Britain.

Tuesday 3rd March – Match 84
Leicester City v Stockport County – League One

It was a wet night, and the game started during a heavy downpour with two goals in the first five minutes. Leicester had a bit of weather assistance for their deflected effort while County responded almost immediately thanks to Chris O'Grady; and that was that!

As always seems to happen when both teams concede early goals, the chances, if not the weather, dried up after that and it finished 1-1. Alongside me throughout the evening was Jitesh Parmar, who'd been covering a lot of football matches for Radio Manchester and he'd asked for some advice about sports reporting.

As soon as I arrived he was keen to impress and very soon I was interviewing Conrad Logan, who he'd spotted in the crowd, just down below us. At local radio level, thinking on your feet and seizing any opportunity that comes along is all part of the job. Sitting alongside me was Tim Flowers, the former City goalkeeping coach, and of course a former Leicester goalkeeper; I interviewed him too, though he didn't believe I'd remembered his days at Leicester!

Jitesh was very keen to learn everything he could and it reminded me of how I'd listened to every bit of advice I could in my early days. I told him how Jack and I had gone to a City reserve game together, many years ago, and had commentated on the game into a small tape recorder. We'd swapped roles, each being the "ball by ball" man while the other was the expert summariser.

It's not always easy listening to yourself, and even now I don't particularly enjoy hearing my own voice, but you get used to it and it has to be done. I've always been my own fiercest critic and I learnt so much from those early, if embarrassing, experiments. Some things work, and others don't, and it can take several listens before you notice your own flaws. It's a bit like prouf reeding, sometimes you can't see the oblivious.

Jitesh was alongside me as I interviewed the County boss Jim Gannon after the game and questioned me afterwards about why I'd chatted to him before and after the interview and how I'd had the nerve to ask one or two quite direct questions. "It's all about building up a trust and being fair", I told him.

It's not possible to teach everyone how to deal with every situation. It's like learning to drive, you can learn how to do the basics, but the subtleties are what makes some people competent and others very good or even excellent drivers.

I ended up speaking to Jitesh for an hour after we'd finished, so it was a late arrival home; a charmer like him will go a long way in this industry.

Wednesday 4th March – Match 85
Manchester City v Aston Villa – Premier League

Aston Villa arrived at the City of Manchester Stadium with an impressive away record and ambitions of breaking into the top four positions in the Premier League, so with Mark Hughes naming a team that was weakened by the absence of Robinho and Craig Bellamy through injury, it seemed like it might be a long night.

What a surprise! City completely dominated a lacklustre Villa team who had gone out of the UEFA Cup, after prioritising their chase for a Champions League place. They'd rested some of their better players against CSKA Moscow and suffered the consequences. I'm not a fan of "resting" players and I think the idea that footballers can't play at the top of their game twice a week is nonsense.

Shaun Wright-Phillips was one of the stars of the show and he'd been brought down for the penalty from Elano that gave City their lead.

It was very fitting that Wright-Phillips added the other goal to round off a 2-0 win. It felt like a turning point in the season. A comfortable win against Aston Villa was nothing to be sniffed at.

Saturday 7th March – Match 86
Manchester City (u18's) v Norwich City (u18's) – FA Youth Cup

What a shame that this game wasn't being played at Carrow Road, as I would have been able to visit my dad again. It's not easy making time to visit him, so I try to take every opportunity I can. I couldn't have asked for a better father, he's always been a great role model, never judging and always showing endless patience.

He was emotionally destroyed when he lost my Mum died in 1977, and I was reluctant to go away to university while he was so obviously in mourning, not to mention my own fragile state of mind. Six months after my mum had lost her battle with cancer, I went to Sunderland Polytechnic to study Geography, although I couldn't find it at first, which didn't augur well. I stayed in digs with a lovely old lady in Seaburn, just a walk away from Roker Park and quite close to the sea.

I'd worried about missing Starsky & Hutch on TV when I moved away, but she was very homely and was happy to indulge me and make me feel at home. The real problem though, was coming home at weekends and finding my dad sat in a dark room, with just a table light on, looking through photo albums of my mum. It broke my heart to see him like that and I wanted to be nearer to him.

It was also proving very difficult to maintain my obsession with City, illustrated perfectly by my efforts to watch City's League Cup tie at Blackpool. For the Wednesday evening trip to Bloomfield Road, I had to catch a train from Sunderland to Manchester, after my final lecture of the day, and then on to Blackpool.

After the 1-1 draw, which now meant I'd have to get back to Manchester for the replay the following Tuesday, I had to make the reverse journey. I was awake all night and went straight into lectures again the following day. The thought of having to do this for the next three years was the final straw, so I spoke to the student liaison officer and asked about the possibility of transferring to Manchester Polytechnic.

There was no space on the geography course for me; my grades hadn't been good enough at A level, so I switched degrees to "Social Science", which included psychology and sociology, subjects I'd always found interesting.

I spent the next few months supporting both my dad and City, home and away. It was in November 1978 that I last missed a City game, through choice; although in truth that was because I didn't have the funds. City were away to AC Milan in the UEFA Cup and student finance wouldn't stretch that far. I would have listened to the game on the radio, but it was postponed due to fog.

The following afternoon, the Thursday, I was sitting in Piccadilly Gardens listening to commentary of City's 2-2 draw. I missed one City game in the 80's; a trip to Brighton in 1980. I'd been a little overzealous in my courtship of Irene and not got home until the early hours of the morning. I slept through my alarm clock and missed the coach from Maine Road and had to listen to the game on the radio while I walked around Oldham market with Irene and her mum. I've never done that again.

In the summer of 1979, I headed off to see Dennis Tueart play for New York Cosmos, knowing that I'd not really got to grips with statistics and economics, which were two of the modules on my course. I'd failed some of the first year exams, so I decided it was time to get a job. I took my dad's advice and got a "safe" job in a bank, which included weekends off, which was perfect for the football.

Slowly but surely my dad's spirits started to lift and things were getting serious with Irene, so encouraged by her mum, who seemed to take a liking to me from the first time I met her, we married in 1984. That was the best decision of my life.

Once I was hitched my dad must have felt that he didn't need to look after me anymore and started doing things for himself again, including return visits to his friends in the Norwich area. It was during one of these trips that he met Sadie, and within a year they were married, living initially in Surrey.

I miss him being part of my day to day life, but I'm happy that he's found love again and has been living a very happy and long retirement. I sometimes wish he could have seen his grandchildren growing up and seen me fulfil my dream of becoming the City reporter, but he's happy and that's the main thing.

The Youth Cup game against Norwich was a 2pm kick-off at the City of Manchester Stadium, on one of the Saturdays when the first team should have still been involved in the real FA Cup. Naturally a bigger crown than normal came along, nearly three and a half thousand were there to see the Blues win 1-0 thanks to a slick goal by Robbie Mak.

Tuesday 10th March – Match 87
Rochdale v Bradford City – League Two

It's funny how every time a club seems to have problems, a win seems highly unlikely and supporters turn up depressed, that the team produces its best performances. City fans say that's "typical City", I'm sure Dale fans say it's "typical Dale" and Rotherham United fans say it's "typical United".

This was one of those days, Dale had named coach David Flitcroft as a substitute, due to their injury problems but they produced one of their best displays of the season. Clark Keltie and Will Buckley were the two stars of the show. Despite failing to score in the first half, they tore their opponents to shreds in the second period thanks to a goal from Rory McArdle and two penalties from Adam Le Fondre.

Le Fondre had first come to my notice as a youngster at Stockport County when I'd heard all about him on their end of season trip to China. Martin Bellis, who was their cheery mascot Vernon the Bear, had never stopped talking about how good Le Fondre was going to be. He was certainly starting to fulfil his potential, though wearing Dale's colours rather than County's.

I'd only travelled out for the second week of the trip to China because City had not played their final league game. I flew out with County's Chief Executive Niels de Vos and his wife, via Heathrow, a week after the team had travelled east.

De Vos even gave me his first class seat because he'd only managed to blag one as an upgrade, and preferred to be with his wife than sit up front on his own. My good fortune meant I could stretch out and even get some sleep, as we headed for Beijing. On arrival in the Chinese capital we found we had a couple of hours to spare, so we hired a taxi to Tiananmen Square where we met a young woman called Xin Ning, and her uncle, who offered to show us around.

Mrs De Vos bought a dress for her daughter but left it in the shop, so I called Xin Ning from the airport and asked her if she'd go back to the shop and look for the dress. I said I'd call her again when we returned from Urumqi a few days later.

We checked into our hotel at one thirty in the morning, as manager Sammy McIlroy argued with various people who'd just told him his team were expected to play two games on successive evenings, rather than the one he was expecting. McIlroy was furious and threatened to play his backroom staff in the second game. At one stage I thought I might get a game myself.

McIlroy played in the game against the Kazakhstan Military and gave me his shirt as a keepsake. That's the nearest I came to playing for County, who lost that game 3-1, not that they were bothered. It was played on the worst pitch I've ever seen.

On our return to Beijing I rang Xin Ning and she told me that she'd been back to the shop but couldn't find the dress. I met up with her and her Uncle anyway and spent quite a bit of time with them during the next few days, when I wasn't on organised trips to the Great Wall or exploring the Forbidden City.

Xin Ning was well educated, like her Uncle, who also spoke perfect English; he was a history lecturer at university. They took me to an authentic Chinese restaurant, outside the tourist areas and I paid for a massage for the three of us in a state-run parlour. Don't get the wrong idea, we all kept our clothes on!

Before leaving England I'd attended a press conference at Manchester City for the launch of their own shops in China, in three different Cities, apparently selling just City merchandise; and this was before Thaksin Shinwatra's name had ever been mentioned at Eastlands.

I extended my stay in Beijing by a day so I could visit the shop there. I quickly realised that the reality was different from the PR briefing I'd been given. The manager of the store, having failed to persuade me to simply meet him in the hotel lobby and talk about the shop rather than seeing it, took me to the shopping centre, to a sports department store. In the basement of the shop, in the furthest corner from the entrance, I found the football department, which had Man United and Liverpool shirts hanging prominently, but no sign of a City shirt or any City merchandise.

Eventually I noticed a signed Sun Jihai shirt hanging in a frame on the wall and one City shirt, last season's, hanging on a rail. There were a few key rings and similar small items on a partially hidden shelf, low down. This was certainly not a City superstore in the Far East, as had been suggested when I was back in England.

I spent the afternoon and evening with my new Chinese friends, followed by a sad goodbye and the long flight home. I tried to keep in touch with Xin Ning by email but her two email addresses started bouncing back my correspondence. I discovered that communicating with someone from the BBC was not allowed. I assume her accounts had been blocked. No wonder she had denied any knowledge of the student massacre of 1989 when I'd innocently asked her about it, soon after we'd met. She'd later told me she wasn't supposed to admit it had happened to westerners.

Thursday 12th March – Match 88
Manchester City v AaB – UEFA Cup

A straightforward 2-0 win for City suggested that their passage to the last sixteen of the UEFA Cup would be a formality. Their team had a couple of familiar faces in it. Striker Luton Shelton had scored the goal for Sheffield United the previous season, in amongst the balloons of Bramall Lane, which had helped knock Sven's City out of the FA Cup. The other player I felt I should know was midfielder Kaka; sorry that should be Caca, but it's pronounced the same way.

City dominated the tie to such an extent that it had even crossed my mind that if they were to score the four or five goals their play had deserved, the BBC might decide, to save money and that I wouldn't need to go to Denmark for the second leg.

Saturday 14th March – Match 89
Sunderland v Wigan Athletic – Premier League

I hadn't seen Joe Royle for ages, so it was a pleasant surprise when he popped up in the press box at Sunderland. I chatted to him for a few minutes and wondered if he missed being involved in management, little knowing that he'd be back in the game very soon. He'd always promised that he had one more job in him, and he felt it would be a team that wore blue shirts, just like City, Everton, Ipswich and Oldham.

Wigan were at their best in this game, with Charles N'Zogbia shrugging off the In'Somnia nickname, he'd been unfairly handed by the Newcastle manager Joe Kinnear, just before his switch to the Latics. As well as scoring, he was impressive throughout, with Ben Watson getting the other goal in a much deserved 2-1 win.

Sunday 15th March – Match 90
Chelsea v Manchester City

One of the proudest days of my life came on the opening day of the 2006/2007 season when my son, Daniel, led out the City team as the mascot at Stamford Bridge. Co-incidentally we had a visitor from Ukraine with us too. My father-in-law was Ukrainian, and had a family back home that he'd had to leave behind during the latter stages of the Second World War.

He was caught between the Russians, who wanted to annex Ukraine as part of the Soviet Union, and the Nazis, who were also not very nice people. He had to get out in a hurry, as did many Ukrainian men at that time, and became a refugee in Austria for a while before arriving in England via Plymouth and eventually Oldham.

He was a very proud man, who always considered himself to be a displaced Ukrainian rather than a resettled Englishman. He'd learnt to speak English and worked as a labourer, often helping build the electricity pylons you see all over the country. Andrij married Gerti, my mother-in-law, who was from the suburbs of Vienna in Austria, so my wife has mixed roots, like me.

While back in Ukraine, Andrij had fathered a daughter, who he'd never seen, as he'd had to flee his homeland while his first wife was pregnant. For many years he couldn't make contact with his first family, because the iron curtain had closed up communications between the countries. Even if he'd been able to make contact he knew that there could be serious repercussions to his family if the authorities knew he was alive in England.

When the cold war ended and Ukraine became an independent country again he found out about his daughter, but decided to keep it a secret because he felt ashamed. He told Irene about his "secret family" years after Gerti died, as he lay in hospital fearing for his own future. He had managed a trip back to Ukraine with his brother who lived near Kidderminster, and who he'd been apart from for 40 years, until the network of British based Ukrainians had brought them back together.

He'd showed us pictures of his family back home, but not truthfully explained who they all were. Soon after he passed away in 2003 we wrote a letter to the family and asked if we could visit them, which we did that summer. They lived in a small village called Kupche, which was about an hour's drive from the city of Lviv, which wasn't too far from the Polish border in western Ukraine.

It felt like we were going back in time when we arrived at Lviv airport, which was simply one austere building with no luggage carousel or any type of mechanical equipment. My suitcase didn't arrive, so I spent the week wearing the same T-shirt and Shorts, until a cow that the family had at their home in the village did it's business all over my shorts. I then had to borrow some clothes from my eldest son Steven, which didn't fit my portly belly!

Irene's new half-sister Sophia, and her mother, had spent several years in Siberia, as punishment for Andrij's escape and life had generally been tough for her.

Their home in Kupche had no running water or flushing toilet and no shower. While we were there I had worked out that there was a football match I could go and see. Karpaty Lviv were to play Stal' Alchevsk from Donestsk. I travelled there in a "clapped out" Lada with one of Sophia's sons and his mate, who had the car.

There were no seat belts and plenty of pot holes to endure during the hour-long journey. We couldn't speak to each other, except through hand gestures, so I sat in the back listening to their cassette tape of Ukrainian comedy, which, just like David Seaman's attempt to keep out Nayim's shot in the 1995 European Cup Winners Cup final, went over my head.

I splashed out on VIP seats for the three of us, which cost £1.50 in total. The game was played in torrential rain, in a huge open air bowl, so paying that bit extra for the VIP seats was well worth it! The match finished 1-1.

Sophia had a daughter too, Maria, our niece, and we'd invited her over for a visit in the summer of 2006, so she came with us to Chelsea to see Daniel walk out alongside Richard Dunne, Georgios Sameras, Nicky Weaver, Ben Thatcher and the rest; a proud moment indeed. City lost 3-0.

The 2009 visit to Stamford Bridge was much less dramatic, but another City defeat. Michael Essien scored the only goal during the first half.

After the game, as we waited for the tube at Fulham Broadway, Chris received a text from Joe Royle, confirming he'd taken the managers job at Oldham Athletic. His exact quote being, "I've returned to the madhouse", which I suppose is how most managers feel about their roles in football.

It was a tiring, but very enjoyable weekend for me, the trip to Sunderland on the Saturday afternoon and then a 1.30pm kick-off the following day at Chelsea, with a night at home squeezed in between. Most people seem to assume I'd have stopped in a hotel somewhere between the two, but I'd rather be in my own bed.

Thursday 19th March – Match 91
AaB v Manchester City – UEFA Cup

Going back to Denmark for a third time made me feel like Bill Murray in Groundhog Day; you know, the film where the same day goes around and around, until Bill gets his love life in order, though I already loved Denmark from my previous trips.

It's a fascinating country and each of the three places I visited were different. Herning was a sleepy, little, and yet special, landlocked and student-dominated town, in the middle of the countryside, while Copenhagen was colder (literally and metaphorically), cosmopolitan and had a bit of everything. Aalborg was different again, with my first impressions being of a cultured and very centralised town.

My journey there had been the most long-winded so far, but the flight-for-a-fiver from Stansted to the Danish coastal town of Aarhus had to be good value, if a little inconvenient. I set off from home just before 1am on the Tuesday morning for the middle-of-the-night drive down to London's third airport and was already red-eyed and nauseous by the time I boarded the 7.10 flight. There were a couple of other City fans on board, who'd booked before they knew if the game was on Wednesday or Thursday - like me.

Once in Denmark, there was a 40 minute bus journey into the charming town of Aarhus before an hour and a half's train journey north, to the opposite coast and Aalborg.

One of the City fans on my flight, Greg, joined me for the journey and he was great company as we chatted about City and the UEFA Cup so far - he'd only missed the trip to Cyprus, because he'd had a heart attack; I guess that's what watching City can do to you!

Once I got to my hotel, I collapsed into my bed for a couple of hours of much needed shut-eye before showering the fatigue away and preparing for a meal at one of Denmark's finest restaurants, the Mortens Kro.

Two of the staff from 'Visit Aalborg' had invited me for the meal and it didn't disappoint. We enjoyed a five course meal, complimented by fine wines, champagne and excellent company, and after monkfish, yoghurt soufflé of shrimps, roasted breast of Bonholm cockerel, veal tenderloin and a selection of desserts, I could hardly move. It certainly beat my usual diet of cheap fast food on these European trips.

My hosts, Maiken and Ulla were utterly charming as you'd expect PR people to be. I suppose they could have cynically bombarded me with brochures and promotional chat, but they seemed genuine and were lovely company; oh and good looking too!

Wherever I'd travelled I'd met people who were prepared to "go the extra mile" – not something I always found in England. It seemed to me that the locals were all rightly proud of their area and wanted to show it off.

I had noticed one uniquely Danish trait, which I'd asked my hosts about, a pattern of speech I'd observed on my three trips there and also to the Faroes (who, of course, have strong links to Denmark).

Almost everyone, from time to time, ends a sentence with an intake of breath that also makes a noise - you'd know what I mean if you'd heard it.

Apparently, they don't know they do it, even when I pointed it out to Maiken and Ulla. Perhaps it's the equivalent of Mancs saying Manchest-oh - and just as charmingly different.

I was discovering that Aalborg was rich in culture. During my second day there I tried to drink in the local ambience, which I knew to most City fans would mean the local beer. I walked along Jomfru Anes, the street which had the pubs and bars along it, but only to navigate my way to the Utzon Center, down by the side of the Limfjorden, the huge waterway that runs through the centre of town.

The Utzon Center looked a bit like the Lowry at Salford Quays but it was billed to be "much more than a museum". It was "a cultural centre, inspired by the interrelations between architecture, design, engineering, art and culture."

What a pretentious load of poppycock; I'd describe it in one word - weird. I couldn't make head nor tail of it. I walked into one room which exhibited the designs for the Finnish Embassy in New Delhi, complete with models and pictures of the finished building.

In the next room was a video, being shown on three screens, in Finnish, but with English subtitles, of a woman in a house who thought her car and a paddle steamer were in there with her. What?

I swiftly moved into the next room to watch another woman talking about her dog dying of leg cancer! I'd had enough and decided to move on to somewhere else - maybe I'm not intelligent enough to understand stuff like that. I think Coronation Street is more my level.

My next destination was a short bus ride away. The Lindholm Høje was the site of a museum and monuments from the Iron Age and Viking periods. This was more conventional and well set out, with artefacts displayed next to re-creations of how the area might have looked a thousand years ago.

That said, even here, there was a touch of the surreal, as I sat with a Danish man and his son in a replica longboat, watching a 3D film, while wearing a Viking helmet which had in-build multi-coloured glasses. Disneyland it wasn't.

The highlight of the day, apart from City arriving for their training session, was a return to the restaurant I'd feasted in the previous evening to meet the chef himself, Morten Nielsen. He told me that he'd "started a fight against the Gordon Ramsay style. A lot of younger people see him on TV here and they are trying to behave like him."

"Chefs are role models today," he went on, "I've had my own TV show, once a week for seven years, and I believe quality is more important than image."

Now there's a philosophical statement I agree with. I enjoyed my chat with Morten, he was charismatic and intelligent.

City arrived at the Energi Nord Arena in early evening, without the injured Craig Bellamy, though Vincent Kompany had travelled, despite a recent toe injury. I suspected he'd be a substitute, only coming on if things started going wrong for City.

After the press conference, at which I also quizzed AaB's Swedish coach Magnus Pehrsson, I was interviewed by a woman from Danish TV, who wanted to know how such a big influx of money had changed City. Now there's a question!

I ran along the Fjord on match day. It was a beautiful sunny morning and refreshing, if a little nippy. I chatted to a couple of City fans, many arrived mid-morning on the day trip, before meeting up with my mate and fellow journalist, Chris Bailey, for a walk up to the Maritime Museum, which wasn't too far from the stadium.

Naturally it wasn't busy, this being the quiet time of year for tourists, so we were able to explore the indoor and outdoor exhibits without hassle, after first enjoying the cheapest thing I'd found in Denmark; a cup of tea for a pound.

The fall of Sterling on the world currency market had produced a less than favourable exchange rate, though even the Danes admit they prefer to take a ferry to Sweden for their shopping, since it's much cheaper there. Seemingly their money, money, money goes that bit further in the land of Abba.

Having explored the inside of a Danish submarine, which even Shaun Wright-Phillips would have struggled to fit into, we climbed aboard a small battleship and looked at a wonderful array of model warships. I had a go at the sailing simulator and crashed into the dock, which surprised me, because I've never done that on the boating lake at Heaton Park.

It was time to sample some opera! Aalborg was staging a week-long opera festival. There wasn't time to see a full production in a theatre so this would be a few selected highlights, at an open-air taster. It was staged in the courtyard of a circular block of flats. I parked my posterior on the concrete wall, overlooking the underground car park, which was more comfortable than it sounds.

The singer, Berit Meland, sang alone, as her partner in 'Duo Amore' was ill, so it was "Uno Amore" for one day only and she sang beautifully. It was easy to forget the unglamorous location as she warbled through songs by Johann Strauss, Bizet and Harald Arlen.

Then it was onto the match, a straightforward game, or so I'd expected. With ten minutes of normal time remaining the story took a twist. The hotel receptionist had suggested she'd love the game to be dramatic and not be settled until the last kick of the game. I'd said I would be happy with a boring City win. The receptionist got her wish.

I thought that the most dramatic moment of match day had been when the diva performed her opera songs which had included her version of 'Over the Rainbow'. I didn't realise at the time that those lyrics would be so appropriate.

"Somewhere over the rainbow - skies are blue and the dreams that you dare to dream really do come true."

Those words might have described the feelings of the City fans after they came through what should have been an unnecessary penalty shootout. Two late Aalborg goals in normal time had extended the game, eventually, to the sudden death spot-kicks, just like the game in Herning.

How fitting that the decisive moment should be a missed penalty by Luton Shelton, who'd broken City hearts a year earlier in the balloon strewn penalty area at Sheffield United, when City had been ingloriously knocked out of the FA Cup.

When you come so close to going out, just like City's first trip to Denmark, maybe, I thought, it was only right to dream of travelling to Istanbul in May, for the final of the UEFA Cup; ever the optimist, like all City fans.

Saturday 21st March – Match 92
Bury v Chester City – League Two

After all the travelling to and from Denmark I was happy to be covering a game close to home, though I would have preferred to have been at Boundary Park for Oldham against Tranmere. As I listened to the build-up to the game, which sounded terrific on the radio, I couldn't help feeling that I was missing out.

Joe Royle's return to the Latics was always going to be special and I could hear the excitement, even though I was sitting in my seat at Bury. Jimmy Wagg was presenting the show from Boundary Park and our Latics reporter John Gilder was out and about interviewing the supporters, something I always enjoy doing. I could hardly complain though, and I still felt lucky to be at my game, Bury against Chester.

This was a huge game for both clubs with Bury pushing for an automatic promotion place and Chester battling for their lives in the football league. One of the interested spectators, sat just a couple of rows in front of me, was the former Bury boss Chris Casper. He'd brought his son. I could be fairly confident it was his son because he looked liked a mini version of dad, who in turn looks the image of his famous father Frank.

Chris is a studious type, and I watched him carefully pull out his glasses and very precisely place them on his nose before pulling a piece of paper out of his pocket as the game began, making notes thereafter. I'd seen him at an Oldham game, earlier in the season, and he'd told me he was doing a bit of scouting, as well as being Youth team coach at Bradford City.

Bury started the game well, with six chances within the first five minutes, but there was no early goal. They took the lead on the stroke of half-time with a scrambled tap-in from Andy Morrell. Early in the second half the Shakers had Ryan Cresswell sent off and from that point on decided to try to protect their one goal advantage.

Heartbreakingly, Chester scored a last minute equalizer and Bury had to settle for a point. I hadn't intended it to be, but my post-match interview with the Bury manager Alan Knill ended up sounding like a disagreement. I'd asked him if his team had sat back too much once they were down to ten men – a reasonable question I'd thought, and not necessarily my opinion.

I do have opinions of course, but I'd asked the question because I guessed that's what some Bury fans would be thinking. Alan wondered what I'd do in his situation and asked me if I'd seen other managers go for it, in that situation. My opinion was irrelevant so I just sat back and let him talk. I knew my question was fair.

It had been a good game, and since Oldham had lost to Tranmere, despite the Royle return, perhaps I'd been at the right match after all.

Sunday 22nd March – Match 93
Manchester City v Sunderland – Premier League

The easy excuse for this plodding performance was that the team was tired by the midweek trip, complete with the extra time and penalties in Denmark. I've never been a professional footballer, so maybe there is some validity in that argument, but I don't really buy it.

I'd overheard a conversation between two Premier League players (not City players in this example) during which one had asked the other about the last time they'd been to Dubai or Spain. "I nipped over for a couple of days last week, when we had Monday and Tuesday off", came the reply. We're supposed to believe that a midweek trip to Denmark, a ninety minute flight away, makes players incapable of being at their best three days later.

I blame managers like Alex Ferguson and Sam Allardyce for creating this "mental excuse" by repeatedly changing teams around "to save their players from having to play twice in a week". The more they, and others, say that, the more the players and the public accept it as fact. Surely it's a state of mind?

The Germans seem to cope better and rarely, if ever, field so-called weakened teams in their domestic cup competitions.

City beat a poor Sunderland team 1-0 thanks to a goal from Micah Richards. If there was ever an example of winning ugly, this was it; but then again if a club is to become successful they have to learn to win ugly, at least that's what the experts say!

Tuesday 24th March – Match 94
Rotherham United v Bury – League Two

Although I'd regarded my trip to Colchester as completing a full compliment of 92 league grounds, technically I hadn't seen Rotherham United at the Don Valley Stadium, although I had seen sport at that venue on many occasions. It was nice to have the opportunity to see a game there nevertheless.

The Don Valley Stadium is designed to be a venue for athletics, built for the World Student Games of 1991, so is not ideally suited for football. I knew that, from my many trips there to watch Sheffield Eagles Rugby League Club in the early 1990's, when freelancing for Clubcall.

The press positions, I won't call it a press box, were right at the back of the main stand, and to see clearly you really need a pair of binoculars; it has to be the worst view in football, apart from the away fans behind the goal at Brighton's Withdean Stadium! The half-time tea was the worst I have ever tasted.

Rotherham were a better team than their league position suggested because they'd had to battle back from a points deduction for going into administration, so this was a difficult game for the Shakers, who earned a very creditable 1-1 draw, thanks to a late equaliser from their skipper Efe Sodje.

The Bury manager Alan Knill, who I'd verbally fenced with after their game against Chester, just days earlier, started our post-match interview by asking me if I'd noticed that Alex Ferguson had gone defensive with his Man United team in their recent game at Fulham when Vidic had been sent off. He wanted to prove to me that he'd been right to be defensive against Chester.

I was flattered that my question, after that game, had made him think about the subject so much!

Wednesday 25th March – Match 95
Chesterfield v Rochdale – League Two

I wasn't unfamiliar with Saltergate after my trips there, earlier in the season, with Droylsden and Macclesfield, but I'm told constantly that you learn something new every day and on this visit, to the town with the crooked spire, I learned that there was free parking around the back of the town hall, which was very useful, because I had no change for the parking meter.

I found myself saying hello to regulars at Chesterfield as if I was a regular there myself. The game was a cracker and the best quality game in League Two I'd seen all season. Rochdale played very well, despite losing 3-0. They were simply outplayed by a team who did everything right on the night. I can't say I enjoyed watching Dale lose, but I can't deny my pleasure at watching such a good game.

Jack Lester had been the star man, scoring twice but terrorising the Dale defence with almost his every touch, Gregor Robertson got the other.

After the game I spent some time talking to Rochdale's assistant manager Dave Flitcroft, who is everything I admire in a human being. He's passionate about football, of course, but he oozes integrity and you can tell when you talk to him that he's a deep thinker and cares very much about his family.

His brother Garry had just taken the manager's job at Leigh Genesis and Dave told me about the ups and downs he'd had with Garry down the years. I'd admired Garry as a player at City, and thought he had the potential to be one of the best in the game but felt he never really fulfilled that potential after his deadline day move to Blackburn Rovers. From what Dave told me, Garry had found ordinary life difficult to readjust to after being a Premiership player, a situation that many top players have very hard to cope with. Sometimes money isn't everything.

Dave's experience in the lower divisions, and his obvious love for his brother, prompted him to act as Garry's advisor as he moved into non-league football, and his unconditional support of his brother was a joy to listen too.

Eventually, as reluctant as I was to leave my second home, Saltergate, I headed back to the car, and then home, ready for the next game.

April

Saturday 4th April – Match 96
Arsenal v Manchester City – Premier League

I felt a little self-conscious driving down to Arsenal for this game, because it was the debut of the "crew van" which had been delivered to BBC Radio Manchester. Unlike the pool cars I had driven previously, this was a white van. I'd driven vehicles like that before, in fact I spent my last few months at the Co-op Bank travelling around the north west in a similar van, but I felt more conspicuous heading down the M1 with Fred sat alongside.

It was an early departure, as usual, and we parked up at Cockfosters tube station, before completing the journey to the Emirates Stadium by train. It's such a pleasure to visit Arsenal that I often forget how many fruitless trips there have been down the years. Most of the games I've seen there, including many at Highbury, have been home victories. The football, especially in recent years, has always been good, and I enjoy good football by any team.

Arsene Wenger has always been courteous. I always think the way someone treats a stranger is a good indication of their character. I'll never forget meeting Alex Ferguson for the first time. My first interview with him was while at hospital radio. I'd requested the meeting shortly after he'd joined from Aberdeen and he was happy to invite me to "The Cliff" where they were training at that time.

He was very kind to me and that first interview, in his office, was about ten minutes long. I asked him if he was a bit "media shy" as he'd arrived from Aberdeen with a bit of a reputation for not being very open with the press. He disagreed and was happy to talk about his personality and his hopes for the future.

I did a few interviews, like that, down at the Cliff, and always enjoyed meeting him. My first interview with the United boss for BBC GMR, as it was then, was completely different. "Who the **** are you? No stupid questions!", was his opening gambit. I was taken aback, but fully aware that I was now a professional. He must have been trying to intimidate me. I didn't expect him to remember me from my days at hospital radio, but I hadn't expected such a crude introduction to my new job.

I've never interviewed him regularly, because I'm the City man, but back then I wasn't associated with any club, on air, so I would be sent to do interviews wherever there was a gap to be filled. I never allowed Fergie to intimidate me, but I respected him less for his actions. I'd like to think I would never introduce myself to anyone in such a bullish way.

Maybe that difference in personalities is one of the reasons Ferguson and Wenger have never been good friends?

The friendliness of Arsene Wenger, who always got on well with Sven Goran Eriksson, another true gentleman of football, stopped when the game started.

Wenger didn't need to be angry or lack courtesy on this day though, and as we waited to speak to Mark Hughes after the 2-0 defeat, he said hello and smiled politely as he returned to his office after speaking to the national media.

Hughes had taken a long time to emerge from the visitors' dressing room, apparently sipping tea as we waited patiently to speak to him. More than an hour after the final whistle he came to give us his views on the game.

City had started strongly, but conceded from a freekick, awarded after a foul by Robinho on Sagna. Fabregas floated in the freekick for Adebayor to head home, unchallenged. Early in the second half Adebayor added a second and City were chasing shadows. There seemed to be no plan "B" for the Blues and Arsenal cruised through to the final whistle, without breaking sweat.

Sunday 5th April – Match 97
Everton v Wigan Athletic – Premier League

Everton's press box is one of the worst in the Premier League, with leg space very much at a premium, so it's always been an uncomfortable experience, shoe-horning yourself into your seat. This wasn't a commentary game, but I still had Paul Rowley sitting alongside me. He'd travelled up from his base at Westminster to watch his beloved Latics and it's always a pleasure to sit with him, even though his contribution on air was not needed.

It costs £10 to park a car close to the stadium, so I decided to head for Anfield, just across Stanley Park, which meant a long trudge back to Goodison Park with my equipment. Just like many Premier League Clubs, there's no parking allocated to visiting press, their valuable spaces being given to corporate fans instead.

As I approached the stadium, I could see them, collar open, shirt hanging loose, strolling, carefree to their entrance, as I struggled to the press door. I'm not complaining, I'm observing!

My first trip to Goodison Park was back in October 1977, a 1-1 draw against City. I'd travelled there by train, arriving at Lime Street station with no idea how to get to the stadium. There weren't many City fans around, so I asked directions and followed the growing numbers of Everton supporters as I neared the ground.

After the match I tried to follow the crowds, but was determined not to speak more than necessary as I had been told that Liverpool was not one of the best places to reveal that you were from Manchester. I was a bit naïve and feeling a bit vulnerable as I headed back towards Lime Street Station.

A teenager, older than me, walked up alongside me and asked me what time it was. I didn't really want to answer but was scared by the threatening tone of his voice. I pressed the button of my state-of-the-art digital watch to read the time from the illuminated red numbers. The lad snatched the watch off my wrist, breaking the leather strap from its mountings with one swift tug.

I said nothing, and just carried on walking. He tried to intimidate me further by teasing me about stealing the watch from me. I refused to rise to the bait, fearing that I would get beaten up. He decided that there was no fun to be gained from my non-resistance, so he accelerated away with my watch as his trophy.

I'd been given the timepiece by my German Uncle Karl, and so it meant more to me than any watch I'd bought myself. I'm sure it was expensive too, as it was one of the first of the new digital watches.

After my assailant had walked off into the crowd with his booty in hand, another supporter asked me if I was okay and waved to a passing police car which quickly pulled over to find out what had happened. He drove me around the area for a few minutes and I spotted the lad, and his mate, walking along. Having identified the culprit I was taken to a local police station while the mugger was picked up by another vehicle and taken to the same police station.

I was asked if I wanted to press charges but I was so scared of the consequences that I refused; I just wanted to go home. In an interview room, somewhere else in the police station, the mugger was being told that I would press charges.

He didn't have the watch in his possession, but he must have been worried about facing legal action, so he told them his mate had it. Within half an hour I was reunited with my watch, minus the strap, and on my way home. I presume the thief was given a warning, which in those days might have been enough to stop him doing it again. These days I'm sure he would have laughed at the police as they told him I wasn't pressing charges.

I arrived home to find my dad a little anxious due to my late arrival. Now I look back on all that, I realise my dad must have been really worried. My mum had died just a few weeks earlier and his only son had been to Liverpool, to a football match, alone, and arrived home very late. If that had been me and it had been my 17-year-old son I would have been beside myself with worry. He just told me he was glad it had all ended well.

The Everton fans who sit near the press box at Goodison Park these days are a friendly lot and I brought out a Mars Bar from the press room for one of the youngsters at half-time. Don't tar everyone with the same brush is my motto; there are good and bad everywhere.

It was a good day for Everton with Jo, on loan from City, scoring two goals, making it five in seven appearances since his January loan move from Manchester to Merseyside. He played well too, with Leon Osman being Everton's man of the match. It was a rare off day for the Latics and by far the worst I'd seen them play all season. The Wigan boss Steve Bruce was gracious in defeat and accepted that 4-0 was a fair reflection of how things had gone.

Wednesday 8th April – travel to Hamburg

I was used to starting my trips to European games two or three days before the game, but once I'd assessed all the options the best plan for this trip was to go the day before.

I wasn't alone on this trip, for the first time, I had my commentary sidekick, Fred Eyre, with me. He'd contributed his comments on a couple of the previous games abroad, but by watching a TV monitor back in the studio; this time he would be beside me.

We flew into Germany via Hannover from Manchester, which I saw as a bit of luxury, having spent many of these European trips heading for far-flung airports at both ends of the journey.

Our trip from Hannover Airport to Hamburg was by express train and we arrived in the city in mid afternoon, immediately becoming better acquainted with the area by meeting up with Thorsten Tschirner, in the tourist office, who recommended a few places to visit. The harbour boat tour seemed a good idea and we decided we'd try to fit that in on match day.

I'd been led to believe that our hotel was close to the stadium and it was, but the wrong stadium! The Arena Hotel was next to the Pony and Trap Racing Arena, rather than the HSH Nordbank Arena. This meant more walking around, with all my equipment in tow, than planned. Fred was worn out by the time we checked in, and his dodgy knee was swelling up rapidly.

We'd called in at the Nordbank for the press conference, where Mark Hughes spoke of his growing excitement, as the competition was reaching its climax and Micah Richards told us that he thought that City could live up to their position as favourites now and go on to win the cup.

There was a noticeable growth in media interest too, now that the competition was down to the last eight, and for the first time, there was a UEFA representative conducting affairs and huge numbers in the audience. It felt a world away from my experiences in the Faroes back in July!

After the interviews, I rushed up to the press box, only to find a security guard telling me I couldn't be there. While I tried to persuade him that I had a right to send my interviews back, I slyly did it anyway, so all was well in the end.

As we came out of the stadium, there were supporters with HSV scarves heading past us, so I asked where they were going and was told there was a big handball game in the smaller indoor arena, next to the main stadium.

After escorting a now limping Fred back to the hotel, I left him watching Liverpool against Chelsea, in the comfort of the bar. I headed back to watch the latter stages of the handball. It wasn't easy to get into the game. I hadn't pre-booked, and there was only about fifteen minutes of the match to go. I raced around the various entrances trying to find someone who would let me in. I asked at the ticket window and they couldn't comprehend why I would want to see the last few minutes of a game that was due to end.

Through sheer persistence, I eventually found a glamorously dressed woman, who looked important, and asked for her help. She was stood outside the arena taking a cigarette break, the only time I've been glad that someone is a smoker! I felt fairly certain that she was the owner/chairman's wife because she wafted in with a real air of authority and showed me to a courtside seat behind one of the goals.

It was worth the effort, with the 12,000 fans packed into the very impressive, steep-sided arena creating an electrifying atmosphere. It was no wonder they beat TBV Lemgo 32-24 with backing like that. It was a sport I'd only seen on TV before, so I was impressed by the speed the ball was moved around by the athleticism of the players. I couldn't help thinking that if the Hamburg footballers got that sort of backing the following evening, it wouldn't be easy for City.

Back at the hotel, I chatted with Fred and Peter Clark, the interpreter who had overseen the Mark Hughes press conference earlier. It turned out that Peter was the personal English teacher to England coach Fabio Capello and had spent three mornings a week teaching him the finer points of conversing with us Brits.

We could all see what a great job he'd done with Capello, so he must have been good at his job. Even though I pushed him on it, he denied that he'd tried to teach Stuart Pearce the same skills, perhaps that task would have been too difficult even for him.

It felt like Christmas Eve as we talked past midnight in the hotel bar, I was as excited as I used to feel as a small boy. City were closing in on a major trophy and there was a growing feeling that this could be their year.

Thursday 9th April – Match 98
Hamburg SV v Manchester City – UEFA Cup

I skipped breakfast and while I contributed to our breakfast programme from the hotel, Fred had headed off to the city, to make better use of his time. I decided I'd have a quick look at the Pony and Trap Arena across the road and wandered through to the open gate, to take a look. It was huge and looked like a really big speedway track.

I took a bus to the City centre where I boarded an old London double-decker for the city tour, which lasted about an hour. I disembarked near the old docklands area where I'd planned to see the world's biggest model railway. You don't have to be a model railway enthusiast to appreciate the scenery, which takes in everything from the ski season in the Alps to the Las Vegas strip. There's a scene depicting an outdoor rock concert and a perfect replica of the centre of Hamburg complete with the Nordbank Arena – I was tempted to add a miniature copy of myself, but decided to leave it.

I'd had a model railway as a boy, probably because my dad had worked for British Rail, so I'd developed a fascination for trains. My dad was a "controller" based at Piccadilly Station, but never a "fat controller"!

After whizzing around the exhibition, I headed back to the dockside to meet up with Fred, who'd preferred the sunshine than the model railway, and we also met up with Bernie and Claudia, two of my German friends, who'd made the trip up from Gelsenkirchen to follow their second team. We discussed the game and all hoped for an away win, or at least a draw. Fred and I then quickly boarded our boat for the harbour cruise, too late to order coffees but with plenty of time to enjoy the warm sunshine, with temperatures in the 70's.

There weren't many City fans sightseeing so I needed to know what they were up to, just in case of trouble – it was part of my job to report on any problems, something, happily, I had not had to do on my trips. Most of the fans were enjoying the sunshine of Germany's second biggest city, up on the Reeperbahn, the street that represents the less salubrious side of life.

Everywhere I looked there were strip clubs, pubs and sex shops, and then, very much out of place, a tribute to the Beatles, who first burst onto the pop scene in Hamburg back in the 1960's.

The City fans were oblivious to anything but the sunshine and beer, but they seemed good natured and in fine voice when I walked among them. Back in 2006 I'd visited Hamburg during the World Cup, and visited the fan park, before watching a game at the AOL Arena, as it was known then.

The fan park was very impressive with stalls representing all the nations involved in the competition and even a fan beach on tons of imported sand. For this trip, the same area was a huge open air funfair and it seemed strangely appropriate that I was suddenly wandering among rollercoasters as we got closer and closer to kickoff time. Life with the Blues certainly has plenty of ups and downs.

The day was passing by very quickly and match time was soon upon us, and I could feel the nerves in by stomach. Fred and I agreed that this was going to be City's toughest test yet. The highlight for Fred, before the game, was sitting on Uwe Seeler's big toe. It wasn't a case of Mr Eyre putting his foot in it, the toe in question was part of a huge, slightly bizarre sculpture of the foot of Seeler, a former hero for Hamburg and the German National Team.

As we enjoyed several pre-match frankfurters in the press room high up in the stadium, surely hamburgers would have been more appropriate, we watched the fans arriving and there was an atmosphere building that reminded us of being at the old Wembley. The Nordbank Arena was certainly impressive and by kick-off time, that atmosphere had built to a crescendo.

We couldn't have asked for a better start, Stephen Ireland starting and finishing a lovely move, that also involved Robinho, and which had City ahead within seconds, but from that point onwards, the blue rollercoaster was heading down hill. City lost 3-1, meaning that it would take something really special to turn it around back in Manchester.

After the game, Ireland accused some of his team-mates of lacking his passion and commitment. I've learnt to expect the unexpected during the 40 years I've been watching City, and as Charlie always says to me, "Always say you don't know". I feared City's European adventure was fatally wounded, but hoped I was wrong.

Saturday 11th April – Match 99
Wigan Athletic v Arsenal – Premier League

Who would want to be a referee? This was a match that illustrated how difficult it is to be a match official. I wouldn't say the whole game hung on one decision, but that's the way some people in the stadium saw it.

Wigan had taken the lead through a goal from Mido, which was a just reward for their domination of the first period. Just before half-time Antonio Valencia made a break down the middle and was brought down by Kieran Gibbs, just outside the Arsenal penalty area as he was preparing to shoot. In my opinion, a free-kick was rightly awarded, with Gibbs being shown a yellow card.

There was an argument to say that Gibbs should have been sent off, but by the letter of the law, with Mikael Silvestre running alongside the incident, the referee, Alan Wiley, showed a yellow. As I described the incident, during off-air commentary, I mentioned the presence of Silvestre and had said I expected a yellow card for the player.

I can't deny that morally, if that's the right expression in football, Gibbs should have been sent off. He knew what he was doing and was prepared to stop Valencia by foul means before he reached the penalty area, but the fact remains that another player was alongside.

I later watched the incident on Match of the Day, having not had the luxury of a replay while at the game. A second viewing suggested that Silvestre was a stride behind Gibbs as his "tackle" went in on Valencia. Was he within playing distance?

As I sit here, with the advantage of time and replays to consider my view, I'm still not certain about whether the player should have been sent off, which can only mean that the decision was correct by the referee, who surely shouldn't send a player off unless he's certain.

Ben Watson hit the post from the resultant free-kick and Arsenal scored four times in the second half to win the game comfortably. Would the dismissal of Gibbs have made any difference to the outcome? I'd seen many games where the manager had claimed that NOT beating a team of 10 men was because it was harder, but I'd also heard others claim it was harder winning WITH ten men.

What that incident showed was how thankless the task of being a referee is. I've been invited to speak to groups of referees and I've always told them how much I admire them. I believe they're honest and care passionately about doing their job as fairly and as professionally as possible.

I understand the anger of the supporters too, and you'd never convince the Latics fans that the right decision was made about Kieran Gibbs. I seemed a lone voice in the press room that day, when I expressed my view that the referee had no other option than to show the yellow card. In the same way that the referee had made his decision in a dispassionate way, my view was not based on any agenda, it was simply the way I saw it at the time.

Sunday 12th April – Match 100
Manchester City v Fulham – Premier League

What a dismal, terrible performance this was by Manchester City. In some ways though, it didn't surprise me, it had been coming. Some of the recent home performances had been just as bad as this one, but the opposition had been even worse. Mark Hughes had been telling us all season that his team would get stronger as the season went along, because of the work he and his coaching staff had done to get the players fitter than their opponents.

There was no evidence of this against Fulham. City lacked imagination, determination and any sort of leadership on or off the pitch.

Partly through injury, the side was completely different from the one that had lost in Hamburg, with Petrov, Etuhu, Garrido, De Jong and Bojinov brought in. The excuse that his team was tired, seemed a bit misjudged since half the team had not played in the previous game.

City had lots of early possession but rarely left their own half and had no idea how to break down Fulham who were well organised and well disciplined. City had taken the lead thanks to a wonderful solo goal by Stephen Ireland.

Fulham got into gear in the second half, with three goals that could all be blamed on individuals but were just as much about collective failure. I'd been puzzled by the absence of Robinho from the starting line-up, especially with a few players not available for selection, but the City boss had been determined to leave him out at some stage, but why was a fully fit and fresh Elano watching from the sidelines?

Almost a year earlier, to the day, Thaksin Shinawatra had brought over some Thai politicians as his guests for the game against Fulham and City had lost 3-2. This was the game when Shinawatra had also wanted City fans to stay behind after the match while he drew out a lottery ticket for someone, in the ground, to win a car. Very few people stayed as City did a very laboured and delayed lap of honour.

It was the final, embarrassing, straw for Shinawatra who met with Sven Goran Eriksson the following day and confirmed his departure from the club in the summer. It made me wonder what sort of pressure the defeat of 2009 must be building on Mark Hughes. I couldn't help thinking that this defeat would mean City would not now qualify for the Europa League the following season. I went home with a heavy heart.

Monday 13th April – Match 101
Darlington v Bury – League Two

Have you ever wondered what "sat nav" is all about? I drive up and down the country watching football matches, going to grounds I've never been to before, without the aid of sat nav. As I pass other motorists I often see a satellite navigation tool suckered to the window and wonder why it's not driving them mad.

"Drive straight ahead for fifty miles", I assume it is saying as they head down the M1 to London, constantly reassuring the driver every time they pass a junction. I have a map reader with me on the long journeys, he's called Charlie, but even without him, and he wasn't with me for the trip to Darlington, I know where to head and, here's an old fashioned concept, I follow the signs.

I arrived nice and early at the Darlington Arena, even though I knew our sports programme didn't start until 2pm. I'd made a schoolboy error though. Having left home in lovely warm sunshine, and after wishing I hadn't got a coat with me in Hamburg, I left my outer wrapping at home.

You would have thought that the experience of Middlesbrough, the season before, would have taught me a lesson. Let me explain. For City's last game of the 2007-2008 season, in May, our jolly little group of travellers had set out for the game wearing summer clothing and sunglasses and by the time we approached Teeside we were hot and steamy, due to our footballing debates and the weather.

Five miles away from the Riverside Stadium the temperature suddenly dropped by ten degrees and it felt like the middle of winter. It was as if we'd been transported to that island in the TV series "Lost". Fortunately I had my coat with me, because watching the 8-1 defeat certainly didn't warm me up.

Having had that experience, you'd have assumed I would be aware of the potential for dramatic temperature drops in the north east, maybe that's what sat nav is for, maybe that bland voice is telling the occupants on the A1, "prepare for a huge temperature drop, as we are now entering Teeside".

All seemed well when I picked up my gear and walked to the press entrance but once sat in my seat, in the shadow, it was freezing. By the time I was interviewing Bury manager Alan Knill after their 2-2 draw I was shivering and desperate to go inside, which is very unlike me because I don't usually mind cool conditions. I'd commentated on City's game in Copenhagen when the temperature was below freezing.

The match had been a thriller, so in that respect I couldn't complain. Bury had taken the lead with a deflected shot from Glynn Hurst, but Darlo, as their fans call them, were level from a corner by half-time. The Shakers, who needed a win to maintain their push for automatic promotion, were back in front when Efe Sodje headed home, but Darlington again equalised.

Only two sides of their new stadium were opened, I had to buy my programme, which covered three games and there was no half-time or pre-match tea or coffee because the club was in administration. I also found out that the Darlington players were not being fully paid, which made their stirring performance all the more admirable.

At least the carvery had been open as usual, though the price had gone up considerably. It was as tasty as ever, and just like my last visit there I sat with Eric, the press steward and we chatted about football. He told me that two of Darlington's better players would be missing because a complaint had been made by one of their opponents that clubs in administration should not field loan players.

Maybe that was why Darlington were so motivated, despite all their problems. I do find it bizarre that a month's wages from some Premier League players could solve all the financial issues of clubs like Darlington.

During the return journey, I listened to the radio and heard that Luton Town had been relegated from the football league. There was no great surprise in this because they'd had 30pts deducted before the season had started, for various financial issues, so their demise had been inevitable.

There would have been a time when I would have been jumping for joy at the prospect of Luton going out of the league but I felt no happiness. The reason for my previous dislike of Luton does not come from "The David Pleat Dance" and Luton's survival at City's expense back in 1983, as you might have thought.

It dates back to 27th September 1986 and a 1-0 defeat for City at Kenilworth; it was also David White's debut. Just over a year earlier, the country had seen Luton's FA Cup tie against Millwall ruined by a riot, with hundreds of seats being ripped up in the Bobber's Stand, these days known as the "conservatory salesroom stand".

The previous month England fans had rioted in Dublin at a friendly against the Republic of Ireland and the 1985 European Cup Final had been the venue for more troubles with deaths resulting from violence between Liverpool and Juventus fans.

The Prime Minister, Margaret Thatcher, wanted to push through a system that would mean all football fans carrying ID cards, not an idea that I ever felt would solve the problem, but I knew would make my life, and the lives of other decent football supporters, much more difficult.

The Luton Town Chairman, David Evans, a Thatcherite and prospective Tory MP, decided his club would take things a step further by banning away fans. I'd had mixed feelings about Luton up to that point. I wasn't a big fan of their plastic pitch, but always had a soft spot for them because the comedian Eric Morecambe was a fan. Trying to stop me watching City there was the final straw.

Evans' creeping to his boss clearly worked, because a year later he became the Conservative MP for Welwyn Hatfield, but I, and other good people like me, had the problem of trying to get into Kenilworth Road when City played there.

The only way to get in would be to have a Luton membership card and to achieve this I would need to prove I was a Luton supporter, even though I lived in Oldham. I visited a football programme dealer in Accrington and bought a dozen old Luton programmes against various opponents, making sure none of them were against City or other north west teams.

I split the programmes with Charlie, and we each sent a few covers with an accompanying letter to Luton's membership office, explaining that we were exiled Luton fans who visited Kenilworth Road when we could. The programme covers were the proof. A few days later we both received our membership cards, and the problem seemed to be solved.

As Luton played their early season home games, rumours began to circulate that other away supporters had done something similar to us, so the Luton computer had been programmed to reject membership cards from fans with non-local postcodes. I was worried that when City visited my card would be rejected, which would then be followed by questions from the stewards and turnstile operators.

I couldn't take this risk, I hadn't missed a City game, home or away, for nearly ten years, and was determined to get in. My next plan was to use my newly acquired list of fellow "92 Club" members to ask for help from a genuine Luton fan. There were two or three Luton fans on the list so I rang one and he was very sympathetic to my situation and hated the membership card scheme as much as me.

He offered to lend me a card that wouldn't be used that day because his friend would be on holiday. We agreed to meet outside the ground on the day of the game. I was still worried that this plan might fail. What if he didn't turn up, or if the police noticed him passing the card to me; I was getting paranoid.

I asked the Chairman at Radio Cavell, the hospital radio station at which I was involved, for permission to use their headed paper to ask for a press pass, something I'd never done before, and he gave me his blessing. Luton promised there'd be a pass waiting for me, so surely now I'd get into the ground by one of the three alternatives?

I drove to Luton with Charlie and another dedicated City fan, Steve Boyd, who I knew well from the football specials, where he was a fellow travel steward. We all knew that this trip was going to be very different from the usual trips by train, and there was a nervous tension as we headed south. Such was our anxiety that we passed the normal Luton exit on the M1, and decided to come in from the southern side of the town.

We parked in the town centre, well away from the stadium, and decided to split up, so we'd look less suspicious. I met the Luton 92 club member, as planned, and he gave me his mate's membership card, which I agreed to send back to him through the post the following week; we were kindred spirits, real supporters who cared more about fellow decent fans than rivalry.

I faced a dilemma, which of my three alternatives should I use to try to gain entry. I saw other faces around that I recognised and watched from across the road to see if any of them got in. I saw one coming back out, having had his card rejected, so I decided I'd try the press pass first. On arrival at the press door I showed a copy of my letter of application and was immediately, without question, handed my ticket.

I was ecstatic, I was in! There were no mobile phones in those days, so I had no way of knowing if Charlie and Steve had got in successfully, so there was still a feeling of unease as I headed for the press room. I noticed a pay-phone on the wall, in a corridor, and it immediately occurred to me that I could ring my friends at Radio Cavell, who were on-air, preparing to do commentary on

Oldham Athletic v Brighton and Hove Albion, at Boundary Park.

I felt guilty that I had a press ticket without any intention of doing something that justified my presence, so I wondered if they wanted me to do a pre-match, half-time and full-time report for our listeners in Oldham. They thought it was a great idea, so I made sure I had three 2p pieces ready, and rang in. Those were the first football reports I'd ever done.

My seat in the press box was next to David Oates, whose move from GMR to Radio Five, years later, would provide the chance for me to join the BBC. After the game, I met up with Charlie and Steve at the car. I caught up with Charlie, as he was walking back, Steve was already stood by the car.

Charlie told me that his card had been rejected at the turnstile because of his Sale postcode but he'd been allowed in anyway because his explanation had been plausible and measured; I suspect the fact that he was a well dressed man in his early forties also helped.

Steve seemed a bit agitated and I immediately suspected he hadn't got into the game. We quizzed him, and although he knew all the details, who'd scored etc, his story somehow felt wrong. A few weeks later, as we travelled together on the football special to Southampton, Steve admitted he hadn't got in at Luton. His card had been rejected, like Charlie's, but he'd argued angrily with the stewards and they'd sent him away.

I felt sorry for Steve, he would have never harmed anyone. He was just an ordinary fan who had been prevented from watching his team by the actions of the hooligans and the overreaction of the politicians and in particular David Evans and Luton Town. It took me a long time for me to forgive them.

Ironically that day proved to be the start of my football reporting career. Every time I went to an away game I'd be looking for phone-boxes close to the stadium and regularly reporting back for Radio Cavell; I'd got the bug.

For the next few years I'd run out of the ground, as soon as the final whistle went, to the nearest pay-phone to do a quick report before heading back to the train station. Usually, I'd watch the game from the City end, but I found that there were occasions when the police wouldn't let me out, at the end of the game, preferring to keep the City fans together so they could escort us back to the station. I started asking for the occasional press pass to circumnavigate the problem.

My overenthusiasm at Oxford, in 1989, almost meant I missed the train. I ran out, as usual, as soon as the game ended (a 4-2 win with Nigel Gleghorn one of the City scorers!) to look for a phone box. I couldn't find one anywhere, and as I headed up and down the streets near the Manor Ground, I was getting more and more desperate and aware that the clock was ticking.

I knew that the train station at Oxford was too far away to reach by foot, so I had to be on the special buses that had been organised for us. This meant I had less time than normal, because I could usually catch the police escort and pass it, by running faster than they were walking.

With no phone box in sight I ran up the footpath to a house that had lights on, which I assumed meant someone was in. I knocked and waited for an answer. A stern looking man answered the door, presumably assuming I was a thug, but as soon as I explained my predicament he offered me the use of his house phone and I did my report on Radio Cavell. I thanked him, offered him 10p for the call, which he wouldn't accept, and shot back out of his front door and ran, like the wind, to the line of buses which were just setting off.

I reached the last bus with seconds to spare, dripping in sweat, but happy that I'd achieved my goal. I could have taken the easier, and perhaps more sensible option, that day and not done the report. My colleagues at Radio Cavell would have understood, but that's not my way.

Thursday 16th April – Match 102
Manchester City v Hamburg – UEFA Cup

City had played a masterstroke ahead of this game by dropping the price of all tickets to all fans to just £5, guaranteeing a full house of passionate, flag-waving supporters; and so it proved to be.

The atmosphere was crackling as the game kicked off and there was a real belief that City could overturn the first leg deficit, but then an early goal by Hamburg seemed to kill off the dream as Guerrero scored after just twelve minutes.

To their credit, the City fans and the players responded impressively and the team grew stronger and stronger. Elano's successful penalty came at exactly the right time, just five minutes later and everyone believed the team could score at least two more goals to take the game into extra time.

Early in the second half Filipe Caicedo gave City the lead and Hamburg were hanging on, looking like rabbits caught in the headlights of a car, but despite trying everything, the third goal never came and Martin Jol's side hung on for a 4-3 aggregate victory.

That match could prove a pivotal moment in City's history though. It was the day that Mark Hughes' team and the supporters came together as one. Hughes is a quiet man, who seems to find it difficult to show his emotions and it has been a slow-burning relationship between the City fans and their new manager, who'd once played for Man United. Maybe that game would prove to be the real start to the management era of Mark Hughes.

Saturday 18th April – Match 103
Bury v Macclesfield Town – League Two

Rochdale and Bury, neighbours and fierce local rivals, were both closing in on promotion, with three games of the regular season to go. Dale kicked off early, so by the time Bury's match was kicking off, the Shakers fans knew Dale had lost to Darlington, which had given them a lift.

It was a strange feeling for me, because I was disappointed Rochdale had been defeated because I wanted both clubs to gain promotion, ideally automatically.

I was looking forward to the game from the moment I arrived at Gigg Lane, nothing new there I suppose, but conditions were good, the pitch was lush and everyone seemed in high spirits. After I'd announced Bury's team news and done the two o'clock scene set on BBC Radio Manchester, I headed for a burger, outside the ground.

I hadn't had a lot of sleep the night before, having sat up until three in the morning talking to my eldest son, who was in a communicative mood, for once. I'd been off work on the Friday and had spent the day in the Lake District with Irene and Daniel, cruising Windermere and relaxing. On the return journey we stopped off in Morecambe, to see Eric Morecambe's statue on the promenade and to sample the best chips in the country from the little chip shop next to the football ground.

Despite the late night, I spent some time in the gym before heading off to Gigg Lane, so I suppose I only had myself to blame for being tired.

I have to admit that I love reporting on games, it actually focuses my mind on the action in a way that watching as a spectator never does. If, or perhaps that should be when, my reporting career comes to an end, I will, of course, return to being a paying spectator, but I'll miss being a commentator and reporter. Hopefully that won't be for a long time and I know I will be one of those people who doesn't want to retire.

I saw Alistair Mann preparing to go in through a turnstile with his son. Ali used to go to Stand Grammar School, and is undoubtedly one of the nicest and most genuine people you will ever meet. He'd helped me out, earlier in the season, when I hosted a couple of stadium tours at City and talked about my role as a commentator. I asked Ali if he'd come along and talk about his role on Match of the Day and his vast experience with Granada TV. Unhesitatingly he agreed, which tells you all you need to know.

I also said hello to my primary school friend Roland Lowe, who works at Gigg Lane. It's a small world isn't it.

The game was a delight. Bury played some wonderful football, passing and moving, as the game should be played, which was all the more surprising, given that the Shakers were into those final few nervous games of the season.

I'm a big fan of Brian Barry-Murphy, Bury's left-footed midfielder, who has skill aplenty and a great attitude to the game. Many managers would play him wide, but the Shakers boss Alan Knill had him in central midfield, which I thought got the best out of him.

Bury won 3-0, thanks to two goals from all-action Glynn Hurst and one from Andy Bishop, though all their rivals, apart from Rochdale, also won. During half-time I briefly interviewed Bury's Mayor, Councillor Peter Ashworth, while afterwards Stephen Dawson, who'd missed the game through suspension, gave me his immediate post-match reaction. I also spoke to Efe Sodje, Bury's charismatic defender, who I'd first interviewed while he was at Macclesfield.

By contrast the Macclesfield manager Keith Alexander was not impressed by his team's performance, proving there are always two sides to every story.

Sunday 19th April – Match 104
Manchester City v West Bromich Albion – Premier League

I feared this game could prove to be an anticlimax after the excitement of the game against Hamburg, and although there were plenty of goals, I was right. West Brom were drinking in the last chance saloon, and had to win, to keep their fading hopes of Premier League survival alive. City needed to win to keep alive their ambition of qualifying for the following season's Europa League.

City started brightly with Stephen Ireland's inch-perfect pass finding Robinho who finished perfectly, his first goal of 2009. When Nedum Onuoha headed home a second, I was hoping to see a convincing and stylish win, but the Baggies got back into the game before half-time with a goal from Chris Brunt.

Early in the second half they were level, Brunt scoring from a free-kick which left Shay Given rooted to his line. The game was much quicker by now and there were plenty of gaps for both teams to exploit. City hit back immediately with Elano converting a penalty, which he'd earned, but by now it felt like I was commentating on a schoolboy game which had plenty of enthusiasm, but little shape.

Despite substitutions, presumably designed to tighten things up, and including the removal of Elano, a decision which was greeted with booing by some City fans, the mistake-ridden game continued as it had been. Close to full time Stephen Ireland broke away and squared for Daniel Sturridge to end the game as a contest.

On the one hand, it was a 4-2 win, in the sunshine, so who could complain? My commentary sidekick Nigel Gleghorn told listeners that the Baggies had been the better side, a view that was hard to disagree with, but at least City were back into the top half of the Premier League; just.

Wednesday 22nd April – Match 105
Arsenal u18's v Manchester City u18's – FA Youth Cup

An apologetic text from Fred, on the morning of the game, told me I would have to describe this game alone as he'd been double booked, without his knowledge. Not wanting to let anyone down and erroneously believing we were only doing brief updates on BBC Radio Manchester, he decided to stay behind.

I'd received the news while waiting at the Carrington training ground to speak to Robinho. It was the first time I'd been invited to speak to the Brazilian and he spoke through an interpreter, which is never ideal for radio.

He shook hands with the four of us who'd been granted the interview and we took it in turns to ask him questions. His answers were diplomatic, as you'd expect, and his body language suggested he was relaxed and genuine. He concluded proceedings with another handshake, and a cheery wave.

I also took the rare opportunity to get an autograph for my son Daniel, who's a big fan of Robinho. It's not generally the done thing, but this, more intimate setting allowed for a different protocol, and he was happy to oblige.

I returned home and sent the recording back to our studios via the laptop I'd borrowed from the BBC, which meant I could visit the gym for a couple of hours and have something to eat before driving into the BBC to pick up our crew van for the journey to Arsenal.

We were underway by half past one; no Fred but with Chris and Tim from City's website, as passengers. There was plenty of "life" discussion, as usual, on the journey down, and we arrived at the Emirates Stadium at about a quarter past six.

City were trailing 2-1 from the first leg, so it seemed likely that Arsenal would win through the tie, especially as Jack Wilshire was in the heart of their midfield and he was the player who'd impressed me so much when Arsenal beat Wigan in the Carling Cup earlier in the season.

Arsenal were 4-0 up, on the night, after half an hour, playing some wonderful football. The boy blues seemed a little overawed. It finished 4-1, 6-2 on aggregate. After the game the Arsenal coach Steve Bould said he was furious that his players had eased off and that if they wanted to succeed and become world class players they couldn't do that. Jim Cassell, City's Academy Director, was visibly upset by the way his boys had capitulated so meekly.

Chris had helped me out with my commentary, with a few comments, in between his own match reporting, via his laptop.

On the return tube journey to Cockfosters, a lady sitting close to where we were standing, suddenly had a seizure and fell to the floor of the train. I was impressed by how quickly the London Underground staff reacted, once someone who saw what happened pulled the emergency handle.

What did disturb me, though, was the number of voyeurs who quickly gathered in close proximity to the incident. Once we realised what was going on we all walked off the train, back onto the platform, to make room for the ambulance crew and to give the woman a better chance of breathing relatively fresh air. As we moved away others immediately stepped into the positions we had vacated.

We noticed one teenager leaning on the outside of the window, which gave the best view, and he stood transfixed by the sight of the woman twitching and shaking as she waited for help. To him, and the others around him, it must have seemed like some sort of reality TV programme or one of those documentaries that follow car chases, the police on Saturday nights or ambulance crews cleaning up the mess after binge drinkers; or maybe he thought he was watching some sort of video game.

We moved well away, further down the platform and waited patiently for the medics to arrive. Twenty minutes later we were on our way again, heading back towards home. I walked back into my house at just after two o'clock in the morning and after winding down to an episode of "Friends", which always makes me laugh, even when I'm tired, I quickly fell into a deep sleep.

The following morning, after dropping Daniel off at school, I was back at Carrington for the pre-Everton press conference. Mark Hughes usually arrives at about 10.15 and sits behind a small desk in front of one of those advertising boards that have become the norm as a backdrop for such events. The problem with those boards, when they don't fall down while the interviewee is in full flow, is that the interview could be taking place anywhere.

The main press conference is usually started by some questions from the journalist representing Sky Sports. Once all their questions are exhausted, the other journalists would chip in with their questions. There's no "pecking order", just whoever dives in first or speaks the loudest, meaning that there's often no flow to proceedings. Then again, the broadcast media generally only want soundbites while the written press can embellish and sew together all the bits for their stories.

After about fifteen minutes the main conference ended and I moved into a separate room with someone from the club's website and the press officer, to record a separate piece. Radio interviews never sound good when recorded off a top table, as the questions sound off mike.

I tried to find another angle for my interview, as this was still two days before the match and all the news stories to come from the press conference would be well known by Saturday afternoon. On this occasion I asked Hughes how he judges the personality of a signing in this era, when so many deals are conducted remotely through agents. He explained that he liked to see the player train whenever possible.

It seems to me that his approach requires a little more patience but is more likely to be successful in the long term.

Typically, after the press conference, I head back to the office, or onto another press conference before preparing the interview for broadcast within a sports bulletin or for programme.

Friday 24th April – Match 106
Stockport County v Crewe Alexandra – League One

My working day was split into two, with a trip to City's training ground for a Mark Hughes press conference kicking things off, before heading home for an hour in the gym, then into the office to do some editing and then onto the game.

Editing can be quite a tedious job, but also very rewarding, and definitely time consuming. I was using a mini-disc recorder with a large storage capacity, which means I can records lots of interviews on the same disc. There are pieces of equipment that have inbuilt microphones, can send the audio back via wi-fi or telephone connection, and they all have their advantages and disadvantages.

I'm not really bothered what the equipment is, as long as it's reliable and does the job. I've met radio enthusiasts who ask me all sorts of questions about the type of microphone I use and the number of ohms it drains, but I can't help thinking they're missing the point or destined to become engineers. Asking the right questions is actually the most important thing; albeit that we still have to record it!

I once interviewed Ron Atkinson for an hour, in an off-air studio, while Allan Beswick was presenting his programme next door. I was really pleased with the interview, but was mortified to find out, shortly after he left, that I hadn't recorded it successfully. I'd ended up with a mini-disc full of Beswick advising an 83 year-old lady how to claim back her pension from the post office. I've kept the disc though, just in case I need the advice, if ever I reach that age.

I arrived at Edgeley Park nice and early, and after checking all the technical stuff, I wandered off to the nearby shopping precinct to pick up a bag of traditional English chips. The queue stretched outside the door so I started to read the match day programme.

The County manager, Jim Gannon, hadn't been speaking to the media for a couple of weeks and hadn't even been writing his programme notes, so when I realised he had resumed, for this last home game of the season, I took particular interest. It wasn't the first time Gannon had turned down requests for media interviews, he'd stopped talking to Sky Sports earlier that season because he'd had a problem with the dish installed at his home.

In his programme notes he explained that he hadn't made his decision to be disrespectful or unprofessional. He also argued that his interviews should be seen as a privilege by the media rather than a right, which I find an interesting point for debate. He pointed out that lower division managers were not contracted to talk to the media and moaned about media misrepresentation and misinterpretation. I have some sympathy with that view, given the sound-bite nature of how things have developed, but maybe his reaction had gone too far.

Perhaps the root of the issue was his unhappiness about what was going on behind the scenes at the club. He bemoaned the fact he'd had to sell some of his better players, due to the club's economic difficulties, and went on to warn County's board of directors that their actions were taking away some of the spirit of the fans and supporters. "Something has to change" he warned.

Elsewhere in the programme the club's chief executive Sean Connolly used his column to talk about how the Stockport County family had not stuck together throughout the season, saying that there had been some highly destructive and ill-informed things put on fans message board sites and that even some of the articles in the match day programme had been unacceptable.

In his notes, chairman Martin Reid warned that the future of the football club seemed uncertain and precarious. This stuff was hotter than the chips I was not being served with. As soon as I got back to the ground I located Martin Reid and he duly obliged with an interview which we transmitted live before kick-off. There was clearly something going very badly wrong behind the scenes, so it was particularly pleasant to see the team perform so well during the game.

Over seven thousand fans were packed into the ground, it was a great atmosphere and proved to be a fantastic game. Crewe needed to win as they were in the relegation drop zone with two games to go. They were up for it right from the kick-off. It was County who scored first though, through James Vincent but Alex were soon level.

Early in the second half County scored two more through Chris O'Grady and Oli Johnson but Crewe couldn't afford to give up and pulled things back to 3-2, before Johnson got his second. Crewe pulled another back in stoppage time, but County held on for a 4-3 win. The spirit of Stockport County was certainly evident throughout, but for Crewe, relegation was now, potentially just one game away.

Saturday 25th April – Match 107
Everton v Manchester City – Premier League

I have to admit I went to Everton with low expectations, though most Blues fans will tell you that's when they're most likely to take all three points. Charlie drove us there, because it can be a bit of a problem parking anywhere near the ground, unless you're prepared to pay heavily.

There was a little bit of traffic congestion close to the ground, because a lorry had crashed into a house, virtually demolishing it. There were cranes and emergency vehicles all around the scene of the accident, which must have happened at least a couple of hours before we got there.

It was the usual heated debate en route with Chris having a "feeling in his water" that City wouldn't lose, but his was a lone voice of optimism. His instinct proved correct, with the Blues putting on a very impressive display. They kept possession well and I thought the midfield trio of Elano, Ireland and Robinho worked very well together and there was more support from the defensive midfielders than usual, giving the "creators" more options going forward.

There was always the excuse that Everton were tired from reaching the FA Cup final and then playing at Chelsea in midweek, but the truth was that City were excellent, hopefully a sign of things to come.

During the return journey I heard that Falkirk had reached the Scottish Cup Final, not something that would usually have been of much interest to me, but the former Oldham Athletic captain Dean Holden was a Falkirk player, so I was excited for him.

I got to know Dean very well while he was at Bolton and Oldham and consider him to be a good friend. He's got a lovely wife, Danielle Nicholls, who used to be a TV presenter on CITV and Dean comes from a good family. It's funny how you hit it off with certain people, there's no explanation for it, but that's how it's been with those two.

Sunday 26th April – Match 108
Blackburn Rovers v Wigan Athletic – Premier League

I was able to watch the start of the Malaysian Grand Prix on TV before setting off for Ewood Park, though I had to enjoy the latter stages by listening on the radio. Blackburn were fighting for their Premier League lives, so I knew this was going to be a very determined performance from them.

I hadn't seen Blackburn for a while so I was quite surprised by the amount the team had been transformed, if not in personnel, then certainly by the way they played. It's easy to slip into clichés in this job, just as many did when Wimbledon were at their height. It was universally accepted that the Dons always played the long ball game, and lazy journalists were still saying that long after they'd started playing a more attractive style.

In the case of Blackburn, the clichéd Sam Allardyce "long ball and set pieces" type of football had clearly started to become dominant. Their left sided midfielder Morton Gamst Pederson, a player who'd always impressed me with the quality of his delivery from set pieces was suddenly taking all the throw-ins too, and looked more like Stoke's Rory Delap than Rory Delap himself!

I'd been so impressed by Wigan throughout the season, that I was still surprised that the Latics weren't playing the way I'd seen them, when they'd been at their best.

Where had the shape and passion of just a few weeks ago disappeared to? I'd heard the rumours that Wigan didn't want to qualify for the Europa League, but I didn't believe them. They lost 2-0 thanks to goals by Benni McCarthy and Ryan Nelson.

Thursday 30th April

No match today, but a sad day, although it was one I'd seen coming for Stockport County. At lunchtime I'd been interviewing assistant manager Peter Ward at their training ground, and he was happy to admit that he didn't know what was going on behind the scenes. I chatted briefly to Jim Gannon, who was still officially not talking to the media. He told me that the players hadn't been paid and he couldn't get any answers from the people running the club.

I headed off to Oldham, where Dave Penney was being revealed as their new manager. By the time I arrived, County had announced they'd gone into administration. A sad day for all concerned at Edgeley Park, while at Boundary Park they were hoping their appointment would signal the start of a new era.

If you've ever watched "Coronation Street", and who hasn't, you'll know that whenever there's a big tragic storyline unfolding, elsewhere in the street someone is blissfully unaware and usually laughing and joking at a party. It's written that way to exaggerate the emotions of the two situations. It was a bit like that for me that afternoon, reporting on the optimism and happiness felt by Dave Penney while feeling sorry for all those connected to another club I know so well, Stockport County.

It had to be Dave Penney taking over too, didn't it? He'd just left Darlington, also in administration, to move to Oldham, so Latics couldn't be accused of Penney pinching and he knew only too well the pain felt at clubs in dire financial difficulties. He spoke about the possibility of signing players from his old club, because, to put it crudely, the strong have always fed off the weak. Would County now suffer in that way too?

May

Saturday 2nd May – Match 109
Manchester City v Blackburn Rovers – Premier League

I've been writing a column, of sorts, in the City programme for a few seasons now, and I used the one in the Blackburn programme to talk about the club's great creative players again. I've always liked writing and it was an article about one of City's great entertainers that started me off.

During a summer holiday to Florida with Irene in 1988 I went to a game between Tampa Bay Rowdies and Boston Bolts. I'd wanted to meet Rodney Marsh, who was the manager/coach of the Rowdies. I'd always loved watching him play for City, although I was aware that his critics felt he over elaborated at times. I wouldn't strongly disagree, but he ticked all the boxes for me.

I wrote to the Rowdies and asked if it would be possible to interview Rodney, and my aim was to write an article based on that interview for "Shoot magazine". Irene and I were given press passes, and were impressed by the facilities, which were much better than those in England at the time. We watched the game from a specially constructed box, high up above the half-way line. It was huge, clearly designed for American football rather than the "soccer", which was only attracting modest crowds.

Rodney was a gentleman and cheerily sat through the interview, telling me about life where soccer was "a kick in the grass". On my return to England I sent off my article and received a cheque, through the post, a few days later for £20. The most exciting moment, though, was when I bought several copies of the magazine to show off my work to my friends and family. I'd made it! If only it had been that easy.

A year later I was back at Tampa Bay Rowdies again, Rodney was still running the club, and had Mark Lawrenson as his number two. Jack Dearden and his partner Margaret, were on the trip with us, and we were given access to the locker room after the game to talk to Rodney, Mark and any of the players. We were impressed by their hospitality and their openess with the media. If only it was like that in England.

I'd expected City against Blackburn to be a really difficult game for the Blues, as this was the first time Mark Hughes and his backroom staff had faced their old club and of course Sam Allardyce was now the Rovers manager. City had struggled against Blackburn in recent years, even if they'd not usually been very attractive to watch.

Perhaps it was a sign of how well City had progressed that they breezed through this game, being 3-0 up at half-time thanks to goals by Caicedo, Robinho and Elano. Rovers got a goal back in the second half, but this win kept City's fading hopes of European qualification alive.

Thursday 7th May – Match 110
Shrewsbury Town v Bury – League Two playoff semi-final first leg

I'd been to Shrewsbury's new ground with City a year earlier for a pre-season friendly, so knew what to expect, or so I thought!

Fred and I were greeted at the entrance by a cheery man who was handing out lollipops, the sort that has a big lump of chewy toffee at the end of a plastic or cardboard stick. I didn't take one, as my hands were full from my bags of equipment and I was also trying to sign the journalists' attendance book.

We found our way to the press box and I plugged in all my bits and pieces ready to start. During a break, on the journey down, I'd chatted to Jack, who was at Rochdale's Spotland Stadium preparing to present "Rugby League Extra", and he'd wondered if I might be able to take over with the football a couple of minutes earlier than the scheduled start time of 7.20pm, as per the instructions we'd both received.

I'd wanted to start at 7pm anyway, because we had so much to try to fit in before kick-off, so we made an executive decision, as I took another sip of my tea at the Little Chef on the A49, to bring the start time forward. The other advantage of starting a little earlier was that it gave us both the chance to talk to some of the personalities attending our two League Two playoff games ahead of kick-off.

Fred soon spotted former Bury goalkeeper John Forrest sat near the directors' box, so we asked him if he'd talk to us at half time. Bury's injured player Paul Scott joined me live before kick-off. I also chatted to Fred, of course. It's nice to make eye contact during an interview, so naturally I was looking at Fred as we discussed what might happen in the game, which was now just half an hour away.

Suddenly people around me in the press box were looking towards the sky or down towards the pitch and a split second later I felt an almighty crash on the top of my head, I'd been struck by a lollipop, just like those that had been handed out when we were arriving. It didn't hurt, but it certainly shocked me. Fortunately it struck the plastic part of my headphones rather than my scalp or perhaps more seriously my face or eye.

It had hit me while I was not anticipating any incoming missiles. I had been fully focussed on my next question and was receiving verbal instructions from the studio, via the headphones. It completely knocked me out of my stride and it took me a couple of seconds to get my thoughts back together, especially because "Lenny the Lion", the club's "lovable" mascot was still throwing the objects towards the press box.

I had to keep my attention focussed on him now, as he continued to throw the lollipops over the heads of the children, which were near him on the touchline, towards the press box at the back of the stand. Why was he doing this? Did he think he was being funny? I have a sense of humour and unlike many journalists I know, I think club mascots generally do a great job, but this was going too far.

I sent an Email to the club's Managing Director Rob Bickerton and their Ground Safety Officer Eddie Hines in the hope that other journalists wouldn't be put in the same situation. Someone from the club rang me a few weeks later and assured me that the guy in "Lenny the Lion" hadn't intended his actions to be so distracting.

The game was a cracker and was played at a fantastic tempo. Bury somehow managed to win the game, the first leg of the tie, 1-0 thanks to an own goal of epic proportions when Shrewsbury defender Neil Ashton lobbed the ball over his own goalkeeper Luke Daniels, who seemed to head it back towards his own goal as he attempted to intercept. I knew the second leg would not be a foregone conclusion for the Shakers, because they'd been more than a little fortunate to get their victory.

During our commentary, Fred had a little more drama than he'd wanted too. As I described the second half action I glanced to my left for some expert analysis, to see his face contorted even more grotesquely than normal. He was clearly in pain. Was he having a heart attack, had he been hit by a missile? All I could do was carry on as all these thoughts ran through my mind.

After a few seconds I realised his leg was the problem, and it transpired he was suffering from cramp. A feeling that someone was tearing the muscle out of the back of his leg was how he described it to me later; as if there wasn't enough drama unfolding on the pitch. I thought it was only quick players who suffered from cramp.

A few minutes later he was back to normal, with me hanging off the side of my seat so he could stretch his leg out into the position I'd been occupying.

Saturday 9th May – Match 111
West Bromich Albion v Wigan Athletic – Premier League

As I set off for Birmingham, I was well aware that West Brom could get relegated, if they got a worse result than Hull City, who were at home to Stoke City. I'd seen several relegations, the hardest, professionally, being the day City had to beat Liverpool at Maine Road to stay up, but drew 2-2 and went down.

I wasn't commentating that day, but I was working as an extra reporter to interview supporters after the game, which I'd hoped would be the great relief of staying up; instead it was the disappointment of going down.

Alan Ball was the manager and it felt like Liverpool were doing everything to help City stay up, although, somehow they still went 2-0 up. City battled back in the second half to 2-2 and then the message went out from the City management that either Southampton or Coventry were losing, which meant a draw would be enough. Bally was on his feet encouraging Steve Lomas to take the ball to the corner flag to waste as many precious seconds as possible.

I was listening to the radio and wondered what was going on, because I knew this wasn't true. Eventually the right message got through but by then it was too late and City were relegated. My job now was to talk to devastated City fans.

I knew how they felt and didn't really want to start approaching supporters who were clearly shocked, stunned and emotional. It was my job though, and I knew that the heartbreak of those fans was what needed to be conveyed on the radio. I found a middle-aged man being comforted by his friend and his wife. He was crying. Before I asked the obvious question, he recognised me, which made my job a little easier because he knew I felt exactly the same as he did.

After I'd spoken to him, and one or two others, who were also finding it difficult to come to terms with being relegated, I returned to the press box and we broadcast the interviews. Only then did I allow myself to sit and contemplate the events of the day. It's not like anyone died, obviously, but if you care about your club it takes the wind out of your sails.

West Brom had to beat Wigan, and probably win their other two remaining games too, and hope for help from elsewhere if they were to stay up. Most neutrals wanted Tony Mowbray's side to stay up. They'd never resorted to long balls and kicking people, despite being bottom of the Premier League for most of the season. Their predicament was probably best summed up by the comedian and West Brom fan Frank Skinner, who I spoke to just before kick-off, though he turned down my request to join us on BBC Radio Manchester for a chat.

"It's like being at the bedside of a relative who's slowly passing away due to a terminal illness." He said it with his usual grin, and probably summed up the mood around the Hawthorns very well. I took my place on the gantry, high above the pitch, and within seconds there had been two goals. West Brom took the lead with a close range header from the aptly named Fortune, who was in the right place at the right time, before Hugo Rodallega's deflected free-kick levelled things.

There were talking points galore. Latics goalkeeper Chris Kirkland had gone off early with a back injury and the linesman had fallen over, after a collision with the corner flag. It reminded me of Paul Alcock's overdramatic reaction when Paulo Di Canio had pushed him over in 1998. That exaggerated stumble to the ground had allowed me to repeat his theatrical fall from grace in the Junior Blues pantomime that year; I went down a storm.

West Brom kept on battling and won 3-1, despite an incident that saw Borja Volero take a dive in the penalty area – perhaps Bolero would have been a more appropriate name because I thought he was skating on thin ice. Hull City also lost that day, so the Baggies lived on for another day.

Sunday 10th May – Match 112
Man United v Manchester City

I wanted to be at three games today, the two play-off semi-final second legs featuring Bury and Rochdale and the derby; I could only be at one.

This was my 52nd Derby, and I'd seen some thrillers down the years. My favourite City goal at Old Trafford was Ian Brightwell's screamer in the 1-1 draw in 1990. He told reporters after that game, "I just wellied it". Another great game was the 2-2 draw, which featured a late City equaliser from Roger Palmer, in 1980; it had felt like a win. Generally though, City hadn't tended to play that well at United and it wasn't until my 50th derby that I finally saw a City win.

The 2-1 victory, thanks to goals by Darius Vassell and Benjani, was very special. For weeks leading up to the game, all anyone seemed to want to talk about was whether the City fans would remain silent for the commemoration of 50 years since the Munich air crash. The City fans were impeccable and the team fought hard for their win.

It was obvious that United would want revenge for that defeat, twelve months later, so this trip to their ground wouldn't have been an easy one under any circumstances, but despite lots of bravado from the City manager, Mark Hughes, before the game saying, "This was the perfect time to play them after four wins in a row for City", this was a lacklustre performance. City never showed any fight and United hardly broke sweat.

I can't remember a poorer City performance in a derby, there was no fight, and for long periods they seemed to be content, when in possession, to go sideways and backwards rather than commit players forward.

I hosted the post-match phone-in, once I'd returned from interviewing Hughes and Vincent Kompany and almost all the fans I spoke to were upset by the lack of passion from the City players.

To make matters worse, Bury had lost their play-off second leg to Shrewsbury at Gigg Lane by 1-0 which had taken the game into extra-time and penalties, with the Shakers going out via the shootout. Later that evening I settled down to watch Rochdale's second leg at Gillingham on TV and Dale lost 2-1; they also missed out on the final.

I was disappointed for both clubs and from a personal point of view I've not been to the new Wembley; it'll therefore be even more special when I go there to see City win, which I'm sure will be very soon.

Wednesday 13th May – Matchday 113
FC Schalke 04 v Stuttgart – Bundesliga

My second trip of the season to Schalke was purely for pleasure, but I still had to use a route that was less convenient than I would have preferred. I'd become used to saving money on my trips to Europe with City, so it was second nature to try to find an alternative, once I realised I couldn't afford the £300+ it would have cost me to fly from Manchester to Dusseldorf, by far the most convenient option.

I found that flying from Birmingham would save me more than £200, so even with the extra parking and petrol costs, it would be more sensible to start my journey by heading down the M6.

It was to be a much shorter trip than those I'd got used to during City's UEFA Cup campaign; in on match day and on the way home again 24 hours later. I could relax on this trip too, as I didn't have to think about blogs, reporting into the breakfast programme and all the build-up to the game. The truth is, though, that all that stuff adds to the fun of the trip, especially doing the commentary.

I watch a game so much more intently when I'm on air, the adrenalin in my system means that I'm studying every touch of the ball, every movement of a player. When I've done a commentary I have an opinion on how every player, from both teams, has played, whereas when I'm watching the game as a spectator there might by individuals, especially those playing for the "other" team, who "slip under my radar".

Given a choice between watching a game normally and doing a commentary, I'd always prefer the latter, which is one of the reasons I helped do the commentary for visually impaired spectators at the UEFA Cup final in 2008 between Zenit St.Petersburg and Rangers. A team of three or four volunteers offer this service at all games, staged at the City of Manchester Stadium and they do a great job, not only when describing the action but also patiently handing out receiving equipment to fans, in all parts of the stadium, before collecting them in again after the game.

On arrival at Dusseldorf I was disappointed to find that the airport monorail wasn't running, I love riding to the train station in the unmanned cabs that glide over the traffic, but on this occasion it was the shuttle bus.

Less than an hour later I was walking up the main shopping street in Gelsenkirchen and felt like I was home again; my second home. As usual I quickly found a side stall selling Reibekuchen and continued to walk down Bahnhofstrasse. Halfway along the street, I looked to my left and saw the flats my Auntie Aenne and Auntie Inge used to live in, while to my right is Weber Strasse where Auntie Lotti lived, until just a couple of years ago.

Sometimes I wander a little further away from the centre of town up Kirch Strasse (Church Street) to see where my grandma lived, but there was no time for that sort of nostalgia on this trip. I went straight to the stadium and collected my ticket from Thomas, my friend in the Schalke press office, who was temporarily in charge, so we didn't have much time to chat.

In the seat next to me was a guy from Stuttgart, Schalke's opposition. He was tucking a card into his wallet from Man United's European scout, who was also at the game. Was he here to look at Stuttgart's German international Mario Gomez, who'd scored four at the weekend? If he was, he was unlucky because Gomez didn't play, due to injury.

Schalke didn't play well, despite the typical "cup final" atmosphere from the fans. They lost 2-1 to end their fading hopes of qualification to the new Europa League. At the end of the game the players didn't race off the pitch down the tunnel, they stayed out for at least five minutes, acknowledging the support of the fans and enjoying some typically German mutual admiration. English football could learn a lot from the way German clubs relate to their supporters.

In front of each stand they held hands and bowed to the crowd, who did the same back to them. Remember this had been a defeat, and it wasn't their last home game of the season, nor was it a local derby, this was just a routine game. It makes me groan to myself when fans in England get upset about players running off down the tunnel, after games, without any acknowledgement. It would be so easy for these players and has become part of the culture at all German clubs; players do it automatically, and without a sauerkraut in sight.

I went to Berlin, in May 2002, with Schalke, when they won the German FA Cup by beating Bayer Leverkusen 4-2. My seat had been away from many of my friends, so we arranged to rendezvous back at the hotel, after the game. The Schalke players remained out on the pitch for forty five minutes, posing for pictures, laps of honour and all the things we see at Wembley after a Cup Final, so as soon as they disappeared down the tunnel I raced back to the underground station to avoid some of the crush.

I sat in the reception of the hotel for over an hour wondering where everyone was. I assumed they'd gone for a celebratory drink or had got stuck in the crowd at the tube station. Ninety minutes after I'd arrived back in the centre of Berlin my friends finally walked in. "Where have you been?" I wondered. "After the players went down the tunnel they put on fresh T-shirts and came back out and we sang songs with them for another hour", was their amazing reply.

Can you imagine still celebrating, with the players out on the pitch after a Cup win, for more than an hour and a half? No me neither!

The most amazing example of their fan culture that I've seen was at Schalke for their game against Bayern Munich on 5th November 2006, a date always associated with fireworks but this was something I've never seen before.

From my observations, the relationship between German football supporters and the players is good, but the Schalke fans weren't happy with the effort of the team, and felt their attitude towards the supporters had deteriorated.

As I listened to what the fans were planning, I was thinking how lucky they were compared to England, but they didn't realise it. They'd organised, via the internet and supporters clubs, to stage a silent protest during the game which would last until 19 minutes and 4 seconds into the game, representing 1904, the year the club was founded (hence the name Schalke 04).

I didn't believe, for one minute, that this would happen; 61,000 fans to remain silent for nearly 20 minutes as the game against Bayern was being played out in front of them?

The build-up to kick-off was just as loud as ever, the flags were whirling around as they sang the club song just before kick-off and then as the game started the ground fell quiet. It was as if the referee had blown his whistle to start a minute's silence.

Schalke attacked, but there was no noise from the huge crowd. After 13 minutes Peter Lowenkrands gave the home side the lead, he received muted, gentle applause. Schalke got a corner and the fans stood on the Nordkurve, behind that goal, turned their backs on the team, as the ball was floated in and headed away by the Bayern defenders. The only noise in the stadium came from the Bayern fans at the other end of the ground.

The Veltins Arena has a huge cube-like scoreboard and replay screen which hangs from the roof in the middle of the stadium and the clock shows every second of the time that was passing by. We could all see it ticking around to 18 minutes gone; just one minute to go until the ground went back to normal.

With about thirty seconds left the crowd started to slowly clap in rhythm and a slow, quiet roar was building, as we headed towards 19.04 on the clock. As it reached 18.55 the ball was played to Levan Kobiashvili, who carried the ball to a shooting position. The roar was building, the clapping was louder, quicker and more intense and at exactly 19.04 he unleashed a 25 yard drive that arrowed into the top corner to make it 2-0. The stadium exploded into the loudest cheer I've ever heard.

You could not make up a story up like that, but it's absolutely true. With the Schalke fans back to normal, Bayern came from behind to draw 2-2! Even more amazing, I attended the after-match press conference and no one asked the Schalke coach how the fans protest had affected the players!!

They made their point though, because the team finished second to Stuttgart that season, missing the title by just 2 points; maybe if they'd won that day...

As usual I'd stayed at my aunties house in Buer, the district closest to the Schalke area of Gelsenkirchen. We'd had a good catch-up, a schnapps or two and the next morning I was on my way back home after another enjoyable trip; my final European trip of the season.

Saturday 16th May – Match 114
Tottenham Hotspur v Manchester City – Premier League

This was the nearest I was going to get to Wembley, for another season, with White Hart Lane being a few miles around the North Circular. There are plenty of City fans, younger than me, who've never seen their team win a major trophy; at least I have seen a City win at Wembley.

For this trip to Spurs, we'd travelled down to London in the BBC Radio Manchester Crew Van again, which by now had the name of the radio station written all over the outside, which I couldn't help feeling would make it more of a target for vandals and hooligans, not to mention the funny looks we were getting from other road users when they passed us.

Fortunately the trip passed without incident and it was a last chance of the season for the four of us, me, Fred, Charlie and Chris, to travel to an away game together. In fact, I knew it might be the last time Chris would come with us, because he'd told us he was accepting voluntary redundancy from the Manchester Evening News.

The game was equally disappointing because City had to win to have any hope of qualifying for the new Europa League, and despite a brave second half performance, which saw them battle back to 1-1, they lost 2-1 due to a late, slightly controversial Spurs penalty, given away by Micah Richards and scored by Robbie Keane. No more trips to far flung European outposts for me then, at least for a while, and no more exciting nights like the Hamburg game.

It was a long journey home.

Sunday 24th May – Match 115
Manchester City v Bolton Wanderers

This was my last working game of the season. I can't deny that I was in need of a break, but then again I love my job so much, that two months without football matches to attend seemed a long time.

I met up with Jack and Alan Gowling, our Bolton commentary team, and Nigel joined us too at the Pavilion Café in Chadderton for a pre-match breakfast, to mark the conclusion of the season. We mulled over the highs and lows of the campaign as we munched on our full English breakfast, before heading off to the City of Manchester Stadium in convoy, chilled out and ready for the game.

The relaxed atmosphere didn't last long. Soon after plugging our broadcast equipment into their usual sockets it became apparent, as Jim Lovell once said, "we have a problem". There was an echo coming back into our ears, when we were speaking on air. Jack was struggling to cope with it and was making even less sense than he normally did, so I tried to work out what the problem was and solve it, while he carried on trying to present the programme.

There were various different technical settings that were tried from the studio but none of them worked. Jackie Oatley, famous for being the UK's first female football commentator, who was working at the game for BBC 5live, offered the use of her spare connection point, which is wired into the stadium independently. The problem was solved, but you can only imagine the stress that had been created while we reached that point.

It hadn't been the best preparation for a game, but with just a few minutes to spare, before kick-off, we had sorted out all the technical problems and the game was underway. It seemed to flash by, and was actually a very good match, especially considering that there was nothing at stake for either club. City won 1-0 thanks to a goal from Filipe Caicedo.
The most significant moment of the match came with just five minutes

remaining when Glauber Berti got his five minutes of fame as a substitute. The Brazilian had sat patiently on the bench for twenty games, warming up periodically but never actually coming on. There had been many questions to Mark Hughes from fans asking when he might play and the City boss showed a touch of sentimentality by bringing him on.

I've not heard a cheer like the one he received since Colin Bell made his comeback from injury on Boxing Day 1977. I'd finished my stint of commentary by the time he made his appearance, because Jack and I shared the role, doing half of each half each, so I made a point of counting every touch of the ball that Glauber or should that be Berti (I guess we'll never know!) had. For the record he had seven touches of the ball and took one throw in, for which he got a standing ovation!

All too soon the game was over and I was packing up my equipment for the final time and heading back to the car park. What would next season bring? How many of the players would still be there in August when it was all due to start again?

Saturday 30th May – Matchday 116
Falkirk v Rangers – Scottish Cup Final

What a great way to end the season; a Cup Final. It wasn't the one I'd really wanted, and not since 1981 had my season ended by watching City conclude the season by going for a trophy. Had Mark Hughes' team reached the UEFA Cup Final it would have been played ten days earlier, but that would have been perfect too. Instead I'd watched, on TV, Shaktar Donetsk of Ukraine beat Werder Bremen to lift the trophy.

I'd chosen to go to the Scottish Cup Final because the former Oldham defender Dean Holden was a Falkirk player. It was a wonderful, hot and sunny day, very fitting for the occasion, as I headed north. It seemed a foregone conclusion that Rangers would win and Dean had told me he was unlikely to play, but as the team had yet to be named, I remained hopeful.

Last time I'd seen Rangers play, was at the UEFA Cup final against Zenit St.Petersburg at the City of Manchester Stadium when Daniel had been on the pitch holding one of the big white balloons during the mini opening ceremony. He'd spent the day before rehearsing in the Regional Athletics

Arena, next door, and was quite nervous on the day.

Irene had a seat on the opposite side of the ground and I was doing the commentary for the visually impaired, sat in the press box. His big moment came when he popped the big balloon to release hundreds of tiny balloons that floated up into the Manchester sky.

On the pitch Andrei Arshavin had impressed and my father-in-law would have been proud to see the winning captain Anatoliy Tymoschuk, a Ukrainian, lifting the trophy as captain.

My memories of the cup finals I've attended include the Euro 96 game at Wembley, when Germany beat the Czech Republic, the culmination of a competition I really enjoyed. Although it wasn't a cup final, City's play-off decider against Gillingham in 1999 was also special. I've heard some supporters describe it as one of the "great games", and I understand what they mean, it was certainly dramatic; but great game?

It was an awful game, only made special by the late drama of coming back from 2-0 down and eventually winning promotion via a penalty shootout. This was a third division play-off though, hardly something to be proud of.

It's a shame I have to go back so far for my favourite final. I was sixteen years old when City beat Newcastle United 2-1 at Wembley and proudly wore the sky blue and white scarf my mum had knitted for me. I pinned onto the thick wool, circular metallic badges which showed the faces of the twelve players who were on duty. They were each about two inches in diameter, and would be regarded as a bit garish these days, but at that time they were fashionable.

I went to Wembley with my dad and we both wore rosettes. My hero Colin Bell couldn't play because of his terrible knee injury, but Peter Barnes and Dennis Tueart were both in the team, so I was happy and hopeful. It proved to be the perfect day, with both of them scoring and Mike Doyle lifting the League Cup after the game, as I sang loudly with the other travelling City supporters, "We won the Cup, we won the Cup, ee eye addio we won the Cup". Ahh, the old days!

The following day there was a homecoming parade in Manchester, so I went into town, resplendent in my mum's scarf, to cheer the boys home. There was Colin Bell on the balcony taking the cheers of his team-mates and the fans and my heroes were on top of a double decker bus; I'd never seen a double decker without a roof before, though I'd seen a tram like that in Blackpool when we'd gone to the illuminations.

As I returned to the bus station, someone tried to steal my scarf, and nearly got away with my Kenny Clements badge, but I hung on grimly and jumped onto the doorplate of the nearest bus to reach safety just in time.

My final match of the 2008-2009 season couldn't live up to that League Cup Final of my youth, especially when it was confirmed that Deano wasn't involved. I have to admit I put my fingers in my ears everytime bagpipes were played, the noise was threatening to give me a headache.

On the journey north I'd stopped briefly for a "comfort break", just over the border. Right next to me, was a Scottish couple wearing City shirts. They were long distance fans, going on holiday. I hadn't expected to bump into City fans on my journey north.

When I arrived in Glasgow I was in danger of getting lost. I wasn't sure where Hampden Park was, but followed a car that had Falkirk scarves fluttering out of the window. I drove past Celtic Park and eventually realised we must be close to Hampden, so I found a side street about a mile from the ground.

In some ways it didn't feel like a Cup Final, the Rangers fans in particular seemed subdued, probably because they had been to so many events like this in the past. English football is in danger of following the Scottish pattern. The dominance of one or two clubs can't be good. I feared I might be looking at the future of the FA Cup in the coming years; apathy from one of the participants.

The match felt flat too. Falkirk tried to make a game of it, but were limited to pot shots, despite the obvious lethargy or perhaps apathy of the Rangers players. I felt that Falkirk's Scott Arfield was the best player on show, though the lads sat near me, who were wearing face masks and holding up a huge banner in support of Michael Higdon, might have disagreed! They were up for his stag do which was taking place that night. Would that have still gone ahead if Falkirk had won the Cup; but then again, that was never going to happen, was it?

Nacho Novo scored the only goal, early in the second half. It was a beauty by Nacho, his crisp shot had plenty of dip on it, just as I like them!

So, that was that, the football season was over, and it was time to recharge the batteries ready for the build-up to another exciting season in July. I think I've got the best job in the world, and there wasn't one game, one trip that I didn't enjoy. No matter where I was to go on my holidays, I'd find some sport to watch.

On my honeymoon to romantic Rome and Sorrento we'd managed to fit in the Italian Cup final – second leg – Roma beating Verona 1-0. I've watched various football matches in Austria, Ukraine, Sweden, Germany and the USA while on my holidays, as well as baseball – I've got a soft spot for the New York Mets.

Maybe I should try to get as far away as possible, somewhere like the Caribbean, although I'd probably end up watching competitive limbo dancing, but surely even I wouldn't go that low?